Dr. Adrian van Kaam is a renowned spiritual writer and professor of formative spirituality as an academic and practical discipline. Ordained a priest in 1947, he studied and taught philosophy and psychology in a seminary in his homeland, Holland. In 1953 he came to the United States, where he taught and studied the psychology of spiritual formation and received a doctoral degree in psychology from Case Western University. For the last twenty years he has dedicated himself to research, teaching, and writing in the field of formative spirituality. Appointed a professor at Duquesne University, he founded the Institute of Formative Spirituality in 1963. Within this institute Dr. van Kaam initiated, along with his colleagues and graduate students, the science of fundamental human formation, or formative spirituality. He is founder and editor of the journals **Studies in Formative Spirituality** and **Envoy** as well as author of 24 books and over 100 articles.

Formative Spirituality

Volume Four

SCIENTIFIC FORMATION

Formative Spirituality

Volume Four

SCIENTIFIC FORMATION

·ADRIAN VAN KAAM·

CROSSROAD · NEW YORK

1987

The Crossroad Publishing Company
370 Lexington Avenue, New York, NY 10017

Copyright © 1987 by Adrian van Kaam

Library of Congress Cataloging in Publication Data

Van Kaam, Adrian L., 1920–
Scientific formation.

(Formative spirituality; v. 4)
Bibliography; p. 283
Includes index.
1. Spiritual life—Catholic authors.   2. Christianity—
Psychology.   3. Developmental psychology.   I. Title.
II. Series: Van Kaam, Adrian L., 1920–   Formative
spirituality; v. 4.
BX2350.2.V185   1987   248   87–13487
ISBN 0–8245–0841–6

Contents

Preface

S cientific formation is the topic of this fourth volume of my series on formative spirituality. Scientific methodology can raise our feelings, intuitions, and customs to a higher level of validated truth. This process purifies experiences from prejudices of which we may not be cognizant.

During my involvement in formation practice, research, and publication in the Netherlands, I became aware of the impact of materialistic and idealistic trends of thought. They had seeped into the sciences of pedagogy and andragogy through psychological anthropologies. As I describe in chapter 9 of this volume, my experience at that time led me to dedicate my life to a critical-creative investigation of such confusing influences. In the midst of this research I was asked by my superiors to temporarily shift focus from formation to psychology in order to help initiate a department at Duquesne University which would specialize in psychology as a human science.

During the implementation of this project, I had to contend with two offshoots of materialistic and idealistic anthropologies: deterministic-behavioristic and existentialistic psychologies at that moment popular in the United States. To preserve the possible contributions of these two movements while correcting their anthropologies I tried to give deeper spiritual meaning to much of their psychological metalanguages. Finally I proposed the establishment of an *anthropological psychology* that would go beyond behavioristic, existentialistic, and other psychologies and would integrate their corrected contributions while changing their assumptions. My original critique of materialism and idealism from the formation research I did in the Netherlands was helpful for my critique of their offspring in American psychology.

My reservations about existentialism do not imply that I reject the Thomistic distinction between essence and existence or its insistence that certain sciences are more concerned with the study of essences than others, and vice versa. Formation science, for example, like many spiritual writings of classical traditions, focuses on the practical ways in which the essence or foundational form of human life concretely expresses itself in human existence. It examines how people receive and give form to this essence in its distinctive humanness. The sciences of metaphysics and of foundational theology, by comparison, are more concerned with the essentials of faith traditions.

While trying to correct and complement the above two streams of psychology, I realized that something more than theory would be needed. It seemed necessary to develop a scientific methodology to examine systematically the anthropological assumptions and their impact on these two types of psychology. This methodology should enable us to reformulate and integrate the possible contributions of both into an anthropological psychology.

When psychology as a human science was sufficiently initiated in the department at Duquesne, the administration of the university allowed me to return to my original specialization in distinctively human formation and to establish in 1963 the Institute of Formative Spirituality. I was no longer obliged to formulate my insights in terms of psychology. The viewpoint of this one science was too limited to explain the complexity of human life in its wide variety of distinctively human ways of formation. Needed was a science that could take into account all sources of formation wisdom. Their contributions could be formulated in a new metalanguage no longer dependent on the metalanguages of psychology or pedagogy alone. Most importantly, I could freely develop a methodology that would transcend yet utilize some of the contributions to methodology developed by behavioristic, analytical, and existentialistic psychologies as well as by other arts and sciences. This volume is meant to acquaint its readers with the history and present stage of the development of this methodology.

Formation science can provide humanity with a minimum of distinctively human formation directives. Significant numbers of adherents of various form traditions may agree on them. Such consensus would be built on the demonstrable reasonableness of scientifically confirmed insights. By themselves alone, however, they cannot cover all aspects of spiritual formation. The deepest wisdom of formation, specifically of transcendent transformation, cannot be produced or reproduced by scientific research. The highest formation knowledge and experience exceeds the domain of empirical science. Faith and formation traditions are the guardians of this wisdom.

Beyond its own general empirical insights, formation science can only suggest *hypothetical* articulations of the wisdom of existing traditions. It can be helpful especially in suggesting practical ways to implement the ultimate wisdom of a tradition in the everyday life of specific common-cultural, segmental-subcultural, or individual situations. Anything scientists may suggest in this area, as distinguished from their own science, carries neither the authoritative nor the theological or philosophical certitudes of the traditions they research or advise. If such suggestions are unacceptable to either the authorities or the approved theological or ideological consensus of the tradition concerned, scientists cannot interfere, no matter what their private convictions may be. They cannot speak authoritatively for a tradition as such. It would be foolish to pretend that they could tell, for example, the Jewish, Islamic, or Hindu religions how and when they should publicly change their age-old traditions. In the fifth and final volume of this series, on transcendent formation, we shall deal at length with the specific service that formation science can offer to formation traditions, along with its essential limitations.

Acknowledgments

I want to express my appreciation to those who assisted me in the preparation of this volume. I thank Dr. Susan Annette Muto, Director of the Institute of Formative Spirituality at Duquesne University. In spite of her work load as administrator of the Institute and at this time as principal author of the forthcoming letter of the American bishops on the concerns of women, she took time to edit this volume as well as she did the former ones. I am grateful to Father Richard Byrne, Ph.D., Executive Director of the Institute, for his helpful suggestions. A special word of appreciation for Eve Bauer, the typist who coped tirelessly with the various new versions of the manuscript, and for Carol Pritchard, Administrative Secretary of the Institute, who patiently entered repeated corrections. Mrs. Helen Douglas corrected the proofs with her usual efficiency. The Reverend John Kloepfer and the Reverend D. Darrell Woomer, graduate assistants and Ph.D. candidates of the Institute, organized the bibliography. Jeremiah McAuliffe, Ph.D. candidate of the Institute, composed the index. I thank them all in genuine gratefulness for their collaboration.

Introduction

The first three volumes of this series made us familiar with the presuppositions and the theoretical and practical results of a scientific approach to distinctively human or "spiritual" formation. This familiarity has prepared us for a reflection in this volume on the scientific approach itself in its methodological operations.

The empirical approach described in the following chapters cannot replace the approaches to formation represented by traditions that are rooted in either religious or ideological belief systems. Scientific analysis of the sources of spiritual experience in human consciousness itself and of its proximate practical implications can never be a substitute for the richness, inspiration, and authority of the great formation traditions, nor of their supporting belief systems. Scientific analysis can only complement, in the realm of proximate practicality, their investigations of the practical implications of theological or philosophical certitudes and probabilities.

Form traditions are not only irreplaceable sources of authoritative wisdom and inspiration. They are also storehouses of information for our science about transcendent human consciousness in its proximate practical implications. What changes is not the irreplaceability of a form tradition but its exclusiveness as the only possible source of insight into all aspects of distinctively human formation. We call this restrictive notion the exclusivist view of formation. Its vision prevailed through most of humanity's history, fomenting countless wars and conflicts. In many cultures people were programmed to consider any directive of their shared formation tradition as the only thinkable one, as in principle universal and unchangeable. Hence their presumption was often that each form directive should guide the detailed formation of all people in all cultures and periods of history.

Recent developments have begun to mellow this rigorous viewpoint.

The emergence of empirical disciplines, the scholarly examination of a wide variety of traditions, the analysis of the experiential workings of transcendent human consciousness put this exclusivist notion into question. An important source of this questioning of the static conception of human formation can be found in the pluriformity of traditions that directly or indirectly guide the formation of human life in pluriform societies.

Let me illustrate the emergent problems of formation in such societies by recounting a recent experience. The office of the chief of chaplains of the United States Navy confronted us with the following problem. Many men and women enlisted in the service ask for spiritual counseling and leadership. The people enlisted by the navy to respond to this need are clergypersons representing 85 different religious and denominational traditions. Each chaplain however, no matter what his or her particular religious affiliation may be, must be available for spiritual guidance to any of the men and women who ask for such assistance. If the counselee happens to be committed to the religion or denomination of the chaplain concerned, guidance should be given in terms of the authoritative doctrine and the corresponding theologies of their particular belief system. But what about the situations where this is not the case, where no chaplain of one's own persuasion is available? What about spiritual concerns expressed by navy personnel who do not feel called to enroll in any organized religion or who are not ready to learn any particular denominational theology? Evidently one cannot impose on them the specialized teachings of one's own religion or one of its denominations as long as the persons who come for spiritual assistance insist that this is not the type of spiritual guidance they want at this moment of their life.

One can ask how this need for a solution to life's problems in light of the spirit emerges in these sailors. One reasonable answer seems to be that human consciousness itself seems endowed with a potency for spiritual transcendence that, awakened under favorable circumstances, may transform in some measure the practical orientation of the person and throw a new light on life's problems and conflicts. Obviously the enclosed environment of a ship or the stress of sea maneuvers on an aircraft carrier may be among the numerous factors that can actualize this given potency for the life of the spirit. As long as this evocation does not lead to an interest in any particular religion or any of its denominations, the only thing the chaplain can do is to respond to this inner working of the spiritual consciousness of the questioner.

Chaplains, or any other religious leaders, will be better able to fulfill this requirement effectively if they can step outside the specific theological content and language of the spirituality formulated in their own religion or one of its denominations. This compassionate entering into the universal realm of spiritual consciousness—as not yet illumined by their own particular theological training—is possible only on the basis of familiarity with the universal spiritual experience that is possible in any human person. To learn about the universal transcendent dimension of human consciousness and its practical implications for human life as a whole, chaplains need special training that goes beyond particular formation in their own religion or one of its denominations. While being rooted in, committed to, and clear about the spirituality of their own religion or denomination, they should also be able to serve competently the spiritual needs of those who do not adhere to their beliefs.

To put this theory to the test, two faculty members of the Institute of Formative Spirituality were asked to conduct training sessions for the chaplains of 85 different denominations. These sessions took place on navy bases at Norfolk, Virginia; San Diego, California; Okinawa, Japan; Pearl Harbor, Hawaii; Camp Le Jeune, South Carolina; Jacksonville, Florida; and Camp Pendleton, California. The training had to be conducted in light of the science of universal spiritual formation with its own transdenominational and transtheological language, research methodology, universal formation theory, and spiritual counseling methodology.

The pilot sessions were followed up by extensive evaluations and descriptions of the effects by all the participants of the represented denominations. Almost unanimously they expressed a deep need for this kind of approach in their work. They suggested that chaplains on all navy bases should be offered this kind of training.

This experience confirmed the original experiences that led to the emergence of this universal science of spiritual formation in the first place. I was compelled to develop this kind of approach when working with a pluriform group of people we helped to hide during the devastating winter of 1944-1945 in western Holland when the Nazis tried to deport our male population and to imprison and kill our Jewish neighbors in concentration camps. Again, when teaching and counseling after the war in the factory division of the Dutch Life Schools for formation of young adults and later in a Dutch detention center for juvenile delinquents, I was faced with the same necessity to counsel spiritually those who did not feel called to convert to my own religion and who could not be familiar with its theological language. It would have been cruel, for instance, to refuse a lonely elderly Jew in hiding who had lost his family the consolation of insight into his own spiritual openness to the mystery unless he would consent to be baptized in my religion.

The pluriform societies in which we live may at times impose on us the duty of social justice, love, and compassion to assist others in their quest for the life of the spirit. They may feel inwardly compelled to seek transcendence but are unable, or not yet able, to enrich and deepen the response to this aspiration by exclusive adherence to one of the great faith and form traditions of humanity.

To enable us to fulfill this obligation of social justice, we have to examine the transcendent dimension of human consciousness and our apprehension of it as it has developed during the history of human formation. To do so with an unprejudiced mind, we have to leave behind the static and exclusivist notion of spiritual formation. Our view should also be empirical. We should envision distinctively human formation as an unfolding historical process or praxis. This creative praxis of the human form of life can be observed in the personal as well as in the common and segmental ranges of the formation fields of populations. The expression of this basic ground or dimension of human consciousness can be traced in, among other things, the various faith and form traditions of specific populations in particular periods of history.

For example, an Islamic tradition may give rise to different expressions of transcendent consciousness in the formative customs of different common formation fields, such as Turkey or Iran. Again within these common populations different expressions may be found in segments of these common fields, such as Sunni or Shiite adherents of the Islamic tradition. Furthermore in the individual Islamic participants in both such common and segmental ranges of their shared field particular customs and expressions may emerge. All of these can shed light on the flow and flexibility of transcendent consciousness and its implications for ordinary life formation.

Empirical investigations show that the directives which give form to our way of life may stay the same for long periods of time. However, they may give way also to increased movements of reformation that emerge under changing historical conditions. In certain periods such conditions may accelerate the change of directives in surprising ways.

Form traditions are structures of shared directives. These structures may not only change over time, they may also dissolve, as is evident from past form traditions such as the Assyrian, Babylonian, and ancient Egyptian ways of life.

When the exclusivist concept of formation prevails, existing formation knowledge of a culture or one of its segments is apprehended and appreciated as final and permanent. Reflection on it is not absent, but it does not include an argumentative appraisal of possible change of form directives. Only the precise meaning and accurate formulation of each form directive, its faithful maintenance and rigorous implementation, are considered legitimate objects of personal and public argumentation.

It is different when formation knowledge is appraised as coformed by empirical and historical dynamics. The empirical view of formation appraises the process or praxis of formation as a spiral movement of reformation and transformation of humanity's journey through the millennia. This movement includes also periods of regression and deformation. Such appraising apprehension enhances our sense of responsibility for the critical direction of this creative praxis. It invites us to reflection on what happens in this process. Knowledge of formation and of its consonant direction is no longer taken for granted. We experience the challenge to give form to our knowedge in a methodical fashion. Sooner or later this challenge is bound to suggest the initiation of a critical science of formation. The development of such a science implies the search for a methodology that can provide us with objective data and appraising apprehensions which can increasingly enhance the probability that we approach our formation journey as effectively as possible within the limits of humanity's unfolding in our time.

The basic methodology of a science consists of a set of fundamental categories that represent clusters of systematic operations. These categories must be foundational and flexible. Otherwise they cannot be adapted and expanded by the scientists in accordance with the unfolding facet or problem on which they focus their attention within the coherence of objects of the science to which they have committed themselves in service of unfolding humanity.

Take, for example, the methodical category of dialogical articulation to be considered in this volume. This category, as we shall see, must be flexible enough to allow for the addition of newly invented creative operations of articulation. Some of these may enable us to articulate more critically our own objectified personal experience. Other added operations may serve the articulation of statistically significant samples of specific populations.

We envisage in this volume eight distinct methical categories: dialogical selection, articulation, elucidation, consultation, translation, transposition, integration, and application. The justification and orientation of each of these methical categories or clusters of methods, as well as their implementation in research designs, are treated in chapters 8 through 26. The first seven chapters of this volume treat general issues such as science, human science, formation science, scientific and pre-scientific knowledge, and the nature of scientific methodology. The understanding of the presuppositions of formation science treated in these chapters will facilitate the comprehension of the eight distinct clusters of methods to be treated in the subsequent chapters. Each of these fundamental categories serves as a model for a potentially wide variety of methical operations that can be subsumed under it.

These methical categories are not taken out of thin air. Like all basic notions of the science they are rooted in its underlying formation anthropology. Their foundation can be found in the subdivision of formation anthropology that treats the basic formation of human knowledge. Many principles of critical cognition-formation have been dealt with in my book *Existential Foundations of Psychology*, where I contrast my own anthropological psychology of that period with existential psychology. Similar principles are elaborated in the first three volumes of this series and in the glossaries published regularly in the successive issues of the journal *Studies in Formative Spirituality*.

In this Introduction we bring some of these principles of cognition formation together. Our aim is to clarify for our readers how they themselves can and should detect these principles at work within their own experience of the development of their own basic processes of cognition. Only then can they apprehend and appreciate how the eight methical clusters flow forth in their basic identity from these universal principles of all human knowledge formation.

Formation anthropology contains the systematic formulation of those basic principles. An inexhaustible variety of particular methods of knowledge acquisition can be construed by the human mind. But one cannot move outside the unalterable foundational potencies for the acquisition of human knowledge that are given once and for all to our species. These inherent potencies constitute the universal condition for the development of any particular method of knowing.

One can only comprehend formation anthropology by patiently tracing in oneself the foundational structures, dynamics, and directives of formation formulated by this specific type of anthropology. This comprehension should precede, accompany, and complement all empirical research in this field.

The primary focus of this volume is thus on the methodology that particularizes the basic knowledge formation of humanity in systematic approaches to the understanding and explanation of its own distinctively human life formation. This raises the question: What is methodology?

Methodology

A methodology can be defined as a directive set of systematic approaches to a specific object of knowledge that increasingly discloses the scientifically relevant facets of that formal object as well as the dynamic interactions of these unfolding facets with one another and with their conditions and consequences.

For example, one of the methodological categories of our science is that of dialogical elucidation. This category gives rise to a variety of creative approaches. Each of them may grant us a systematic or well-structured access to the dynamism of human formation. Each of them discloses increasingly for us scientifically relevant facets such as the sociohistorical, vital, functional, and transcendent aspects of this dynamism. Elucidated also are mutually coforming relationships between these aspects and between them and their obstacles and facilitating conditions in the formation field.

Foundational Principles of Knowledge Formation

In the first three volumes of this series and in the editorials and glossaries of *Studies in Formative Spirituality* we have repeatedly referred to the foundational principles of any knowledge formation. We highlighted them in passing, according to the specific topics under consideration. We did not consider them primarily from the viewpoint of knowledge formation as such. In this volume we bring them together and examine them primarily insofar as they relate to the methodical categories for knowledge formation in this science.

These fundamental sources of all human knowledge formation are: dialogical attention, apprehension, appraisal (affinitive, affective, and argumentative), affirmation, and application (communicative and executive). We can make ourselves familiar with each of these operations by a sustained attention to what happens in our own intrasphere and in its expressions in the other structural spheres of our field of formative consciousness when we receive or give form to any kind of knowledge.

We should make focal in our own consciousness the successive operations of knowledge formation in which we are usually engaged prefocally. We can only gain understanding of how our human knowledge comes to be if we disclose for ourselves the operations of our consciousness in regard to our own ordinary praxis of knowledge formation and of its unfolding in successive phases. The principle of disclosure of our own experience of our basic potencies and processes is the condition for the possibility of an intimate understanding not only of knowledge formation but of all aspects of human formation as expounded in formation science.

As we shall see later in the discussion of the methodological category of "topic and event selection" this principle of in-touchness with our own formation experience gave rise to the requirement that the researcher start out from a personally experienced formation event.

Each of the basic phases of our knowledge formation orients us to a specific aspect of our object of cognition. We call this the form-cognitional direction of our consciousness to an aspect of an object in our field of formative consciousness.

These form-cognitional operations in the field are performed by what we have identified in earlier volumes as the subjective intrasphere of our field. The intrasphere is distinguished from the other spheres by its capacity for self-awareness. The intrasphere not only receives and gives form to knowledge, it is somehow aware that it is doing so. Hence these formative operations of cognition not only make available to our subjective intrasphere the objective forms in the field; they also enhance simultaneously in the same act our awareness of our intrasphere as formative. In other words, all disclosure of objects of cognition implies some self-disclosure.

Formation science thus distinguishes intraspheric from outer-spheric objects of knowledge. To know a house or a rock is different from knowing an inner thought or image or from knowing oneself implicitly as knowing a house or a rock.

While both kinds of objects appear in the formation field that we are, the type of directed attention we can give to each of them is not the same. The forms we objectify in the outer spheres are attended to, apprehended, and appraised by the intrasphere. The intrasphere is implicitly aware of itself as attending, apprehending, appraising, and affirming forms in the outer spheres. Yet simultaneously it can and does attend to what appears in these outer spheres of the field of its formative consciousness. While I am typing this Introduction, I am focally concentrating on my typing, yet at the same time I am indirectly aware that I am the one who is giving form to my typescript.

Awareness of our intrasphere as form receptive and form productive is thus not a separate operation explicitly and deliberately added to our forming attention to the outer appearances in our field of formative consciousness. Outer form reception and donation implies inevitably some awareness of our intrasphere as formative. This spontaneous self-awareness is a specific type of knowledge formation distinct from that of outer knowledge formation. This awareness of intraspheric presence is not acquired by a looking into ourselves in the same way that we direct our focal attention at outer-spheric forms. For one thing, we cannot give objective form to our forming consciousness as such and as a whole, as we can do for outer forms. I can objectify a tree or a car as a whole. This objectivation implies a distancing from these forms. I cannot in the same way distance myself wholly from my own consciousness as such, for I am identified with my consciousness. I can only give objective form to what happens in my intraspheric consciousness. Only in this sense can we make the intraspheric subject and its operations into a "subject-object" of our knowing. In this Introduction, for instance, we give objective form to those basic intraspheric motions that initiate, deepen, and expand human knowledge.

Successive Motions of Knowledge Formation

Let us look in this light at the successive motions of knowledge formation mentioned earlier.

First, the motion of attending: without any implicit or explicit selection of some object of attention, no formation of knowledge is possible. Following our sustained attending to some object is the motion of apprehending it. Apprehending is a movement of sensate and rational cognitive presence to the object we selected for attention. It seeks to answer the question: What is the form I am attending to? This movement of apprehending is primarily an operation of active form reception. We strive to receive knowledge about the form that is the object of our attending. It results in an apprehension or insight into that to which we are attending.

This is followed by the three main motions of appraising, namely, affinitive, affective, and argumentative appraising. We shall see that these operations become in our science motions of evaluating the formative meaning of what we are apprehending. We seek for an answer to the question emerging in our distinctively human mind: What is the formative significance of our apprehensions for our unfolding life within its field? This search for formative meaning may be initially guided by an inherent sense of congeniality or of "affinity" to what we apprehend and by the affects or feelings which this experience of affinity evokes. However, our final affirmation or nonaffirmation of what we apprehend depends on argumentative deliberation or rational appraisal of the consonance or dissonance of our affinitive and affective appraisals. Such appraisal gives rise to a knowledge of various possible courses of formative presence and action. Even if one of them seems the most desirable one, we are still relatively free to affirm or reject this appreciative apprehension in a definite judgment. Hence the necessity to close the operation of appraising argumentation with the formative motion of affirmation by which we affirm or deny in a decisive judgment one or more of the cognitive appraisals we have made.

Finally, we need the motion of formative application. It is a response to our need to know how to implement in life by communication and execution what we have disclosed in appreciative apprehending. This movement toward communication and execution of what we have affirmed as formatively consonant operates also as an added test of the truth of the formative knowledge we acquired through the other operations of our mind.

The motions of knowledge formation described so far are accompanied, moreover, by those of dialogical consultation, translation, transposition, and integration. These are rooted in the interformational quality of the human life-form. Humans do not act and think in isolation. They are social forms of life. This social characteristic implies that they influence one another in any formation they give to life and world. This applies also to knowledge formation. People consult implicitly with one another when they make up their mind in the ordinary course of living. In science this implicit consultation becomes explicit and methodical. In our science it gives rise to the methodical categories of consultation, translation, transposition, and integration: consultation of other sources of formation knowledge insofar as they may disclose something about the object to which we attend; translation of their relevant insights into the language of the science; transposition of such translated findings into its theoretical frame of reference and therewith their integration in its system of scientific knowledge about formation.

In the everyday course of living these basic movements of cognition formation may remain implicit. Yet when we give persistent attention, apprehension, and appraisal to our various everyday processes of knowing it becomes evident to us that these successive phases are somehow operative in all of us.

Only when we have grasped this universal potency for cognition formation in its successive phases can we appraise the scientific particularization of these processes in the methodical categories of formation science. Insight into the rootedness of these methodical categories in a universal formation anthropology can facilitate also for specialists in other sciences the adaptation of these methodical approaches to their own research.

As in the first three volumes of this series, the content of this volume cannot be assimilated without personal engagement and effort. We must familiarize ourselves with the metalanguage of a new science. This is a requirement of every discipline. It is more demanding, however, when a new science has to be mastered. Few of its lingual forms are assimiliated yet in the general language of educated people as is often the case with the terms of older disciplines such as medicine, physics, philosophy, psychology, pedagogy, sociology, or the numerous theologies of various religions or their denominations.

An added requirement for the personal mastery of a human science is that we must trace back in our own consciousness the basic intraspheric operations that underlie the particular elaboration of its methodical categories. Given this steady recourse to the experience of our own cognition as well as our life formation, we are confident that this book will offer all who study it much food for thought.

CHAPTER 1

Formation Science as a Human Science

T he rise of science is a crucial event in our history. It enabled people to shape life and world in a whole new fashion. Scientific and technical progress is changing humanity in dramatic ways through new modes of labor, leisure, health care, telecommunication, transportation, and habitation.

Among the sciences, those called *human* are concerned with the typically human aspects of our unfolding lives. One of these is formation science. It differs from the other sciences in its focus on distinctively human emergence. It looks on our life as a whole—not only from the viewpoint of typically human characteristics we share with other forms of life and matter, but from the distinctive quality we find only in people.

All aspects of life are considered in this light of distinctive humanness. Many of them have been explored by other sciences. Some have been the object of reflection by the various traditions of human formation that emerged over the centuries. Others are described by the humanities and the arts in general. Formation science pays attention to their findings. It consults them as auxiliary sources.

To make clear that formation science is indeed a science, we must first ask ourselves what science is. Then another question emerges: What are human sciences and what is the place of formation science among them?

Scientific Disposition

Science emerges in human history. There must be a predisposition in the human race that has led to this emergence. A predisposition of curiosity, of longing to know, of discovering truth has been alive in humanity as far back as we can trace its history. This predisposition to gain knowledge became a well-organized disposition. People began gradually to develop methods that would guarantee a higher probability that their ways of knowing would correspond with reality.

1

In this way the scientific disposition was born. Certain people, called scientists, develop this disposition to a high degree. They specialize in the scientific investigation of one or another aspect of reality. They do this not in isolation but together with others who share the same interest.

Our First Way of Knowing

Evidently science is not our first way of knowing. Scientists, like all of us, learn about reality first of all by means of everyday experience. Our first knowledge is prescientific. It is lived rather than thought.

Scientific knowledge is secondary. It emerges from this first way of knowing. Without an everyday perception of the stars, astronomy would never have been born. If we had not met with animals and plants, biology would never have been initiated. Our experiences with the bodies of people and animals led to anatomy. Problems we encountered in daily life gave rise to psychotherapy and its theoretical systems of explanation. Everyday questions of exchange of property made us reflect on the right answers. Gradually we started a science of economy.

Scientific knowledge does not mean the end of prescientific cognition. New questions are raised constantly by everyday experience. Science can pick up these questions and approach them from its theoretical perspective. The theoretical considerations of science go beyond this initial experience. Everyday experience is the point of departure and by no means the ultimate or exclusive or fully accurate source of scientific knowledge. But this starting point is unavoidable. Without prescientific knowledge there would be no scientific knowledge.

While in some measure this process is true for all science, it is more obvious in the human sciences, for their object of study is human life itself. Let me illustrate this point for the science of formation.

It would be impossible to grasp fully what we mean in scientific statements about distinctively human life if we could not relate them to original experiences. How could we fully understand, for instance, theories about love and anger if we had never experienced these emotions?

Like all human sciences, that of formation necessarily develops theoretical propositions. Such formal enunciations do not erase or distort the experience to which they point; otherwise, this science would become irrelevant to life. Hence students immerse themselves in concrete human experience, in this case, the experience of formation.

Research in this field must preserve an intimate relationship with concrete human formation. At the same time scientific research presupposes some distancing from formation as it actually happens; otherwise, no critical appraisal would be possible. We would be at the mercy of popular opinions that may be true or false. Research in our science takes as its point of departure an actual formation event. After obtaining our scientific results, we must constantly ask ourselves whether our theories are still in touch with the basic truth disclosed in our original experience.

Experiential and Theoretical Apprehension: Appraisal Level

Formation scientists apprehend and appraise what is going on within people's everyday field. Only on the basis of this appraisal can our intellect devise concepts that are relevant to the explanation of the events we have experienced.

Formation scientists work, therefore, on two levels: the experiential and the theoretical. So long as one is involved in the first or experiential phase of this science, one can only disclose the immediate apprehension and appraisal of events by means of methodic description. We can, for example, describe in common words what "feeling understood" means for a significant number of people in our culture. Even in this phase, some kind of confirmation of our description by others is mandatory. We should ask fellow researchers to interrogate their own spontaneous awareness of feeling really understood by a person. Their disclosures should be in dialogue with our tentative descriptions about our personal experience. Then we can together strive to develop a first topography of the event under study. We may choose also to expand this interrogation to statistically significant samples of a population.

In the second phase of research, this tentative description may be confirmed, complemented, or corrected by theoretical reflection in accordance with the scientific methodology to be discussed in more detail in later chapters of this volume.

Prescientific methodic disclosure is thus the link between our spontaneous awareness and scientific knowledge.

Scientists who lose touch with their experience of life may be tempted to give priority to scientific methodology. They may omit the prescientific, methodic disclosure of their own and others' experience that precedes an elaboration of theoretical concepts and constructs. Theoretical preconceptions may conceal relevant facets of human formation awaiting exploration. Hence, scientific methodological refinements should not preoccupy scientists at the expense of their starting with the events themselves.

An exclusive preoccupation with scientific methodology breeds a certain sterility, which may distort rather than disclose a given event.

Primary Disclosure Method of Formation Science

This caution against the premature introduction of scientific methodology does not mean that researchers in the pretheoretical phase of their research should approach formative incidents without any kind of methodology.

Prescientific methodology is characterized by its aim to disclose the basic structure and meaning of the occurrence itself. Scientists must try to describe their own apprehension and appraisal of the event. We call this the phase of *primary methodic disclosure.*

At this pretheoretical level, we preclude as much as possible the use of scientific concepts, constructs, methods, and theories. Our immediate task is to make explicit the structure of what is originally given. This first phase provides a first conceptual clarification.

Formation is always prior to any scientific information or theory *about* formation. Formation theory itself, to say nothing of the theories and information offered by auxiliary sciences, can never provide in and by itself a trustworthy point of departure. These theories are always secondary to pretheoretical disclosure.

Formation scientists should not preoccupy themselves exclusively with secondary scientific theories and information; if they do, they will rarely, if ever, arrive at full understanding of events as they appear in daily life. Having lost access to concrete life, they may become preoccupied with endless refinements of scientific methodology. Yet no refinement of method in the second phase of research can make up for a lack of methodical disclosure in the first.

What actually results is an increase in knowledge of the subtleties of theories and methodologies and a decrease in understanding of human formation as it occurs concretely.

Human Life as an Embodied Formative Presence in Its Field

To grasp how science is rooted in the human form of life, we must reflect on the way we are in our field of presence and action. We move in nature, culture, and society as a disclosing formative presence. In the act of disclosure we receive form and become aware of the kind of form we give to our surroundings. Now we must ask ourselves *how* we are present in our environment *as* a disclosure of directives that will guide our life?

At this point we need to speak not only of *primary methodic disclosure* but also of *primordial spontaneous disclosure.*

We are always present to our environment in and through our body. Our dispositions become effective only through embodiment. We are neither a disembodied spirit nor a mechanical organism. We are a living unity, a body permeated by spirit. Because we are embodied spirits, we experience ourselves as a concrete formative presence in a sense-perceptible field. The body is lived as that in, with, and through which we receive and give form within a field of formation.

Our body is our spontaneous entrance as human spirit into all that surrounds us. We could not perceive anything without this bridge that is our body. Our body makes things available to us.

Bodily Formative Presence Is Limited Presence

The fact that we are a bodily presence of disclosure has various implications, the first being this: the presence of human life is always *limited.* Hence the range of what we can disclose is limited, too. This is true of all three modes of disclosure: the prescientific spontaneous, the prescientific methodical, and the scientific-methodical.

The bodily character of our life limits our position. We cannot see and touch at once everything that is visible and touchable. What we perceive depends in part on the position of our body. When we see some form from the back, we cannot simultaneously perceive its front. The various positions we take give rise to various limited visions.

Our bodily presence has many modalities, the main ones being seeing, touching, hearing, smelling, and tasting. We cannot perceive all facets of an object with all of our sense modalities at the same time or with the same intensity. Each bodily modality discloses a different facet.

For example, when we look at people, we apprehend primarily other facets than those perceived when we hear, touch, or smell them. We say primarily, for by a kind of "interformative synesthesia" the other facets may be at least prefocally present to us via our memory, imagination, and anticipation. In looking at the fine texture of a silk scarf, we may be prefocally aware of its soft, tactile qualities. When our fingers feel the soft, smooth folds of this scarf in the darkness, we sense prefocally that it will not appear to our eyes in daylight as heavy or rough. The quality of our experience, and therefore the disclosure of what a silk scarf is like, depends on the modality of our presence.

We may attempt to transcend the limitations of a restricted bodily position and a single sense modality. We may, for example, move around persons. We try to perceive them from all sides. We may attempt to be present to them through all of our sensate modalities. We may touch, smell, see, and hear them. We may ask ourselves how they feel about their movements, about what they attempt to communicate by their actions. In this way, we try to understand them more fully.

Even this more well-rounded approach will never result in a complete, immediate knowledge of such people in action. Sense knowledge no matter how comprehensive cannot escape bodily limitation. By shifting positions we can obtain knowledge by a variety of altered perspectives. Even so, an assemblage, montage, or aggregate of these sense perspectives will lead to a knowledge that will remain fundamentally fragmentary. It will retain the character of a collection of partial sense perceptions. It will not provide by itself alone an immediate, integral sense knowledge of all the facets of the object we observe. For sense knowledge is the result of various bodily positions and sense modalities, and this very bodily mode compels us to perceive objects in always limited ways.

Limitation of Thought by the Limitations of Bodily Sensation

The limitation of sense knowledge is evident. But is thought also affected by this limitation?

Thought is coformed by sense perception. We may think, for example, about the meaning of the gestures of people. Such thought is coformed by our perception of their gestures. Without it we would not even know about their bodily expressions. Consequently, our thinking approach is fragmentary. We cannot maintain all possible viewpoints in thought at the same time and with the same intensity. Our knowledge is limited by the finiteness of our corporeal presence.

Implications for the Scientific Disposition

This limitation has far-reaching implications for the development of the basic scientific disposition of humanity. It explains first of all the differentiation of this disposition into many scientific postures giving rise to many scientific disciplines. Furthermore, the same condition causes such specific scientific dispositions to differentiate themselves again and again in subdifferentiated areas within the same field. This breakdown gives rise in turn to many fields, schools, and specializations within each science itself. Hence each scientific enterprise will be marked by increasing differentiation. Each science and each of its subdifferentiations is defined by its own limited perspective.

The same insight provides the rationale for the establishment of a comprehensive integrational science of distinctively human formation. Ours is an attempt to integrate, among other things, the formationally relevant insights and findings of the arts and sciences and their subdifferentiations. This critical integration is meant to serve the integral formation of human life within its field of presence and action.

Bodiliness and Human Interformation

There is another implication of the fact of our bodiliness, namely, it is a necessary condition for the possibility of interformation with others. Interformation in turn is a condition for the possibility of the emergence of science as a social enterprise.

Our sensate life enables us to meet people. They, too, disclose objects of knowledge in the field we share. They communicate such disclosures by perceptible oral, written, and other expressive signs. We respond to these communications. In this way we constantly teach one another. In some measure the communications of others enhance our knowledge and our communications enhance theirs.

Certain persons may decide to join one another as scientists. They commit themselves to a life of collaborative disclosure of a certain aspect of reality. They select and delineate specific profiles for critical research. They agree also to be guided by a specialized language and by valid methods of critical inquiry. Such associations of specialized scientists tend to continue their investigations over generations, each one building on the disclosures and methodical refinements of their predecessors.

The social facet of our life is thus conditioned by our sensate presence to one another. Such presence is also the condition for the possibility of science as a collaborative endeavor. Formation science, for instance, emerges from an association of people committed to the study of distinctively human formation.

Prefocal and Focal Formation

People are spontaneously involved in the ongoing formation of their life. This formation implies form reception and form donation. Form reception discloses increasingly the myriad forms we encounter in our field. Form donation increasingly reforms this field.

Already, before we focus explicitly on certain significant events, they form us and we give form to them. Prefocally we attend to, apprehend, appraise, and affirm (or do not affirm) what happens in and around us. Prefocally we are familiar with events, things, people, and other forms of life as participants in our field. We may not focus on them explicitly. Yet it is only by focal reflection that we come to know certain aspects of them more fully. Such focusing enables us also to express our prefocal awareness in concepts and words.

In focal reflection we conceptualize our prefocal experiences. We focus our attention on a particular experience. In this reflection we become more distinctly aware of what is going on in our formation. Only now are we able to put our experiences into words.

Science is a methodical-critical mode of focal thematization. This means that we make an experience such as "feeling understood" a special theme for our focal attention and investigation in accordance with the demands of scientific methods. Like all focal modes, it presupposes prefocal modes of experience.

Not all focal modes of attention, however, are scientific. For example, we may explicitly think about a personal problem. We also share with people around us many prescientific focal modes of everyday apprehension and appraisal. For example, we may share a certain dress code with people who work or live with us in the same community. We maintain certain manners of eating within the same culture and may be focally aware of that. We call these the *common focal* modes of everday life.

Interaction between Prefocal, Common Focal, and Scientific Focal Formation

Our prefocal, common focal, and scientific focal modes of formation are interconnected. We can focus in a common way or in a scientific way on what we have apprehended prefocally. For instance, after repeated traffic accidents on the same road curve we travel daily, we may discuss with others the dangers of this spot. We may realize that we were already implicitly aware of the hazards of driving there.

Science necessarily presupposes either prefocal or common focal apprehension, or both. Scientists are at least implicitly concerned with some facet of prescientific experience, even if they are no longer focally aware of this point of departure.

Scientific focusing places us at a certain distance from the particular facet of the field we are researching. After such focal scientific attention, however, we may resume our prefocal and common focal interaction with our everyday ambience.

For example, we study scientifically certain facets of our spontaneous everyday interaction. Let us say we describe and analyze the formative and deformative facets of parental dealings with children. We can do so by utilizing the theoretical concepts and constructs of our own science and by consulting those of other sciences. After this scientific work is complete, we can then resume within the family our prefocal mode of interaction with our children. Ideally, this spontaneous interformation should be enriched and deepened in the course of time by periods of focal scientific study. Its findings should gradually sink into our prefocal and common focal formation.

For example, in everyday interformation with adolescents in a family, parents may sense prefocally their increasing resistance to admonition. Spontaneously they may respond with anxious concern. Later, in a moment of reflection, they may focus in a prescientific fashion on what is going on. They realize that something happened to their adolescent children that makes them different from when they were preadolescents. They are not quite sure how to respond more effectively now. Hence they may turn to formation science for some guidance.

Formation scientists have focused *scientifically* on this problem in relation to distinctively human life directives. It is one of the themes of their research. They have also critically consulted available theories and data from arts, sciences, and formation traditions. They have asked themselves from a transcendent point of view what such data can teach us about the most effective response to rebellious adolescents. Communication of the resulting insights to parents may help them to complement their own appraisal of the situation. Such expansion of insight may seem at first not wholly integrated into their daily spontaneous response and therefore somewhat artificial. Gradually, however, it may sink into the domain of spontaneous prefocal interformation with their children.

We could neither do our research well nor advise parents wisely without first understanding the problems between parents and adolescents as they offer themselves to prefocal and common focal knowledge.

Science as Focal Theorizing

Formation science thus implies a shift from prefocal and common focal formation to scientific formation. This does not mean that prescientific formation is without structure. A certain pretheoretical structuring of formation is evident, for instance, in the prescientific formation programs developed in probably all formation traditions. Such structuring can be elevated to scientific theorizing.

In the past this was rarely the case. Often missing were: the critical-rational requirements of data gathering from *all* relevant arts, sciences, and formation traditions; the explicit-systematic definition of terms that transcend the popular, confusing connotations of common language; the integration and mutual delineation of concepts and constructs in a coherent basic framework of a more general probability; the critical appraisal of the theoretical concepts by methods agreed upon by the scientific community; the testing of the findings in a sufficiently wide variety of formation settings; and the articulation of the theory, if desirable, in terms of one's own formation tradition by critical methods of articulation research accepted by fellow researchers engaged in the same endeavor.

Prescientific Structuring of Formation

The prescientific structuring of formation tries to order prefocally or in a common focal way a situation with which one is directly faced. The primary intention of prescientific structuring is not so much to gain insight in the more general meaning, dynamics, and conditions of formation. Rather, we want to grasp what is of immediate, practical relevance to our problems.

Prescientific structuring is, therefore, immediate-practical; scientific structuring is proximate-practical; philosophical-theological structuring can be ultimate-practical.

Prescientific structuring of formation should never be underestimated. Many prescientific intuitions and sentiments may disclose or partially hide profound insights into the problems at hand. Many prescientific formation projects are based on real life experience. They may contain an immediately practical wisdom. This wisdom of life should not be dismissed arbitrarily but critically examined. We will discover that many formation projects or principles imply valuable suggestions for scientific theory. They ventured already beyond the realm of mere hearsay, custom, spontaneous experience, sentiment, and intuition. Moreover, such programs, projects, and principles often embody the ultimate directives of the faith tradition to which their initiators are committed. These directives should be respected, even if science may have to question some particular concretization of the ultimates. The ultimates as such are the proper object of the philosophical-theological sciences, not of formation science.

We should also be aware that such practical structuring contains an implicit record of prescientific experiences. As we have seen, science and its theorizing must take its starting point from such prescientific awareness. Hence we should not neglect this source of information about prescientific experience and practice in the area of formation.

Prescientific Formation Structures in Uniform and Pluriform Formation Fields

Prescientific formation structures seem most effective and least contested in a uniform formation field. This is a field dominated by one underlying formation tradition, such as the Jewish, Christian, Buddhist, Hindu, Islamic, or tribal. Such dominance determines to a high degree the features of the field to which its participants will be exposed. Hence potential problems are limited. They can usually be met by most people on basis of solutions proposed and practiced by the dominating tradition over many generations.

Prescientific formation structures seem, however, less effective in pluriform formation fields. This type of field is coformed by a variety of traditions and by arts and sciences that exercise directly or indirectly an influence on all their participants. All fields tend to become pluriform at this moment of history. There are many reasons why traditional prescientific structures may be less effective in this new pluralistic situation. Let us mention only a few.

Contemporary participants in a pluriform field are liable to hear about other life directives not sufficiently considered in the prescientific structures of their own tradition. This may undermine their trust in these structures. The pluriform field, moreover, evokes questions and problems that have not been faced by the prescientific traditions. They may have covered the main problems when the field was uniformly dominated by one tradition. But these solutions do not suffice in the new pluriform situation. Contributions of the sciences relevant to formation, learned in the schools and via the media, make participants aware of the possible insufficiency of some of the traditional prescientific life directives.

The nature of pluriformity evokes another question: Can we find formation directives that are valid for all people regardless of differences in their faith and form traditions? Such a question is usually not raised in a uniform field dominated by the same tradition. For example, the uniform field of the Soviet Union, bound by a socialist faith and form tradition, does not form people sufficiently in concern for individual rights. When they come in touch, however, with pluriform societies, they may begin to question if respect for individual development should not complement social concern as another directive valid for all people.

Finally, participants in a pluriform society are usually already exposed to pluriform influences before they are fully formed by the prescientific directives of their own faith and form tradition. Children who adhere to a Christian tradition may already have imbibed a secular profit motive as ultimate before they have assimilated well the Christian view.

Hence we see the necessity to cope with formation questions and problems evoked by such often popularized views of arts, sciences, and non-adhered-to form traditions. They cannot be satisfactorily answered by merely prescientific considerations. For these do not take critically into account the formation questions raised by the influences of people adhering to different faith and form traditions and nourished daily by the popularizations of sciences, arts, and humanities.

Lasting Necessity of Prescientific Formation

The necessity of scientific theory does not make superfluous the prefocal and common focal wisdom of formation. For example, parents in an emergency may need compliance from moody adolescents. They have no time to consult a textbook in formation science. Their immediate need mobilizes their appraisal of the situation. They recall spontaneously their own and other's *past* dealings with difficult adolescents. On this basis they try the best they can to obtain the compliance required within the next moment of the crisis. Before they know it focally, they may find themselves already engaged in formative functioning that placates their moody offspring.

Scientific insight by itself alone is thus less effective in situations that demand an immediate response. The reason is that scientific reflection takes us out of the concrete situation. We confine our attention to only the facets that are the object of our research. We appraise the situation from a specific perspective and with the categories of science. This focus compels us to leave out other aspects of a situation as it appears in everyday life. When we have to respond effectively to an immediate situation, we must take into account all facets that are relevant to our practical performance. For instance, only a person who has experiential contact with personnel demoralized by administrative mistakes and who knows them in their uniqueness may be able to deal wisely with their resentment while taking into account some relevant suggestions of formation science he or she then adapts uniquely to the situation.

Abstractions of Formation Science

Our research aims at the identification of generalizable facets of formation. We gradually abstract these from any individual concrete human life uniquely operating in its field. We are not concerned with the particular worries, hopes, dreams, and loves of this unique person. We detach from his or her situation only those facets which are relevant to our study of more general directives. In daily life, however, where we interform immediately with our spouse, children, friends, and colleagues we are spontaneously open to many other aspects. It is impossible to abstract from them and still do justice to the immediate demands of a unique situation in its totality here and now. This is one of the reasons why formation counselors do not usually work with members of their own family. It is almost impossible for them to shift from their daily involvement with them to a more detached scientific appraisal of their problems.

As we shall see in later chapters on the methodology of the science, researchers are advised to start out from a formation event, to describe it first concretely, but then to identify its general structures and dynamics. This is a first step from prefocal or common focal formation insight to scientific focal distancing.

CHAPTER 2

New Standpoint of Formation Science

A s scientists we adopt an entirely new standpoint with regard to formation. This shift grants us a specific viewpoint, which in turn produces a specific type of comprehension. By it formation events are apprehended and appraised as sources of insight into the general conditions of distinctively human formation, or of a common formation field, or of a particular segment of the population.

This shift in comprehension moves from prescientific understanding to scientific explanation. Necessary for this shift is the art of detaching more general facets of formation from their natural context. They are no longer conceived in relation to a particular event as personally lived by one individual. They are now articulated in dialogical interaction with patterns of the field shared with others.

The general insights thus disclosed become either theoretical concepts or constructs within a theory of formation. As such they are related to other concepts and constructs within the same theory. They are thus no longer uniquely intertwined with a concretely lived situation. Rather, such general facets are now inserted as concepts and constructs in a theoretical field developed by formation scientists as a universe of scientific discourse.

The scientific focal mode, as we have seen in chapter 1, differs greatly from either the prefocal or common focal mode. The scientific mode as such cannot function as an implicit, spontaneous guide for immediate implementation in a concrete situation. It provides only a proximate direction and general rules to be particularized in each unique ambience.

A concrete situation is brimming with unique meanings. As scientists, however, we select only certain generalizable facets as the focus of investigation, yet we relate them dialogically to all other relevant aspects of the contextual situation. This selection gives rise to a specific well-organized system of apprehensions and appraisals.

We also restrict our apprehension by asking only certain well-defined questions. The possible replies of concrete happenings to these questions are limited by the specificity of the questions asked. Consequently the answers of the event will disclose only certain of its generalizable facets. Finally, all these specific answers together will be gradually integrated within a specific system of meaning, a comprehensive theory, a body of scientific truth, a science, in this case, a formation science.

Analogous Application to All Sciences and Their Unique Languages

The same principles apply analogously to all sciences. No science can disclose everything in the universe. The limited realm it can disclose is defined by the focus of the science concerned. Hence every science creates its own universe of discourse by means of its own language. This language is necessarily different from that of any other science. It also differs from our common, everyday language. The differences among the sciences and among their unique languages are thus based on the differences among the questions they ask and among the profiles of reality they disclose. Hence a complete conformity in formal object, method, language, or results of the sciences is in principle impossible. Impossible too is a complete conformity between scientific languages and the languages of everyday popular intercourse.

Fundamentally different questions lead to fundamentally different answers or systems of meaning that cannot be added together. For the same reason, it is impossible to reduce one scientific system and its unique language to another: for example, political science to physiology; biology to physics; formation science to theology or psychology.

If the reduction of one science to another still seems possible, that science has not yet found its own focus or has not yet sufficiently developed its own language. Another possibility may be, of course, that it has abandoned its own quest or its search for its own language. In such a case, it is not yet a specific science in its own right with its own theoretical system, its own methodology and terminology.

Translation and Transposition versus Blind Indentification

The attempt to reduce one science to another should be clearly distinguished from translation and transposition. The findings of one science can be translated into the language of another. Such findings may be relevant to the translating science. Formation science, for instance, because of its integrative nature, translates findings of other sciences into its own scientific idiom. During this translation or immediately after, it integrates such translated contributions by a process of transposition in its own theoretical system, correcting, complementing, and reforming them in light of its own formal object. All sciences today consult findings of other sciences when relevant to some research of their own. Such consultations make a science by no means *interdisciplinary* but merely *discipline related* as formation science is.

Implications for the Science of Formation

As formation scientists we confine our attention to generalizable facets of distinctively human formation. This reflective theoretical presence implies that we assume a specific stance. Doing so in a critical methodical way, we lay the foundations of a specific science, in this case, the science of distinctively human formation which is also called at times foundational formative spirituality. The term *foundational* in this context refers to the transcultural and transdenominational basis of this human spirituality. The precise delineation of this domain of research from any other area of inquiry is a first step in the development of a science.

Formation science, like every other science, differentiates its domain of research in subdomains. These differentiations are constituted by the various perspectives which one takes in regard to the common object pole of the science. They imply, in short, a differentiation of the common perspective. For example, formation science differentiates itself in such subdomains as formation dynamics and phases; formation counseling; preformation, intra-formation, inter-formation, and extraformation; sociohistorical, vital, functional, and transcendent formation; form traditional articulation, and so on.

Every new event that offers itself for scientific consideration is examined to the degree that it conforms to the normative object-coherence of formation science. For example, the sociohistorical structure of the field is examined only to the degree that it is relevant for distinctively human formation. If we choose, for instance, to complement our research in formation science with consultation of an auxiliary science, let us say sociology, then we have to translate its related formational implications from the language of sociology into that of formation science and to transpose them in our theoretical frame of reference. Beyond this, the study of sociohistorical structures of the field is left to sociology and other disciplines, such as political science and cultural anthropology.

Similarly, Christian, Jewish, or Buddhist religious populations may be studied insofar as their faith and form traditions affect the concrete life formation of their members and indirectly that of others. The theological language of these populations, if it points to concrete aspects of their formation, is translated into the language of our science. Beyond this, the faith tradition as such remains the domain of theology and such sciences as comparative religion, history of religions, and religious education.

Criteria of Selection of a Formal Object Pole of a Science

As scientists, we restrict ourselves necessarily to one of many possible viewpoints which emerge in our encounter with reality. It is scientists who decide to prefer one facet of the field to other facets as the focus of their investigation.

There are many factors involved in the selection of a scientific viewpoint, such as an implicit or explicit philosophy; the zeitgeist as related to the sociohistorical pulsations; practical needs manifested in society; the temperament and intellectual disposition of the scientist; social pressures, and the cultural language with its built-in preference for certain object poles, values, and goals.

Object Pole Selection as Possible Beginning of a Science

The selection of an object pole as a focus of investigation is only the beginning of a science. It must be followed by a careful delineation of the area of inquiry. Such delineation continues during the development of the science. Usually it is not clear initially what the exact aims and proper methods of a specific science are.

A science is fully formed in its own right when its scientists have disclosed to their own critical satisfaction which formal object, corresponding methodology, and language make their science different from other sciences and their languages. As long as this delineation of object, method, and language is not yet achieved by a science, there is always the danger that its representatives may exceed the limits of their proper interest, language, and competence.

If a science does not clearly comprehend its own proper mode of questioning and using language, it will remain unaware of its own limits. Consequently it may become involved in questions and language habits that do not pertain to its own primary focus. These lie outside its competence and lingual tools. This happens, for example, when theologians who can be experts in *ultimate* questions of spiritual formation within their own tradition attempt to tell empirical scientists in detail all proximate-practical directives for the basic spiritual formation of all people of all faiths and persuasions.

Relationships among the Sciences

Representatives of a new science may not yet be clear about the object pole, method, and language of their science. They may be tempted to borrow the methods and language of an older successful science. They may overlook the fact that any other science discloses a quite different profile of reality. We do not refer merely to being enlightened by the methods and language of other sciences or the attempt to adapt them by translation and transposition to one's own domain of exploration. This is commendable. Nor do we refer to the obvious fact that research in our own domain can benefit from information obtained by other sciences.

We have in mind the situation in which the insecure representatives of a young science allow themselves to be seduced by the objectives, methodology, and language of an established older prestigious science. They may momentarily lose sight of the formal object of their own scientific enterprise. Early physicists, for example, were at times philosophers of nature; alchemists became mythologists; psychologists sometime slipped into mere physiology or biology; formation scientists may slip into theology, psychology, or education.

There is nothing blameworthy about showing interest in another area of scientific investigation. We should be clearly aware, however, that we are leaving our own field of expertise. We should make it explicit to ourselves and to others that we are no longer speaking as, say, acknowledged physicists, psychologists, theologians, or formation scientists. We may otherwise mistakenly imagine that we are still speaking as experts in our own field while we are in fact disclosing other philosophical, mythological, physiological, theological, or psychological facets of the field. Worse than this, we may use other metalanguages uncritically as if they were our own. However, what we may disclose as amateurs in these other fields is not necessarily useless or invalid. For example, formation scientists may dabble in systematic theology of some denomination as a hobby. They may even make some contribution, but they should not too easily claim to be expert in this foreign field.

Briefly, when we shift to another science and its metalanguage, we should not pretend that we are disclosing a distinctively human, empirical facet of formation in its dialogically articulated totality. Such pretense would delay the development of formation science itself. It would obscure its status as a science in its own right with its own object and language, irreducible to any other discipline. We should persevere in the endeavor to establish the identity of our own science. We must patiently bear with the ambiguities, uncertainties, and awkward formulations of new beginnings. These cannot be avoided when humanity embarks on a new adventure of exploration.

It is in the definition of its own formal object and in the development of its own metalanguage that a science explicitly expresses its own unique apprehension of a selected profile of investigation and its proper mode of questioning reality. By gradually disclosing and defining its own limits, formation science will avoid trespassing on the proper object of another science, such as theology, philosophy, psychology, or education. Respect for these limits will prevent us from dissipating our talents and energies in areas which do not pertain to our area of inquiry under the pretense that we are doing formation science.

Criteria of Science

Formation science, like all sciences, we repeat, is rooted in human life itself. Science is not merely or primarily a theory existing only in books, graphs, and manuscripts that stand outside the scientists themselves. It is a human disposition. Records of science are unthinkable without people composing them on the basis of critical presence to the object of their science.

Science is research and theory. Each aspect is related to the twofold human formation potency. Scientific *research* is rooted in the *form receptive*; scientific *theorizing* in the *form productive* aspect of this potency.

The form receptive potency enables us to study the formation of life and world by receptive openness to what can be known. One articulation of this receptivity is the scientific disposition for research.

Scientific theorizing and its communication and application are rooted in the form giving power of the same potency. This aspect enables us to give form, conceptually, verbally, and practically to what is disclosed to us in our receptivity. Science is thus not only a mode of form reception but also one of form donation. Human life, as scientifically disposed, seeks to give intelligible systematic form to the data received in research.

Science participates, therefore, in our basic formation dynamics. Accordingly, the scientific enterprise itself is dynamic. It manifests the continual change from current form to current form characteristic of human formation. The primary mark of science is thus its foundation in human life itself. What are some other characteristics that flow from this rootedness in human nature?

Critical-Methodical

Scientific form reception and donation are critical-methodical. Every human being receives and gives form to knowledge. However, our everyday collection of knowledge and its application is not critical-methodical in the strict sense. Our prescientific method approach is rarely raised to a systematic concern protected by critical safeguards and strict methodological cautions as it is in science.

Form receptivity becomes critical-methodical in science by devising correct research methods that can be repeated, refined, tested, and validated by fellow scientists.

Form donation becomes critical-methodical by a strictly logical structuring of theoretical explanations based on validated data, on the critical appraisal of the outcomes of logical reasoning, and on the exact formulation in the metalanguage of the science concerned. Scientists must, therefore, follow an increasingly coherent, consistent, and logical systematization of scientific theory. They must also strive for a metaformulation that lends itself to precise discourse and scientific validation.

The scientific disposition thus demands critical planning, systematic organization, and orderly execution of projects of validation. It requires a coherent unfolding of explanatory theories that are logically consistent and expressed in an appropriate, precise language unique to the science concerned. This enables one to transcend prescientific knowledge, which is often naive, inexact, and influenced by custom, myth, folklore, sociohistorical pulsations, and personal idiosyncrasies.

Explications of Assumptions

All sciences start out from certain assumptions that, more often than not, remain prefocal. Many scientists are not focally aware of the basic ideas about reality that underlie their own scientific approach. In the meantime these hidden presuppositions influence their procedures, conclusions, and formulations, and could possibly falsify them. Hence the importance of bringing them to focal awareness, of making them explicit. (For a consideration in depth of this topic, see my article "Assumptions in Psychology," in *Foundations of Personality Study: An Adrian van Kaam Reader.*)

The basic implicit assumptions may be of a philosophical or theological nature. To understand them well may necessitate a consultation of the discipline of philosophy or theology. Here we encounter a real difficulty. As stated earlier, the distinctive mark of all mature sciences is the establishment of their own language. This applies also to the disciplines of philosophy and theology. Therefore, it is necessary to translate and transpose propositions that seem relevant to the particular assumptions of a specific science or discipline from their unique language into that of the science in question.

Formation science, too, may consult philosophy as an auxiliary discipline. In the light of philosophy, it may examine its own implicit assumptions. In that case it selects what seems relevant, translating it into its own language.

If, beyond this procedure, formation scientists engage in the articulation of the findings of their science in terms of one or another religious faith and form tradition, they may use the theology of the religion concerned but only as an auxiliary discipline. In its light they probe the ultimate form directives of that theology, which should underlie, as assumptions, this specific articulation research. To do so they must reformulate such relevant propositions into the language of their own science.

We should note here that this is not the only use formation science may make of philosophies and theologies of different religions, denominations, and schools of philosophy. If certain propositions of these auxiliary disciplines seem relevant to the body of proximate form directives established by formation science, they are translated and transposed in its own language. If they then prove to be factually relevant, they will be transposed and integrated into the science's theoretical frame of reference.

Attachment and Detachment Rhythms in Science

In the third volume of this series we discussed the rhythm of attachment and detachment in human life from birth to death. The scientific disposition, as rooted in human life, shares in this characteristic. In chapter 1 of the present volume, we explained how scientific reflection necessarily takes its point of departure from prescientific involvement. This first involvement implied certain attachments to our spontaneous experiences. This is especially true for a human science like that of formation. It deals with our more immediate, distinctively human interwovenness with our field.

In this everyday engagement we have invested much dedication, feeling, energy, affection, and enthusiasm, perhaps during a considerable period of time. Subsequent attachments have given form to our life, yet the scientific mode of formation compels us to distance ourselves from these. When research and theoretical explanation force us to give up certain cherished opinions and customs, we can be faithful to science only by detaching ourselves from them, no matter how disconcerting this may be.

Because of the same human dynamics, we will become attached to the new apprehensions, appraisals, and so forth formed in us by scientific inquiry. Such attachments provide the drive and energy to expand and deepen these apprehensions as well as their implications and connections. Yet to remain true to scientific formation, we must be willing to distance ourselves again if new disclosures of our research compel us to do so. In short, we must detach ourselves from a current scientific view so as to be reattached to a wider vision.

The same attachment-detachment dynamic applies to the language of our science. We are naturally attached to the everyday, less precise and more malleable language that we have spoken since childhood. To enter into the metalanguage of any science makes us initially feel like children again. We feel, to use another comparison, like immigrants in a foreign country who have to learn a new language whose meaning they initially cannot fully understand. We may resent the precision scientific language demands because it is so unlike the free-floating common language whose meanings we can manipulate to suit our purposes and feelings. We need detachment to cope with the inner resistance we feel in the face of this humbling and disturbing experience. Once we are attached to the language of a science, we must again detach ourselves when this language is expanded, refined, and corrected under the pressure of new disclosures.

A similar detachment will be demanded whenever we shift to another science. Each science has its own language; otherwise it would not be a science in its own right, unmistakably distinguished from prescientific thought and parlance, and from other existing sciences.

Certain human sciences, formation science included, demand that its scientists, as practitioners, be bilingual. This means that they must be able to detach themselves enough from their metalanguage to translate some of its findings and insights back into the common language of the people whom they interview, teach, direct, or counsel. Doing that for some time, they may become attached to this popularization, to its appeal and applause. They may feel reluctant to return to the metalanguage, which by its very nature is always less popular. Nevertheless, it is only metalanguage that can *initially* expand the theory to realms not yet covered by common language. In the beginning popular parlance had not yet made available its own expressions for the new perspectives the scientist discloses. If it were otherwise, neither scientific research nor theory would be necessary.

Valid Form Generalization

The forms encountered in our field cannot be known by science in their uniqueness. Science knows only of forms and their facets insofar as they can be generalized. Formation scientists, for instance, start out from an event in its uniqueness. Their first description of that event, as rendered by their spontaneous apprehension, appraisal, and implicit prescientific explanation, is not yet generalizable. Hence it is not yet science. Only when they are able to identify facets or moments that have potentially a more general probability are they on the way to scientific explanation.

Formation science seeks the generalizable facets either of all distinctively human formation or of the formation of certain segments of a population. Only in this way can the science come to general propositions, which by definition abstract from the concrete and unique. Together they form an interconnected theoretical system or subsystem that can be applied with sufficient probablility to particular events, subsumed under these theoretical generalizations.

Formation science, like many other human sciences, thus begins with induction. This induction aims at a generalization of certain aspects of formation made by abstraction from particular events. Conversely, valid generalization of such facets enables us then to use the method of deduction. We can apply the generalized aspect of human formation to particular events that manifest a similar general facet.

Inspirational Generalization

This method does not seem to apply in exactly the same fashion to one subdivision of formation science: namely, the study of unique, exemplary lives that precisely in their uniqueness have influenced the formation of humanity. Examples would be the life of Christ, Buddha, Muhammad, Lincoln, Luther, Gandhi, Wesley, and the lives of heroes, saints, spiritual masters, or initiators of influential formation trends. The science of formation seeks what is generalizable, also in these unique lives. However, this kind of generalization is different from that which is sought in formation events.

Clearly the inspiring uniqueness of such exemplary formation journeys cannot be applied as such to others. Their generalization is of a different nature; their life has a general inspirational quality. Formation science can show that these lives in their uniqueness do have an inspirational influence on significant form traditions or formation segments of the population. Subsequently, they affect indirectly the formation journey of individuals who are committed to these same traditions or segments.

Something similar could be said of the significant form traditions studied by formation scientists. The Christian, Hindu, Buddhist, tribal religious, Islamic, humanistic, or Hellenic traditions like many others have influenced the formation journey of humanity. They have inspired also other form traditions that are not merely imitations of them. For example, Judaic messianism gave form uniquely to Judaism. The secular messianism of Karl Marx was influenced by Judaic messianism but by no means was it a literal imitation. Because of this generalized inspirational potential, formation scientists can scientifically examine the mode and measure of this influence on formation traditions and segments of populations.

CHAPTER 3

Scientific Dispositions

Scientific Obedience

In Volume 3 of this series, the disposition of obedience was highlighted as a main expression of our striving for consonance. The word obedience comes from the Latin *ob-audire*, meaning to listen attentively. It points to a disposition of listening carefully to what is really given, accompanied by a willingness to subordinate one's thoughts and actions to what is received in this receptivity.

The scientific disposition is rooted in human life, its dynamics and dispostitions. This applies also to the obedience dynamic. Science is valid only when its practitioners listen obediently to what is given in their scientific presence to the formal object of their science. They must be directed throughout their endeavors by this givenness, no matter what detachment it may demand in regard to cherished prescientific notions, sociohistorical pulsations, or outdated scientific theories. Scientific obedience is a disposition that belongs to the scholarly asceticism of scientists. It should permeate their scientific attention, apprehension, appraisal, and affirmation in regard to the epiphanies of reality in the cosmic or cultural ambience of humanity.

To remain obedient is more difficult where the human rather than the physical sciences are concerned. This is so because the appraisal by human sciences influences more directly the everyday life of the scientists themselves. It involves their families, friends, neighbors, and colleagues. In day-by-day prescientific dealings with influential events, listening to them is often distorted by cultural pulsations, vital pulsions, and inordinate ambitions. To become a critical listener to what is given may demand extraordinary effort on the part of scientists, sometimes almost heroic obedience to the truth, even if it renders them unpopular in everyday life.

Scientific Interformation

Volume 1 of the series on fundamental formation demonstrated that our life is always identifiable with a field. This field and its horizons encompass directives that have become formative for a unique human life. The formation field of a human being is not exclusively its own domain of interaction with reality. It is coformed by other influences, among them especially the impact of other people.

The effect of others on our life is not a one-way street. Our own formation affects them in turn. In countless ways we form each other, correcting, complementing, mutually enriching our particular one-sidedness. This most influential kind of coformation is called *personal interformation*. This term points to the relatively free and insightful formation that takes place continuously and mutually between people. It is essentially different from the coformation that happens between people and the cosmos, animals, plants, things, and events.

The scientific disposition, as we have seen, is an outflow of our basic humanness. Hence it also shares in this characteristic of interformation between persons. Specifically the critical-methodical approach, attachment and detachment, validation of generalization, obedience, and other marks of the scientific disposition to be discussed in what follows, are safeguarded and promoted by interformation. In fact, prescientific interformation becomes scientific when it takes the demands of these other marks into account in interformative interaction with fellow scientists. Free-flowing interformation in everyday life then becomes critically and methodically organized.

For instance, certain rules have been devised and enforced for scientific debate. Interformative critique of undue attachment to obsolete positions or to ambiguous language will be pointed out if it shows up in the papers of a fellow scientist. His or her paper is critiqued in accordance with established directives of scientific integrity. Premature generalizations are questioned. Deviation from strict obedience to what is given is soon detected. Popularization of scientific findings in the common or segmental idiom of people is scrutinized for its fidelity to the metalanguage in which these findings were first formulated. Without this critical-scientific interformation, the scientific enterprise would be unthinkable.

Horizontal and Vertical Scientific Interformation

Scientific interformation, like interformation in general, has two dimensions: horizontal and vertical. Horizontal interformation happens between contemporary scientists in academia, through scientific journals and publications, and at conventions. Vertical interformation is served by scholars, libraries, and publications enabling present-day scientists to interform with those of past generations. The vertical differs from the horizontal in that the scientists of the past can no longer actively interform with those of the present. Still there is, analogously speaking, some kind of interformation between them. Critical-methodical attention of scientists today may disclose implicit leads in former scientific findings that were unnoticed before. The scientist then lets the findings of the past give form in a new way to his or her insights and findings, which are subsequently recorded for posterity.

Scientific Transmission Potency

Interformation presupposes that we can in some way transmit to one another our experiences and reflections. Hence the transmission potency is as typically human as the interformation potency itself. Accordingly, scientific interformation implies the potency to transmit and subsequently to develop competence in the mode of transmission proper to the specific science in which one specializes with others.

There are many ways of transmission, for example, repetition of experiments in the laboratory; mathematical formulas, such as in nuclear physics, bodily signs, or computers. The main mode of scientific transmission, especially in the human sciences, remains the metalanguage developed for the science concerned.

The common or segmental language used in everyday formation fields covers only the apprehension and appraisal of life as it is lived from day to day. This language has been developed by past and present generations to transmit what people see and aspire to in their shared world.

Scientists, by contrast, reflect on what is not yet known by this common or segmental apprehension. Otherwise science would be a useless duplication of what people already know and express in daily life. Hence the language of everyday understanding cannot exactly cover what they see beyond the confines of a common or segmental understanding and explanation.

Moreover, science as a critical-methodical approach must in principle be detached from popular pulsations. It requires a precision of expression not found in everyday parlance. Common or segmental language has to be a pliable instrument, rich with ambiguities and connotations, always developing. Only such a language enables people to be sensitive and open, yet guarded and indirect when necessary. Common and seg-mental language must enable people to hide what they do not want to re-veal without appearing secretive; to highlight what they hope to empha-size without being too obvious. Such ambivalent language makes it possi-ble to spare each other's feelings while still communicating what seems necessary. People can be humorous without being offensive, convincing without being overwhelming. They can use words with multiple mean-ings. By means of them they can disclose feelings in such a fashion as to test the response of others and in time step back, claiming that they really meant something else. Without the ambiguities and connotations pecu-liar to common and segmental language, smooth and sensitive daily in-teraction would become impossible.

The precision of scientific terminology cannot be attained by such multilevel intercourse. Scientific parlance aims at precision; everyday parlance at smooth, flexible interaction. Scientific language serves the one-dimensionality of the logical mind; everyday language the full play of mind and heart. It takes into account whole ranges of feelings, partly hidden and partly revealed, as well as pre-, infra-, and transfocal conno-tations vaguely suggested at the border of focal verbalization. Everyday language is almost always a diplomatically contextual and referential language, hence its ambiguity.

The specialized language of science prevents indistinctness, obscurity, and confusion with other sciences and with the pliable, less distinct mean-ings of language as used in everyday communication. It enables scientists of one field to interform with those representing related fields, without endangering the identity of their own specialty. It provides a lingual-theoretical framework to integrate findings and insights from comple-mentary areas of inquiry through methods of critical-creative translation and transposition.

Scientific transmission potency thus means, first of all, that the science concerned develops a precisely defined theoretical language or a constel-lation of mathematical symbols that, without ambiguity, superfluous detail, or vague connotations, guards the interformative validation and elaboration of the words used by scientists involved in the same theoret-ical enterprise.

Second, this metalanguage or mathematical constellation must be such that it can be learned by competent initiates in the field or by other inter-ested people if they receive proper instruction, orally or in written form, and study carefully the terminology or mathematical symbols.

Finally, a number of scientists should be bilingual. This means that they should develop the ability to translate and transpose their metalanguage into the common or segmental language of the population.

Reformation Potency

The theory of formation stresses the openness of human life, its growth from current form to current form. This movement is characterized by progressive reformation. As an articulation of the human life-form, the scientific disposition must share in the same reformation potency. This dynamic assures that science does not become a closed system. Its ongoing development depends on our willingness to question the current form each science has attained at a given moment of its history.

The theory of formation also stresses the crucial role that imaginative anticipation plays in human life. This, too, finds an articulation in the scientific disposition. The reformation of scientific insight is served by prescientific anticipations of possible elaborations of the science. The source of such anticipations is the creative imagination of certain gifted theorists. Their tentative anticipations will be subjected in due course to interformative validation by fellow scientists in accordance with the techniques proper to their work. An outstanding example is the relativity theory created by the imaginative theorist Albert Einstein and increasingly validated by his fellow scientists.

The scientific disposition thus implies a readiness to reform any attained insight, formulation, or theoretical statement. Scientists should be ready to discard whatever form they have given to knowledge if it is no longer probable in the light of new disclosures.

No Absolute Relativity

Scientists are not compelled to assume that truth is absolutely relative. The formation dynamics of human life are rooted in an implicit faith that all formation is a search for the ultimate consonance or truth we cannot yet possess empirically. We grow from current form to current form on basis of partial disclosures of this truth. The scientific disposition participates in this dynamic via the disclosures that make science itself grow from current form to current form. Its tireless critical quest is sparked by the implicit faith that the fullness of consonance or truth will be increasingly approached via all kinds of sciences combined with other ways of cognition. Science tries increasingly to play its limited role within the concert of human ways of cognition. It contributes by its own small steps to the approximation of the ultimate consonance that continually attracts humans in their quest for knowledge.

Relevance to Formation Praxis

Human life is fundamentally a power for free form reception and donation. It is embodied and embodying. Science, too, participates in this basic orientation. Any embodiment of scientific insight is a kind of praxis. Embodiment is not a sudden event. It is a step-by-step process that leads gradually to increasing concretization.

For example, students of philosophy may embody the mental formation they receive into effective embodied dispositions that lead to a deeper understanding of life. The exercises they go through to attain this embodiment involve practical steps. Each science and discipline fosters its own style and process of praxis interpenetrated by theory. Scientific formation at this point begins to interact with prescientific practical formation.

While all sciences are in some way practically formative, there is a considerable difference between the practicality of the exact and the human sciences. Such exact sciences as physics, biochemistry, and anatomy are remotely or peripherally practical when considered from the viewpoint of either typically or distinctively human life. The human sciences are proximately practical. They are more directly related to either typically or distinctively human unfolding. Philosophical and theological disciplines are ultimately practical in relation to human existence. They provide us with ultimate principles for distinctively human living. These ultimates should penetrate the proximately practical directives of the human sciences.

Distinguished from scientific modes of praxis is the immediate practicality of everyday life which calls for the concretization of ultimate, remote, and proximate directives. These are gathered from arts, sciences, and numerous formation traditions directly or indirectly via the integrational science of formation. Each immediate applicaton is unique. Hence it cannot fall as such under any science. As we have seen, science deals only with facets that can be generalized into transindividual propositions. Such propositions should be equally probable for all the members of a certain population and in some cases universally probable for humanity as a whole.

Intra- and Interintegrational

The striving for consonance characteristic of human life is also articulated in the scientific disposition. This striving expresses itself in the realm of science as a striving for integration. Scientists are innate seekers for consonance. They search for a coherent comprehension of their manifold findings.

Every science seeks for understanding and explanation. Explanation aims at a consonant comprehension of each object of investigation. It wants to clarify its consonance or dissonance with its other findings as formulated in its theoretical frame of reference. Consonant comprehension can only be approximated. It is based on a disclosure of the probable unifying factors that can bind disconnected insights and findings together. By means of these factors they are provisionally integrated within a logically consistent system. In every science integrational theory performs this task of unification.

We can distinguish between intra- and interintegration. Intraintegration theory unifies systematically and logically the findings and insights of scientists within one and the same science. Interintegrational theory complements the latter by integrating within it those findings of other sources of knowledge relevant to its own subject matter. Interintegration demands a methodology of translation and transposition of relevant contributions.

Many sciences are only incidentally involved in methodical interintegration. Certain practical sciences, such as medicine, education, pedagogy, and formation science, are, by their very nature, more interintegrative. Among them formation science finds an abundance of relevant findings in numerous arts, sciences, and formation traditions. These touch upon the consonance of human life, its dynamics and conditions, in their potential relevance for distinctively human formation.

When we use thus the term *integrational science* we usually refer to a science in which interintegration plays a crucial role. As mentioned, this does not make such a science interdisciplinary but merely discipline related.

Congeniality, Compatibility, Compassion, Competence

In the third volume of this series, we identified congeniality, compatibility, compassion, and competence as the basic consonance dispositions of human life. The scientific disposition shares also in these four expressions of consonance.

A distinctively human, scientific disposition should select for specialized scientific interest only those sciences that are congenial to the persons doing the selecting in terms of their pre-, intra-, inter-, and extraformation. One must experience a congenial affinity to the matter and method of the science one chooses as a specialty. For example, doctoral research seminars in the science of formation only admit persons who manifest congenial affinity for this branch of science. On top of this, students are encouraged to select as a dissertation topic an event congenial with their preformation and personal history.

Compatibility in researchers refers to their willingness to engage in scientific interformation with fellow researchers. The increasing complexity of science has made it desirable and often necessary that scientists work in teams. Such teams are more effective if the participants strive for compatibility with one another, at least on the level of polite yet forthright scientific discourse. Doctoral research teams in formation science are composed on basis of this principle. Its participants are encouraged to foster this type of compatibility.

Compassion in the realm of scientific teamwork or publication implies the readiness to be of assistance when fellow scientists or team members fail in their efforts, have difficulties in sustaining their scientific dedication, or need new information or explanation that helps in the solution of a research crisis.

Striving for competence is a necessary goal of effective scientific research and practice. Competence means in effect that we choose to do our scientific task in as excellent a way as possible. Scientific commitment thus implies striving for competence in the area we have chosen to pursue.

Collaboration, Confirmation, Concelebration

The dispositions of collaboration, confirmation, and concelebration of a consonant human life must also be articulated in the scientific disposition. Collaboration flows from the will to foster compatibility among scientists. It differs from compassion in that it is willing to seek for cooperation in research and publication, even when a fellow scientist is not perceived to be in need of support because of failure or crisis. Collaboration remains in effect even when fellow scientists or team members are successful. One outgrowth of the human pride-form is envy. Its offshoot is competition (as distinct from stimulating emulation)—that is why collaboration with successful scientists may be more difficult to maintain than compassion with those who fail.

Confirmation goes further than cooperation. It wholeheartedly encourages, confirms, and praises fellow scientists in their attempts. The scientific enterprise is often a lonely endeavor. One does not enjoy instant applause that sustains athletes, entertainers, politicians, public speakers, broadcasters, or performers. Nor does one share in the popularity of novelists or preachers, or the palpable daily effectiveness of a lawyer, administrator, salesperson, teacher, physician, counselor, or journalist. The monetary rewards, too, are often negligible in view of the time and effort spent. Hence mutual confirmation is a desirable ingredient in the type of scientific enterprise that may turn its devotees into "monks or hermits of science." Without it, commitment to the ascetical dedication needed to complete a research project in relative solitude is difficult to maintain.

Concelebration is also basic to sound human interformation. It crowns the solidarity and mutual generosity of scientists. If one of them succeeds, others should celebrate with him or her. Life itself is a gift to be celebrated and concelebrated. What is life without celebration? It tempers envy and envious competition. When one's tedious search is finally rewarded with new insight, one needs and deserves the uplift of concelebration. It serves to remind all concerned that the ascetical existence of a scientist can lead to results that benefit all human life. The breakthrough made by one scientist is only possible because of the self-forgetful commitment of many over the generations. Every breakthrough is cause for rejoicing, but not only the lucky scientists who finally make the breakthrough should be congratulated. In them we should honor all the nameless ones who prepared for this result by their tedious dedication that initiated, maintained, and developed the science. The success of one among us is the success of all of us.

Social Justice, Peace, and Mercy

The theory of consonant human life translates the dispositions of congeniality, compatibility, and compassion in regard to personal relationships into social presence in justice, peace, and mercy toward society at large. The scientific disposition participates in these social dispositions.

Formative social justice is concerned with the optimal conditions for congenial formation of the maximal number of people in society. Scientists ought to be concerned with the selection, formulation, and propagation of their research and its results in regard to their impact on the congenial development of as many people as possible. Such sciences as nuclear physics, biogenetics, and medicine have immense social ramifications. The same applies to formation science, perhaps even more so, because of its concern for life as distinctively human. Its promotion of the distinctive quality of life can enhance the social attitudes of scientists in all fields of inquiry.

Compatibility among whole populations and their segments contributes to social peace. World peace between populations and peace between diverse segments of populations is another concern of science and scientists, who are beginning to realize that their scientific disposition should include a commitment to social peace. Without it scientific pursuits may become severely limited or even extinguished. Science has at times served the cause of war. It may now serve the cause of peace, a service inherent in the notion of a distinctively human scientific disposition.

Compassion becomes social mercy if it turns to those who fail or suffer in society, be they large segments of the population or countries as a whole. The direction a science takes can aggravate or alleviate this suffering. The scientific disposition implies a responsible stance in regard to its selection of research, and its results and their propagation, insofar as these affect the suffering of specific societies or groups.

In this chapter we have considered the distinctive marks that identify formation science as a science. In the next chapter we will look more closely at this science in relation to other existing disciplines.

CHAPTER 4

Formation Science and
the Other Sciences

Our journey through life is clouded by shadows. Our field of presence is filled with obscurity. Our apprehension and appraisal are restricted by the embodiment of our mind in a sensate, finite body, limited by sense perception. Neither our field of presence nor our life is known by us in ultimate depth, as the following examples may show.

We see in our surroundings countless manifestations of matter, but we do not know what matter ultimately is. During our formation journey we discover a basic orientation, a foundational life-form, symbolized by our soul. Yet we cannot fully understand what this inner challenge ultimately is in its uniqueness, nor do we grasp how it is interwoven with our bodily presence in a formation field. When we grow in transcendent receptivity, we cannot escape the announcement of a mystery that pervades us yet goes beyond our life and its power of cognition. We cannot comprehend this transcendence and its mysterious immanence in our existence and its ambience.

Science is one of the ways humans enter this land of unknowing. It is one of humanity's means to escape engulfment by the chaos of comparatively formless energy out of which we emerge.

The radical initial formation of the universe took place aeons ago. This formation continued in an ongoing formative evolution, culminating in the rise of the human race. Formative evolution is characterized by this gradual emergence of order out of chaos. Human science is a mode of participation in this ongoing emergence, this unfolding of the cosmic and human epiphanies of the formation mystery.

Science is one attempt to further formative evolution by consciously pushing back the shadows of unknowing, by letting light come through.

It creates the conceptual tools and conditions for the progressive reformation and expansion of the human field and its vast horizons.

Some men and women are called to commit their life to the scientific enterprise. They are sustained in this rigorous endeavor by the faith that the achievements of science in their great variety shall not be made void. Formation scientists assume that the mystery itself operates in the many levels and shapes of the unfolding scientific disposition of people and the wide variety of disciplines it generates. All science serves the self-disclosure of the formation mystery in any facet of reality. It supports the hope that there will be granted to humankind a gradual disclosure of the mystery in its intelligible epiphanies insofar as the human spirit can receive such disclosure. Due to the necessity of specialized focal attention, a multiplicity of sciences is necessary to approximate this vision. Every science must select a specific profile of the field and a corresponding angle of apprehension. Sciences are means used by the mystery to disclose some of its epiphanies to human apprehension and appreciation.

No science can reduce reality to its own perspective. For example, we cannot shrink the fullness of human life to a mere succession of atomic particles. Equally if not more destructive is the attempt to shape one's life on the basis of one limited perspective. No matter how impressive it may be, its truth is only partial. Scholars and practitioners of formation science strive to integrate certain mutually complementary disclosures of all sciences in service of a proximate formation that is distinctively human or spiritual.

Science of Matter
Physicists have chosen as their object of scientific attention concrete matter. What matter ultimately is they cannot disclose. Its deepest secret remains a hidden domain. Formation science distinguishes between form potency and actual formation. It seems as if prime matter is sheer form potency. Yet it could not be at all if there were not already a minimum of form direction inherent in this prime matter. Prime matter is potential formation energy. This energy has some actual form insofar as it carries in itself an implicit direction toward the dynamic formation of the universe.

Let us look more closely at the scientific explanatory models and theories of physicists. They see energy in matter. They do not apprehend this energy as devoid of any form or formation. This energy is conceptualized as given some kind of form by ordered motion. This form may be conceived, for example, as a rotation of negative electrons around a positive nucleus. Energy in their theory may take the basic form of a fluctuation of electron waves. No matter what image they use, it evidently implies some form or formation of the energy that is matter.

The scientific focus on this energy-in-formation leads necessarily to disclosures that are not covered by the common language of everyday life. The ambiguity of daily parlance would inevitably distort their discoveries and explanations. Hence physics, like all sciences, cannot exist without a metalanguage. This language is so far removed from common parlance that it has to be highly abstract. This explains why the preferred metalanguage of physics has become mathematical symbolism.

We may ask ourselves: To what does this language point? Surely it cannot refer only to mere matter, to mere form potency or potential formation energy. This form potency cannot exist without some minimum form or formation, be it only that of a certain inherent directedness. In and by itself matter cannot be known at all. The focus of physics is thus on the form or formation of matter. This form may be imaged as the dance of electrons around the proton or through similar models of physical formation.

The science of foundational human formation is interested in physics as a science of the formation of matter. We utilize physics, therefore, as an auxiliary science. For example, in tracing the initial formation of the human race, our science is guided by the assumption that one and the same formation mystery appears in all formation. Another assumption is that this mystery directs subhuman formation toward the unique formation of humanity and the emergence of the spirit. It makes humanity's formation emerge at a certain point in the formative evolution of the universe, which itself emerged out of the almost shapeless sea of primordial form potency.

Prescientific and Scientific Apprehension
in Physical and Biological Sciences

The physical and biological sciences disclose to us some of the lower forms in our environment. These sciences abstract certain profiles from what is given to us in prescientific apprehension.

Prescientific apprehension, no matter how sensate, makes a certain focal or prefocal selection that plays a significant role in science. Meaningful forms are isolated out of the swirl of sensate impressions that enter our mind. They are related rightly or wrongly to forms we already know.

Because of a lack of methodical rigor at this prescientific stage, one may be mistaken as to the order, importance, or meaning one assigns to these spontaneously selected forms. On this level our procedures tend to be rudimentary and insufficiently critical.

The positive sciences take up these prescientific apprehensions and appraisals, correcting, complementing, and vastly expanding them by means of exact methods of observation and validation. Characteristic of the positive sciences is that their methods are mainly related to functional -analytical reason rooted in the functional dimension of human life. Because of this limitation, which is at the same time their strength, they must assume ultimate postulates.

Functional rationality cannot disclose such ultimates as the formation mystery or the meaning of human life. Nor can it disclose the full meaning of the cosmic formation field in its totality and finality, or of the nature of matter. Other disciplines, such as philosophy and theology, which are guided by transcendent reason, must deal with such questions.

Formation science studies in turn the formative implications of such ultimates as well as those of the findings of the positive sciences. It also explores the experiential transcendence dynamic inherent in human life. Because this innate dynamic is available to experience and its objectification in expressive forms, it is potentially available to comparative scientific examination and interformative validation. The experiential manifestation of the transcendence dynamic, as objectified in oral, written, taped, or videotaped records, can be a point of departure for rigorous scientific inquiry.

Consonant and Dissonant Anthropomorphisms

The findings of the positive sciences can help our science in its critical appraisal of mistaken directives that may have been developed as dissonant accretions of traditions over the centuries. To give but one example, we turn to the use of anthropomorphisms by various religious traditions.

We distinguish a consonant and a dissonant anthropomorphism. That which is consonant uses metaphors of human life to facilitate the comprehension of nonhuman appearances in the universe. We may say, for instance, that the forming power of nature itself is like a mighty intelligence. Dissonant anthropomorphism is a misguided use of metaphors from human life. They falsify our comprehension of that to which the metaphor points. One example of such a mistaken anthropomorphism is the image of the mystery as an enlarged human person hovering over our world, arbitrarily interfering with the laws and processes of cosmic and human emergence. The positive sciences help our science to eliminate such deceptive metaphors and their crippling impact on our vision of life and its mystery.

Another example is our awareness that deformation is not exclusively the consequence of willful sin. The findings of the positive sciences regarding the forces of heredity and environment, of pre- and infrafocal strivings and traumatic incidences, explain many unintentional failures in the art of living consonantly.

Functional Sciences

The positive sciences of matter and life are concerned with the physical-vital dimension of our life. The sciences that deal mainly with the functional dimension could be called functional. They examine how people practically shape their life in interaction with the functional aspects of their environment.

Technical Sciences

Among the functional sciences are those which investigate how we can handle material objects and instruments in such a fashion that they become most useful for the effective functioning of people within their environment. These sciences encompass technology in all its ramifications.

From the viewpoint of our science, human persons should not be exclusively guided by the directives of functional usefulness. A truly human technology must take into account also the transcendent directives that respect and foster the distinctively human quality of individuals and their societies. Otherwise a dehumanizing functionalism could overtake our lives. Technology would then become a deformative rather than a formative force.

If technology would take its proximate directives also from formation science, it would enable humanity to give form to matter in a distinctively human way, thus serving the victory of the human spirit over matter. It would provide a means for the approximation of consonance between mind and matter.

The functional dimension of our life should be made subservient to the transcendent one. Similarly, functional technology should be subordinated to the demands of the conditions for a distinctively human existence for a maximum number of people. Technologists have invented and perfected conditions that can facilitate this humanization.

We can see in a humane technology and its creations an epiphanous reflection of the mystery fashioning matter or energy via enlightened experts into servants of a life that is distinctively human. To be sure, such technical sophistication in and of itself is not enough. It can and should contribute to the consonance and ascendance of human life under the implicit direction of the mystery.

For example, technical control over things can facilitate our practical implementation of transcendent directives of faith, hope, and consonance as embodied in social presence in justice, peace, and mercy. The production and distribution of sufficient food, medicine, and shelter for the people on our planet may be made possible because of progress in the technical sciences. Thanks to them, we can now accomplish in principle what was impossible for highly motivated religious cultures in the past. They had ideals and the right human directives, but they lacked the means for implementing them concretely as we can do today. For example, we need to direct our technology with a proper concern for those who suffer want and oppression. In other words, concrete implementation of transcendent ideals needs sufficient technical organization of the human field.

One necessary condition for the average human intrasphere to unfold itself consonantly is the joyful apprehension, appreciation, and affirmation of its form potency. This is possible only when there is sufficient scope for this potency to actualize itself. The creations of technology should never make the exercise of human potency impossible for any person. We should be concerned with the establishment of new opportunities for form potency fulfillment when and if technological progress leads to the closing of traditional opportunities for employment, study, art, and recreation.

Functional-Directive Sciences

A second type of science rooted in the functional dimension comprises the sciences that give direction to our potency for effective functioning. Among them are functional ethics—to be distinguished from transcendent ethics—and the functional social sciences.

Functional Ethics

Functional ethics, as distinguished from transcendent ultimate ethics, is primarily the science of effective functioning in variable situations. Hence its directives manifest the variability and pliability that allow for adaptation to different life situations. In a consonant life, such functional ethics should be subsumed under transcendent ethics. The latter is rooted in the higher transcendent dimension of our life.

Functional ethics gives rise to directives that manifest a certain pliability in accordance with the functional demands of a situation. This pliability finds its boundary in absolute, foundational directives, which are ultimately rooted in transcendent attention, apprehension, appreciation, and affirmation. They manifest an intrinsic direction that is independent of the changing conditions of functional situations. Examples are the transcendent directives of a gentle and firm implementation of faith, hope, and consonance in congeniality, compatibility, compassion, cooperation, confirmation, concelebration, justice, peace, mercy, and competence. Their mode of implementation can be modulated by functional ethics in response to changes in this dimension of one's actual environment. However, their basic orientation should not be changed by such adaptation to functional variations.

Another invariable transcendent directive is that of fidelity to our dimensional hierarchy, which is based on the ascending order of sociohistorical, vital, functional, and transcendent dimensions of human existence. Each one generates its own corresponding directives. Fidelity to this hierarchy implies that the directives suggested by the lower dimensions should be subordinate to those generated by the higher.

Lowest are the sociohistorical directives that are blindly borrowed social pulsations in society. Slightly above them are the vital directives that emerge from our vitalistic pulsions. These tell us how to care for our sensate bodily existence in ways that are biochemically advantageous, vitally pleasant, and conducive to physical wellbeing. Above them are the functional directives, covered by functional ethics, directing us how to perform functionally, responsibly, and effectively within varying situations. Their demands may compel us to temper the directives that are merely the outcome of sociohistorical pulsations and vital pulsions.

Above these functional directives are the transcendent. These comprise a wide variety of directives, such as the transcendent-intellectual, aesthetic, and ultimate ethical form directives. Included in them also is the transcendent directive to apprehend, appreciate, and affirm this consonant hierarchy of directives and our fidelity to it. At the summit of this hierarchy is the transcendent directive of obedient consonance with the mystery, giving rise to the awe-filled faith, hope, and consonance that should illumine and animate the other directives in this hierarchy.

In this light we see more clearly the meaning of the science of functional ethics. Transcendent faith, hope, and consonance are invariable in their essential orientation. They cannot be embodied, however, in our changing life situations in the same way under different functional conditions. Human fields of presence and action differ functionally because of their emergence in different times and places, in different individuals and societies. Hence there is a contingent and relative character to functional ethics in and of itself. This type of practical ethics considers the changing functional conditions in which transcendent directives must be realized. As such it belongs to the sphere of functional sciences.

Most directives of functional ethics are implied in practical sciences such as political science, economics, law, medicine, and business administration.

Functional Social Sciences

Functionally oriented social sciences should be distinguished from humanly oriented social sciences. Social sciences can focus on the functional facet of life. They may also concern themselves with either typically or distinctively human facets while taking into account the findings of the functionally oriented social sciences. In the latter case they would belong to the class of human sciences.

Formation science considers itself to be a distinctively human science. It distinguishes itself from other typical human sciences by its focus on distinctively human formation as a whole and by its interintegrative concern.

For this reason it is important to consider in more detail the human sciences as our science understands them and to identify the specific nature of our science in relation to them. Before we can do so effectively, we have to complement our earlier consideration of the nonhuman sciences with a brief reflection on the functionally oriented social sciences.

We have already seen the meaning and scope of functional ethics. It is the science that orders practically the functional facets of one's action in the relative and changing circumstances of one's life as practical. We have also discussed how the directives of functional ethics may or may not be related to transcendent ethics.

The functionally oriented social sciences can be sources of effective direction of our life in society, examined as an intricate organism of functional interaction. Such social sciences as political science, economics, law, psychology, psychiatry, sociology, journalism, business administration, cultural anthropology, education, and medicine can choose to orient their research exclusively toward findings and insights that enable us to function more effectively in those areas of practice selected by them as their preferred realm of inquiry.

The main objective of social sciences *as* functional is the material, practical, and educational development of human life and society, including our functional intelligence, perception, aptitude, pragmatic appraisal, and vital sensitivity.

The same profiles of life can be examined within these sciences from the viewpoint of either typical or distinctive humanness. To demonstrate the typically human orientation for one science I started the first graduate program in psychology as a human science at Duquesne University— without, however, denying the importance of a functionally oriented psychology. On the contrary, in my book *Existential Foundations of Psychology*, a critique of certain aspects of existential psychology, I took a strong stand against any attempt by humanistic or existential psychologists to underestimate the value of psychology as a functional science or to neglect its important findings and methodologies. I proposed the term anthropological psychology instead of phenomenological or existential psychology to emphasize among other things that psychology as a human science should not restrict itself to the results of only one type of research nor neglect the contributions of functionally oriented psychologies.

This openness in principle for the relevant results of research methodologies in functionally oriented psychologies applies a priori to formation science, which is primarily about distinctively human or transcendent formation. In formation science this openness of anthropological psychology for all kinds of psychology expanded to include the formationally relevant results of the research methodologies of all sciences, not only psychology. Formation science itself is basically a human science. Thus the question arises: How are the humanly oriented social sciences distinct from the functionally oriented social sciences?

Human Science

What we today call human sciences were originally named moral sciences by the philosopher John Stuart Mill as far back as 1843. They were considered to be sciences about human nature. Under the impact of the success of the methods developed in the physical sciences at the beginning of the nineteenth century, it was proposed that such moral sciences should follow the same path.

Around the same time in Germany certain thinkers began to use the term *Geisteswissenschaften*. They gave it initially the same meaning the term moral sciences had in England. It was Wilhelm Dilthey who extended the scope of the *Geisteswissenschaften* and changed their methodology. For him the *Geisteswissenschaften* included sciences such as philosophy and aesthetics, psychology, anthropology, political economy, law, and history. He held that the methodology of these sciences should be different from those of the natural sciences. He insisted that such new methods, while appropriate to the subject matter of the *Geisteswissenschaften*, should manifest methodical rigor, general validity, and availability to ongoing critical self-validation. They should have a theoretical-critical foundation.

English speaking authors later inaugurated the term human sciences. I introduced into the psychology department of Duquesne University in 1958 the first American graduate program in psychology as a human science. In a series of books published by the Duquesne University Press, other authors used the same terminology. Stephan Strasser entitled one of his publications in this series *Phenomenology and the Human Sciences*. In the same series, my book *Existential Foundations of Psychology* argued that this type of approach was solidly scientific. Realizing that this position implied the assumption of an enlarged base of scientific knowledge, I wrote many pages to demonstrate how and why and under which conditions a human science could be correctly identified as a science in the broader yet proper sense of the term science. After the book appeared in paperback, it was widely distributed on the college and university campuses, giving rise to vigorous debate. My view was supported later by Dr. Amedeo Giorgi, who wrote a book entitled *Psychology as a Human Science*, where he reiterated some of the main positions of *Existential Foundations* and corroborated them with his own research. Paul Ricoeur's work on hermeneutics and the human sciences acknowledges independently a similar view of this broader meaning of science. In the same vein many French authors speak about *les sciences humaines*.

After nine years in the psychology department, I was able to return to my earlier scholarly concern with distinctively human formation as a dialogically articulated whole. In 1963 I initiated at a separate institute of the same university the new science of distinctively human formation. This science adapted some of the main presuppositions of my original approach in psychology to this new, more comprehensive object of inquiry.

Consequently, formation science holds that the human formation field can be researched with methodical rigor, general validity, and critical ways of interformative validation. To be sure, the methods of the human sciences as such do not yield absolute certainty, but they may increasingly approximate the limited certainty that is presently available to us by the rigorous establishment of high probabilities attainable at this moment of the development of methods of inquiry. As has been shown in *Existential Foundations of Psychology*, recent developments in the philosophy of science have demonstrated that we have to acknowledge at present that the natural sciences also operate within similar limits. They, too, give us no absolute certainty, only high probability.

Formation Science as Distinct from Other Sciences

Formation science as a human science tries to understand and explain the formative connections between and among the pre-, intra-, inter-, and extraspheres of the human formation field, each with their own sociohistorical, vital, functional, and transcendent dimensions, and in their common, segmental, and personal ranges and regions of consciousness. Formation science takes its departure from the observable objectifications of the distinctively human presence that permeates this field as a whole as well as all its facets. These distinctively human foundations of formation cannot be derived from the mere physical facets of human life when studied in isolation from this human presence, its formative impact, and its direction. The human object of study differs also from the facets studied by a functionally oriented type of psychology. Hence, the methodology of formation science cannot be identical with the methodologies demanded by the natural sciences or by functionally oriented psychologies developed along the same lines of inquiry.

This does not mean that formation science as a specific human science does not take into account the formationally relevant findings of these other sciences. On the contrary, the specific interintegrative nature of formation science makes the critical-creative translation and transposition of such findings a mandatory aspect of its methodology.

The methodologies and the findings of other typically human sciences are by their very nature nearer to the distinctively human science of formation than those of the natural sciences. Hence they offer more findings that may prove potentially relevant for our science. Critical-creative translation and transposition is also necessary here. The reason is that none of these other human sciences explore the human field as a dialogically articulated whole in light of distinctively human formation and in terms of the latter's proximate meanings and directives. Nor do they take into account as critically and systematically the findings of the arts, sciences, and traditions in terms of our particular object of inquiry and its projected limitations.

Rejection of Idealism and Romanticism in Science

Formation science, like other human sciences, considers as insufficient certain approaches of both idealists in the social sciences and romanticists in literature. Both argue, often eloquently, against the attempts to understand the uniquely human in terms of the categories of the natural sciences. Some of them, perhaps in overreaction, would even go so far as to doubt the possibility of any critical scientific approach to the phenomena of human life. Serious students of the human sciences strive to replace or complement such idealistic and romantic criticism with the development of rigorous research methodologies proper to their distinctively human subject.

The human sciences and their subdivisions approach a chosen aspect of life with a variety of research strategies. We share the general framework of the human sciences, yet our own distinct object of inquiry demands the development of an appropriate methodology. Our research designs serve our aim to understand and explain distinctively human life within the dialogical articulation of its field. Such exploration takes into account critically whatever may have been disclosed about this unfolding life by any science, art, or tradition.

Like other human sciences, this one finds itself unexpectedly at the frontier of innovation in scientific research. This is due to the fact that the methods of the natural sciences, thought infallible in the past, are now shown to be limited in the certitude they can provide. Their assumptions are not as unassailable as was originally assumed. The fact that the approaches of the human sciences were already known to have similar limits is no longer a reason to consider them less scientific than those of the natural sciences. For the latter must now acknowledge that they, too, are burdened by boundaries they cannot escape.

Limitations of Functionally Oriented Research Methodology

Life formation is central to human experience. The methods of positive science are limited. They do not enable us to explore fully what is most central to this experience. Using them exclusively would mean that we would have to forgo the most significant questions about distinctively human formation.

The acknowledgment that we need different methods to complement those of the positive sciences does not mean that we undervalue the methods and results of these disciplines. On the contrary, we respect them in their own realm of inquiry and integrate their results when they prove relevant to a better understanding of human life. The point is not that we want to replace these methods by others. We simply want to complement them by the methods developed in our science as well as in other already existing sciences.

Our science holds that knowledge provided by any empirical or experiential approach is never absolute and ultimate. It represents the best understanding and explanation attainable at this moment in the history of knowledge. We see science itself as but one instance in the formation history of humanity.

This history is marked by encounters with old and new events. Such happenings challenge our powers of understanding and explanation. Humanity responds to this challenge by means of conceptual tools already formed or by those that can be given form at a particular phase of the history of intellectual development. Subsequent new knowledge has then to be confirmed by other experts in our area of inquiry. People need to be convinced that its application represents an improvement over previous practices. Such confirmation depends on the reasoning implied in making practical decisions.

Our science could be described, therefore, as a creative-critical search to understand and explain distinctively human formation. It utilizes the results of any approach that clarifies the particular facets we have to address. The ultimate criterion of its own specific methods is the confirmation of results by people seriously involved in such applications, based on their critical observation that the newly disclosed directives are more effective and consonant than the previous ones.

CHAPTER 5

Complexity of Formation

Human formation presents us with numerous complex problems, as the following summation may show.

First of all, human formation is never static. It entails an intricate history of formation, reformation, and transformation. Second, it unfolds within a field constituted by pre-, intra-, inter-, and extraspheres; personal, segmental, and universal ranges; focal, pre-, infra-, and transfocal regions of consciousness; sociohistorical, vital, functional, and transcendent dimensions; and foundational, core, current, apparent, and actual integrational forms. People interact with all of these facets in countless ways.

Formation, moreover, is influenced by sociohistorical and lingual symbols that carry a great variety of meanings.

There are manifold dynamics of formation. These can be subsumed under sociohistorical pulsations, vital pulsions, functional ambitions, and transcendent inspirations and aspirations.

To make it more complex, social directives are instilled, maintained, and reformed in us by continuous interformation. Added to this is a mysterious transcendence dynamic moving us to go beyond our familiar structures.

Because of the complexity of our predicament, effective research needs to remain in a state of openness to any insight offered by various sources and methods. The pull toward a single science or toward one school or branch and its exclusive methodology must be resisted. None of them is capable of covering the multifaceted quality of human life.

We may be tempted to choose one or the other science as the exclusive explanation of distinctively human formation as a whole. The aberrations resulting from such a choice prior to the rise of formation science are evident as people move from one "sure" set of solutions to another.

48

Formation science, therefore, mandates, next to its own methodology, an openness to the methodological pluralism of other sciences.

Our Own Limits of Formation Knowledge

Part of the complexity of this study is the fact that our own approach is always conditioned by our prescientific and scientific knowledge. Our mind-set is limited. It is restricted by the phase and the place in which we find ourselves. We can only try to overcome this limited perspective to some degree by being open to the formation knowledge and wisdom of other cultures and other times.

Four Sources of Formation Directives

To decipher the complexity of this field, it may be helpful to realize that there are four main sources of directives.

First of all, such directives arise from the elementary strivings in each human life. These strivings can be sociohistorical, vital, functional, or transcendent. These innate strivings provide us with the basic energy needed for the maintenance of their corresponding dynamic directives. For instance, functional strivings are one of the sources for the directive to develop our marketable skills.

Second, directives are influenced by the patterns prevalent in our field. They are usually rooted in traditions. Such patterns modulate in some way the directives arising from our basic strivings, their first source. For example, the patterns of Japanese community-mindedness modulate the functional striving for success in the market with elaborate rituals of politeness. These patterns are rooted in Shinto, Buddhist, and Confucian form traditions.

Third, the directives are modified in some measure by the unique life call of each person. It moderates the expression of the innate strivings already altered by the patterns of the community. For example, an individually aggressive or shy employer or employee may experience the directive meaning of this mood for his or her life in a different personal fashion.

Fourth, we have ultimate directives that are transcendent. These may affect in some measure all the other directives in their orientation and expression. For example, many people may feel guilty about their misuse of others. The kind and intensity of guilt directives and the way they handle them depends on the quality of their transcendent conscience as influenced by their religious or ideological traditions.

Ascending Hierarchy of Directives

Another complexity of formation is due to the shift of influence from the lower to the higher directives.

The four kinds of directives described above influence each other. Life becomes more consonant to the degree that the directives of the higher dimensions modulate the lower ones. For example, the directive of functional effectiveness should control the vital directives sufficiently to prevent life from being dominated by unchecked passions and pulsions. A consonant hierarchy of directives thus implies a descending (from higher to lower) rather than an ascending (from lower to higher) pattern.

In the beginning of life, however, the pattern is ascending. This means that higher dimensions only gradually disclose themselves when we grow older. In the meantime, we are not in sufficient control of the directives of the lower dimensions. Different kinds of strivings disclose themselves only successively at various phases of life. Each of them gives rise to corresponding directives.

For example, children are first moved by spontaneous directives that spring immediately from their strivings, beginning with the vital ones. Soon they are compelled to accept some functional control instilled by the pressures and invitations of people around them. Growing into adolescence, they begin to experience their call to a relative uniqueness. They become aware, at least implicitly, of a need to modulate personally the common directives.

If the circumstances are favorable, they become increasingly open to ultimate directives. If they adhere to a faith and form tradition, their understanding of this tradition is deepened in the light of this awakening experience of the "more than." Conversely this tradition facilitates the awareness of ultimate directives. The philosophy or theology of the tradition, its symbols and rites, also facilitates this awakening.

Descending Hierarchy of Form Directives

Once these phases have led to an awakening, life formation should become descending. Ideally the order of responsiveness should now start out from the top of this pyramid of strivings and their directives. The vital pulsions and the sociohistorical pulsations at the base line of the pyramid should no longer provide decisive directives by themselves alone. On the contrary, the transcendent aspirations and inspirations at the top of the pyramid should be decisive. In other words, ultimate directives should illumine one's life direction. Our call to uniqueness, too, should be modulated in consonance with the formation mystery, disclosing itself in this transcendent dimension in dialogue with the whole of our field with its transcendent horizon.

Subsequently one should engage in the ongoing reformation of life directives that emerge from one's basic strivings.

Specification of Formation Experiences by Dispositional Form Directives

Dispositional form directives influence our experiences. They lead us to interpret appearances in a certain way. For example, a church tower has a different meaning when it is apprehended and appraised under the influence of a Freudian libidinal directive, a religious awe directive, or one that is architectural, historical, or technical.

A cultural or subcultural form tradition may foster one or more of these dispositional directives. We retain, at least in principle, the freedom to reform them and, therewith, the meaning which they impose on what appears to us in our environment. Much counseling is engaged in the reformation of dispositional directives that threaten to encapsulate the counselee in a field of meaning experienced as less than beneficial for consonant unfolding.

Form Traditional Complement

Our research can be complemented by the study of form traditions. Form traditional articulation goes beyond the science as such. It studies either a religious or an ideological faith tradition in its formative implications. Such implications give rise to formation traditions.

The promotion of such research, for those interested in it, prevents formation science from being perceived as a kind of new faith or form tradition that posits itself over against already existing traditions. Nor does this science want to give the mistaken impression that it presents a sort of common denominator. It should not pretend that its body of knowledge comprehends all possible formation principles and conditions offered by all possible faith and form traditions.

Formation science is not a superformation tradition. The limits of the scientific method make it impossible for any empirical science to cover all the formation directives and especially all the animating transcendent motivations that could be beneficial for one's formation. Many directives and inspiring motivations, especially the ultimate ones, fall outside the domain that can be disclosed by any scientific method. Formation science wants to establish a cooperative instead of a competitive relationship with such traditions. In this way science and tradition can enrich one another.

CHAPTER 6

Form Appreciative Apprehensions

In this chapter we would like to go more deeply into the kind of apprehension that has a formative influence on our life.

We may be touched by a death in the family, a failed examination, a book, a movie, a poem, an illness, a fight, a victory, and so on. How we appraise what we apprehend will determine how it will give form to our life. Hence we may say that an apprehension that is appraised in such a way that it gives form to our life is a formative apprehension.

We could condense this process in the expression "form appreciative apprehension." This is an apprehension that implies an appreciation of the form that it can give to our life. As such, it is different from a merely informative apprehension. For example, I may see on television that farmers have lost a crop because of excessive rainfall. This may be merely a piece of information to me. It may not affect me personally. When I myself become the victim of flooding, I begin to appraise what it means to lose my possessions. I am forced to reform my thoughts, feelings, and actions about what victims of natural disasters suffer.

Prefocal and Focal Appreciative Apprehension

We are not always clearly aware of our form appreciative apprehensions. For example, we may not notice a person's relaxed face, shiny eyes, smiling lips, and upbeat movements. We do not infer from these signs that the person is happy. Instead we apprehend and appreciate immediately the presence of a happy person and may feel good about it.

Such global impressions and their influence on us are prefocal. But we can make them focal. This may happen, for instance, when this happy appearance evokes in us wonder, curiosity, or perhaps suspicion. Then we may feel inclined to question it. We may then engage in a prescientific focal examination of our spontaneous apprehension.

Formation scientists may in turn correct and complement the results of our prescientific reflection. The general approach of the science to the disclosure of a form appreciative apprehension begins when the researcher examines the subject and object pole of an event and notices the relationships that shape the way in which the apprehension of the object pole makes it meaningful for a person. For example, the loss of a child in an accident is an event that is not merely something a mother feels informed about. It has a profound impact on her thoughts, feelings, memories, and family relationships—briefly, on her whole life.

In regard to her subsequent formation history, much depends on how the loss of the child affects the mother's life. Her form appreciative apprehension will be coformed by the pre-, intra-, inter-, and extraconditions of her personal field. Let us say that a relationship of mutual loving confirmation existed between them. In that case, the loss of the child, though deeply painful, may be less traumatic in the long run than it would have been had the home situation been one of estrangement and conflict. In the latter case her apprehension of the event may be different.

Also, the preformation of the mother as well as her intraformation will modulate her apprehension. For example, genetic preformation may have left her excessively vulnerable to any kind of upheaval. On top of this, her childhood preformation may have been so lacking in confirmation that the loss of any loved person would rekindle feelings of false guilt. Such feelings may have been implanted in her during a childhood that was perhaps too demanding and accusatory. As a result of this irrational guiltiness, she may reproach herself destructively about anything she might have omitted that would have possibly prevented the child from incurring the fatal accident.

Once researchers have provisionally identified form appreciative apprehensions by the best disclosure methods available to them, they go on to the next step. They try to complement and correct their tentative findings by comparison with pertinent insights developed by the auxiliary sciences, disciplines, arts, and form traditions. They then try to lift out of the conditions peculiar to the event the basic elements that can be generalized and applied to a wider population. In this example they may try to reach consensus on general or potential patterns of form appreciative apprehensions and their conditions in Western people, who are confronted with the loss of a loved one.

Researchers interested in form traditional articulation may expand this investigation to include the formative influence a particular faith and form tradition may exert on the form appreciative apprehensions they are studying.

Symbols and Form Appreciative Apprehensions

Symbols play a crucial part in the shaping of form appreciative apprehensions. Faith and form traditions, myths, proverbs, and works of art express in symbols possible links of formative meaning between the subject and object poles of events that take place within a shared sociohistorical field. People in such a field are exposed to these symbols of meaning. This exposure modulates their apprehensions. Hence a critical study of such symbols and their influence is relevant to the research at hand.

Other sources of formative symbols that influence form appreciative apprehensions are legal codes, constitutions, and social conventions. Understanding their implications for the emergence of apprehensions can help to explain the responses of people in the events and situations under study.

Formation scientists themselves are affected by the symbols and settings they explore. In one way this is helpful. Their embeddedness in the same field enables researchers to participate in the apprehensions of the people they study. Coformed by the same field, they can start out from empathic understanding. This makes their point of departure different from that of scientists in the physical realm of cosmic formation. Unlike the latter, students of human life are not limited to an observation of relationships that remain mainly external and abstract. Obviously physicists cannot enter into the relationships they discover between physical elements. Formation scientists, however, can be part of the relationships they disclose between people. They can in some measure enter into other human situations because of the basic strivings they have in common with any form of human life. By empathic imagination they try to grasp the directives such strivings may initiate in any setting.

Primacy of Form Appreciative Apprehension for Formation Science

The science of formation is dependent on a primary mode of apprehension different from the informational apprehension on which the positive sciences are built. This primary mode is the act of form appreciative apprehension. In this act, one recognizes instantly, even if nonfocally, the presence of some formative direction in one's own or others' response to an event.

Every happening or appearance can become formative for us or others in a distinctively human fashion. It may be an encounter with a person that somehow touches us, with a book, a film, or in relation to simple everyday things, such as doing the dishes, making the beds, stopping for a traffic light, changing the baby's diapers. All of these actions imply the perception of physical objects. Yet we may see more than these mere physical manifestations. We may apprehend appreciatively the formative direction they imply for our own life or that of others.

This act of spontaneous appreciative apprehension of forms and directions is the basic building stone, the point of departure, for our science. While the knowledge it gives us has to be checked, complemented, and corrected by strict procedures of critical validation, the initial act of recognition itself cannot be replaced by something else. Without it we would simply not have any awareness of forms and their implied directions to begin with. This is the only initial means at our disposal to start a science of formation.

Every time we want to expand the science, we have to fall back on the disclosure of certain acts of form appreciative apprehension. The word appreciative refers to the fact that to apprehend something as formative or deformative implies a value judgment. We judge spontaneously that something is not simply a physically observable event or a piece of neutral information. We appraise it also as something that has its own humanly meaningful form. This form can be contemplated receptively. It is potentially relevant also for form donation in our life.

Analysis of the Act of Form Appreciative Apprehension

Let us try to analyze further the act of form appreciative apprehension. The process concerns itself with humanly meaningful forms and the directives implied in them. Its primary concern is not the measurable and perceptible information that can be gained from our sensate observation of events.

For example, one has no form appreciative apprehension of a rock when one approaches it only as a geologist. When it is approached as a potential source of formative meaning—for instance, by a religious poet —it can give rise to an image of God as the rock of one's life in whom one trusts. This image is open to contemplation. It is also formative because it can direct one's life journey concretely in faith, hope, and love.

To give another example. When one's wife is seriously ill, one can approach this event from the medical viewpoint, gaining the necessary information about her malady, the prognosis, the medicines to be obtained.

But also one's potency for form appreciative apprehension may be awakened. In a sudden flash or in a prolonged process of reflection, the husband may apprehend the meaning of her suffering and the potential directives for their life together that are implied in this occurrence and in their contemplation of its meaning.

Formation science starts out necessarily from this spontaneous apprehension. The choice of a form appreciative mode of cognition is appropriate for studying the formal object of the science of formation. The objects studied by the physical sciences, insofar as they are limited to their sheer material measurability, do not disclose potential human meanings. The latter are examined by the human sciences. Among them, only the science of formation has as its formal object of investigation the formative meaning directives appreciatively apprehendable by people as relevant to their distinctively human life.

Conditions for Scientific Critique and Validation

Formation science takes its departure from such appreciative apprehensions, but it does not rest there. It subjects them to a rigorous scientific critique and validation; it explores their dynamics, conditions, and consequences. Such scientific study implies openness to interformative validation. Therefore, it presupposes the critical study of comparable communications that objectify in some measure the apprehensions under investigation.

What are the conditions for a critical study of apprehensions, objectified in these records? We can identify three conditions.

First, the formation scientist must be familiar with the processes through which forms and their implicit directives are appreciatively apprehended and communicated by people. This familiarity can be fostered by a study of the theoretical frame of reference of formation science as it has developed since its inception. The study of auxiliary sciences, such as semiotics, linguistics, psychology, medicine, cultural anthropology, and sociology —insofar as they touch on this form apprehensive process—can expand the knowledge already available in formation theory. The same applies to the study of arts, traditions, and social institutions.

Second, formation scientists need to explore the particular field in which such an apprehension takes place and finds expression. They must appraise the influence of the unique pre-, intra-, inter-, and extraspheres of this field on the apprehension concerned and on the concrete response of a person or group.

Third, the formation scientist must be familiar not only with the processes of form appreciative apprehension and communication but also with comparable apprehensions and records by other persons in the same and in other fields as already or not yet recorded in the existing body of scientific knowledge.

Formation scientists use their own appreciative apprehensions, those recorded by others, and the initial articulation of both *only as a starting point* for their scientific inquiry. They have to integrate within the provisional results of this initial approach the validated findings of all other modes of scientific cognition, for example, those obtained by experimentation and by means of statistical techniques. If necessary, they correct and revise their provisional conclusions in the light of the validated results obtained by other reputable scientific methods.

Formation scientists must realize that a full concrete understanding and explanation of distinctively human formation is impossible without a critical analysis of appreciative apprehension as its starting point. For this reason they must return continually to the immediately given apprehension of formation directives.

Introspection Not Basic to Formation Science

Access to one's own form appreciative apprehensions requires a methodic focal attention on them. A serious problem is that such attention interferes with the very form appreciative apprehension we seek to understand. We find similar limitations in the physical sciences. By the very act of focusing our attention and instrumentation to explore atomic and subatomic constellations, we interfere in some way with their formation.

It is for this reason that scientists in the field of human formation rejected the method of methodic focal attention to one's own formative apprehension as the foundation of their science. This method is called introspection. Instead they turn to the critical study of the objectively comparable expressions of such apprehensions and of their objective parameters in other ranges of the field. Beyond this point, they develop also techniques of comparative appraisal of the related results obtained by other auxiliary sciences. The contemporary availability of movies and videotapes enables them to expand their techniques of critical articulation and elucidation to nonverbal expressions of form directives in facial expressions, gestures, movements, and actions.

Briefly, an idea I expressed in my book *Existential Foundations of Psy-*

chology applies also to this science. This thesis is that an exclusive introspective, existential, phenomenological approach to psychology would constitute an extreme position. Instead I argued for an integrative position that I then provisionally named anthropological psychology. This prepared the ground for an integrative approach as most appropriate for a fruitful science of human formation.

Provisional Listing of Main Propositions of Formation Science

We can now list twelve of the main propositions of the science of formation.

First, human life and its formation always unfold in the pre-, intra-, inter-, and extraspheres of a field, its ranges, regions, dimensions, integrational forms, and horizons. This field is at the same time unique and shared. Therefore, a balance should be maintained among studies of the contributions of each one of these facets, whether they are done integratively by this or another science.

Second, human life keeps forming itself in and through its inherent vital, functional, and transcendent dimensions, all of which are pervaded by the sociohistorical. All spheres mentioned above are affected in their unfolding by each of these dimensions, and they affect them in turn. Hence a balance should be maintained among the contributions of these dimensions within each of the spheres. Auxiliary sciences that can give special information about one type of dimensional contribution to the overall picture of human development should be mined, as it were, for their insights and findings.

Third, human life integrates its own formative attentions, apprehensions, appraisals, affirmations, and applications in lasting, or relatively lasting, integrational forms. These are the foundational core, current, apparent, and actual forms of life. They are partly consonant, partly dissonant with one another and with the field. A balance should be maintained among studies of each of these integrational forms. Their mutual relationships should be examined. We should explore their effect on appreciative apprehensions. Conversely, the effects of such apprehensions on the integrative forms should be an object of our study.

Fourth, human life is a structural dynamic whole of continual mutual interaction. The formative modulation of any range, sphere, region, dimension, integrational form, or horizon can have some modulating influence on all others.

Fifth, each form appreciative apprehension is a structural whole, too. It modulates the various coformants that are implicit in the apprehension. These should be articulated.

Sixth, each response elicited by a form appreciative apprehension may express itself in various observable ways, including facial expressions, gestures, actions, spoken or written words, aesthetic or symbolic presentations. Such manifestations also indirectly disclose apprehensions and dispositions that underlie the response.

Seventh, other sources of knowledge about form appreciative apprehensions, directives, and subsequent dispositions are the responses expressed in public communications, such as music, songs, movies, pictures, dances, plays, diaries, poems, and stories.

Eighth, the thematic and concrete directives that give coherence to the development of a human life are not necessarily present focally to the person's awareness at the time the directive becomes manifest in behavior. Hence the necessity of studying not only the focal but also the pre-, infra-, and transfocal consciousness in regard to such directives.

Ninth, human formation is historical. This means that the integrational forms of peoples' lives are reformed and transformed during their formation journey. Consequently, these forms cannot be presumed to be static. The reason is that the form directives of humanity and individual persons do evolve. They constrict, expand, refine, deepen, or drop out. They change their mutual hierarchical position. They are different in various phases of the history of the common, segmental, and personal ranges of their fields.

Tenth, ascending human formation is centered in directives generated by the transcendent dimension of life. The directives that flow from the sociohistorical, vital, or functional dimensions are distinctively human to the degree that the direction of the transcendent dimension is at least minimally implicated in their forming influence. Scientists in auxiliary fields may focus their research exclusively on sociohistorical, vital, and functional directives as isolated from any influence by those of the transcendent dimension. They may study biochemical or biophysical coformants, reflexes, sensations, instincts, or behavioral reactions. In this case, we have to relate their findings to human formation. Otherwise the subject matter of our science, distinctively human formation, will be missed.

Eleventh, formation scientists subsume formation directives, along with their conditions and consequences, under general categories applicable either to humanity at large or to particular populations. They systematize them within an open, progressive theoretical frame of reference. Before this generalization and systematization takes place, they must engage themselves in detailed descriptions of complex events. Such occurrences include the form appreciative apprehensions and the further responses that constitute them precisely as events of formation.

Twelfth, a crucial source of expanded information and of critical validation of their own findings is the validations of other sciences, arts, disciplines, and traditions that are relevant to the topic under study.

CHAPTER 7

Field Approach of Formation Science

Our field approach originated in the observation that the impact of events cannot be fully appraised without taking into account all the forces that coform the event and our appreciative apprehension of it. Human life is a field of forces that interact with one another. An analysis of any facet of the field or of any event or its apprehension in isolation will not yield a sufficient understanding. No particular event, apprehension, or direction is a self-sufficient unit. Any one of them is only what it is because it is coformed by other forces.

Take, for example, the directive to utilize yoga as a servant source of our consonant unfolding. The meaning of this directive is coformed by other directives operative in people engaged in yoga. If they happen to be Hindus, the directive will be coformed by transcendent religious tenets. If they are Western people with a humanistic concern for bodily relaxation, the directives of vital and psychological wellness will color their interest. Such apprehensions modify the inner way of yoga, alter its results, and may affect the selection and execution of particular exercises. Hindus may primarily experience religious growth in the transcendent dimension of their life, and secondarily enjoy health benefits. Western secularists may primarily appreciate the physical and psychological advantages.

Dialogical Field Thinking

Thinking in terms of the field of life as a whole differs from logical reasoning by means of which we deduce the truth of a particular statement. It differs also from causal thought in which we explain an effect by tracing it to one cause.

Dialogical field thinking, instead of focusing on a particular cause or reason for a happening, tries to comprehend it as emerging from life as a whole. It considers each event or directive to be open to the influences of other facets of the field.

For example, the directive that forms a young person's attitude toward the other sex will be modulated by interformation, by situational sexual formation via the media, by new disclosures of one's hormonal preformation during adolescence. We cannot fully understand what directs people in this or any other area of life without taking into account such factors. Reducing the meaning of the directive to vital-physical, sociohistorical, or interformative "causes" would necessarily lead to misunderstanding.

Each coformant interacts with the others and is modified by this interaction. Formation is thus to be understood in relation to the field as a whole with its interactions. For this reason, we distinguish formative field thinking from informative thinking.

Exemplary Application to the Subfields of Formation Segments

We can illustrate the difference between these two types of thinking by applying them to segments of a population. Each segment constitutes its own field. Segment and field originate in shared exposure to similar challenges. As a result, people similarly exposed may search for similar appropriate responses. Professional athletes pursue goals that are of no interest to professional biochemists. Particular problems confront executives that do not arise for blue-collar workers. Their concerns are not concretized in the same way.

People belong to various segments. Some are based on shared interests, such as an affinity for music, poetry, figure skating, or great books. They meet similar challenges in the area they share. Together they form a segment that cannot be identified with, for instance, their occupational segment. Affinity segments cannot replace those that are occupational. They cannot offer shared solutions for the specific challenges one has to meet in one's occupation.

Let us now apply the difference between informative and formative field thinking to this concept of segments. Informational analytic thinking would view a segment as a collection of individuals. To gain information, the researcher may use methods of quantitative analysis to discern the ways in which different individuals bring personal patterns to the segment.

By contrast, formative field thinking, based on the concept of dialogical coformation, recognizes that a segment and its field are more than the sum of individuals with their various patterns of life. Shared form appreciative apprehensions and directives are a result of the coformative relationship. This relationship emerges when participants face similar problems together. They do not remain the same as when they faced such challenges in isolation. Each new directive disclosed to the participants as effective may be shared with others.

Concepts like "formation segment" and "subformation field" require the use of dialogical field thinking. This type of thought recognizes the unique demands of fields and subfields and the mutuality of their coformants. It understands that a field consists of more than the sum of the individuals who constitute it.

The directives of the segment cannot be deduced exclusively from the original patterns of the participants. They can only be disclosed by studying the segment as a whole through methods of dialogical articulation and elucidation. By breaking down a field into its facets and then examining these in isolation, one loses sight of the directives that are characteristic of the field as a dialectical whole.

Emergent Formation as a Result of Field Dialectics

Human life is marked by emergent events, apprehensions, and directives. Radical reformation, surprising transformation, and discontinuous leaps are to be expected. These cannot be accounted for by the logic of informative thought and rigorous deduction.

Dialogical field thinking aims to comprehend such changes on basis of a consideration of the interaction of all facets. Guiding this interaction are the transcendence and integration dynamics of human life. For example, the emergence of antiwar directives in segments of Western populations can partly be understood in light of interactions taking place between soldiers and victims of recent wars. The media alert us to the devastations caused by war. Reappropriation of spiritual traditions make us long for peace. Elementary fears of extinction are disclosed under the threat of nuclear war. People long for a prosperous, healthy, safe, and happy human life. All these facets together give rise to antiwar directives.

The field as a whole is neither static nor closed in upon itself. Creative types exercise continuous pressure at the boundaries in an attempt to expand them. Conservative types evoke counter pressures to preserve the foundations. Dialogue between them is meant to bring about a gradual expansion, consonant with both the identity of the field and with the newly disclosed realitites. For example, in recent years various Christian churches have manifested more than usual pressures on their boundaries to change; as a result, subsequent counterpressures have emerged to guard basic tenets.

Transcendence Dynamic and Restabilizing Integration Dynamic

The formation field is thus directed by two dynamics: that of transcendence and that of restabilizing integration. The transcendence dynamic moves the field to go beyond its present state. The restabilizing integration dynamic seeks the maintenance of its identity. It does so by congenial integration of the reformations and transformations that are the result of the transcendence dynamic.

Both dynamics can assure the consonant unfolding of the field if mutual dialogue and balance are preserved. Such transcendence and integration cannot be accounted for by examining various events, apprehensions, and directives in isolation.

Dynamic forces drive the field onward, resulting in new forms. Such forces are not simply the sum of all the events that occur. Events cannot be considered simply as so many independent happenings. On the contrary, an event is modulated by the field as a specific whole with its own identity. This identity tends to express itself in formative events. They are beneficial insofar as they realize this identity. It is thus not a question of one event giving form to another. Instead, events, apprehensions, and directives reciprocally form each other. They are truly coformants.

Articulation Complement of Analysis

Dialogical articulation is essential to field thinking. Insulating analysis belongs to informational and logical thinking. To insulate is to isolate the facts to be studied from the web of interactions in which they are embedded. This has its benefits. The methodic isolation of a fact enables the researcher to focus on the properties that can be disclosed within the fact itself and to measure immediate conditions and consequences. It is the preferred method of the exact sciences.

While formation science appreciates such validated findings, its task is to apprehend and appraise how these findings affect and are affected by human life as a whole. It translates them into its own language; it transposes them within its comprehensive theoretical vision; complementing and integrating them in service of transcendent formation.

Dialogical articulation explains events by the part they play in the field; by the manner in which they interact; and by the way in which the field interacts with its horizons and with other fields. Dialogical articulation insists, therefore, that each facet fulfill some formative function. For example, one of the many functions of festive celebrations in a shared field is to alleviate the tensions generated by a onesided promotion of functional performance and production. Traditions of national celebration may strengthen a felt unity between diverse subfields and segments and the wider formation field of the country to which they belong.

Formation Traditions

A formation field can also be described as a dynamic set of interacting patterns nourished by the dispositions rooted in religious or ideological traditions. These recurrent patterns are formative in and through the events they structure. For example, certain religious directives yield patterns of formative expression, which structure such events as memorial services, special sessions of government, national mourning of heroes and soldiers. People expect these ceremonies to unfold according to such patterns. Without them they would feel that something was missing with respect to their religious convictions or ideological feelings of patriotism. These patterns of general form donation are different from those practiced in the subfields of one or another specific religion or denomination, where the pattern of form giving can be understood only in light of its interaction with other patterns characteristic of that group. A national religious pattern is traceable to certain common elements of its various religious faith and form traditions. For example, the monotheistic terminology that is part of some patterns—such as "in God we trust" inscribed on American coins—can be attributed to the rootedness of this terminology in various traditions that share a monotheistic outlook.

Potential and Actual Formation; Intentional and Effective Formation

Earlier we distinguished between what is actually and what is potentially formative. To return to our example, general religious patterns manifested at national celebrations can be potentially formative for the participants. For many, however, they may not be actually formative. Many may apprehend and appraise what is happening as merely an external ritual, an interesting ceremonial without relevance for their religious life.

A distinction can be made also between what is intentionally and what is effectively formative. The intentions of individuals may not coincide with the effect of their actions. For example, the federal authorities who express the religious patterns customary at national celebrations may be people of faith. They may intend to inspire the participants in the ceremony. Yet the effect that occurs may be different from what was intended. For instance, what they express may evoke only a mythical sentiment about the secular greatness, ethical standards, and uniqueness of a country and its historical role in the world.

What is effective but not intended may be recognized or not recognized as such. Formative effects may be unanticipated. They can contribute to distinctively human presence or detract from it. An example of an unintended effect would be a compulsive-obsessive pattern of behavior, such as a guilt-ridden addiction to overly detailed religious prescriptions in accidental matters. Those who devised rigorous codes pertaining to nonessential practices may have intended to safeguard spiritual values. It may take time before the deformative effect is recognized.

An example of the opposite is the intention of a dictatorial regime to give an atheistic form to society by executing religious leaders. The effect of making martyrs may be the opposite of what was intended. A rather vague and decaying faith may be revitalized by the creation of martyrs. Here again it may take time before the rulers recognize the difference between their intentions and these unanticipated effects.

From such examples, it may be clear that we cannot be satisfied with merely mentioning manifest intentions. An exploration of the effects should complement our study.

Intentions of Formation Segments and Individual Participants

A related distinction is that between the intentions of segments of the population and of the individuals who belong to them. A religious segment of the population, for example, may institute positions of leadership to safeguard the fidelity of its adherents. Some individuals, however, may strive for such positions in order to satisfy their need for power. This personal direction is contrary to the original intention of the community.

To give another example, a segment may organize protest actions against social injustices in order to assure that minorities will attain the material conditions conducive to a distinctively human life. Some protesters may join the movement mainly as an opportunity to live out the resentment and rage they did not dare to admit to themselves or to express within their family, community, or neighborhood. Under the cover of the positive intention of the justly and reasonably protesting segment, they may use this protest as an outlet for lifelong nurtured, explosive antagonisms. They may be unaware of what is really moving them to participate so passionately in the common cause. This nonfocal motivation may turn their protest into violence the moment an occasion arises to attack opponents with the remnants of their repudiated rage. Their personal directives clearly deviate from the intention of the segment concerned.

Dialogical Articulation as Such

It may now be possible to understand more clearly the term dialogical articulation. It provides a mode of interpretative explanation that accounts for events by relating them dialogically to their function within a field. Dialogical articulation holds that no event can be explained as formative in rigorously deductive or inductive terms only. The full direction of such events must be understood first of all in terms of the function they perform: Do they serve or frustrate the consonant unfolding of the unique foundational form of a shared or personalized field as a whole? The term articulation refers to a whole to be articulated. Articulation presupposes not an absolute but a relative separation from a wider context.

We may clarify this process by comparison with a more familiar area of articulation, that of speech. Speakers may focus attention on words within their speech by articulating them emphatically. Still, the words articulated receive their meaning from the context of their speech. Similarly, the scholarly articulation of a facet of a field would not make sense outside the context of the field. The articulated facet must be kept in dialogue with other facets that modulate its meaning.

Dialogical Articulation and Rigorous Induction and Deduction

Dialogical articulation thus does not subsume human events under a uniform law, as traditional physicists did with physical events. Unlike lawful causal or logical explanations, dialogical articulation is explicating. Explication shows how an event under investigation serves or frustrates the consonant unfolding of human life as a unique dynamic whole. Once this explication has been accomplished, it may be possible to come to certain general directives that illumine consonant or dissonant responses to similar happenings. While this latter procedure may seem identical with the inductive and deductive processes of the positive sciences, there are differences.

Induction in exact science proceeds directly from a number of identical isolated facts. Analogous induction in formation science does not follow directly from identical isolated occurrences and responses but from a gathering together of explications pertaining to these incidents as articulated within the whole of a field. What is induced is not an exact law but the probability of certain general patterns of formation that should be taken into account when examining similar conditions in any human formation field.

Researchers keep in mind that such probable patterns, when transposed to a specific field, will always be modulated by other facets typical of each unique field. Such nuances render the pattern never totally identical with patterns established thus far.

This latitude of flexible application makes the deduction of formation science only an analogous deduction in comparison with the uniform deduction of the exact sciences. We must add to this that recent developments in the exact sciences, especially in atomic physics, have raised considerable doubts regarding the possibility of uniform induction and deduction in all areas of physical inquiry.

Relative Methodical Separation in Service of Articulation

The demands of articulation do not exclude methodical separation. What is excluded is an absolute, not a relative, separation. It is evidently impossible for researchers to describe at once, simultaneously, all the field influences that coform the incidence they are trying to articulate. The limitations of human intelligence oblige them to separate for methodical reasons each one of the influences. Yet at no moment should they lose the awareness of the dialectical nature of such influences, even if they are not yet fully articulated. Researchers, therefore, should return time and again to the original whole of the initial form appreciative apprehension in order not to lose their openness to the total field. Only then can they articulate the incident in its probable links. After this articulation they consult the possible contributions of auxiliary sciences, disciplines, arts, and traditions. These may confirm or contest their hypothetical findings. In the latter case they return to their provisional descriptions, articulations, and elucidations in order to eliminate subjectivistic distortions or unessential accretions that are to some degree present in each initial report. By this repeated process, they may disclose a more general probability pattern that is relatively applicable to similar situations.

Dialogical Articulation by Formation Counselors and Directors

Formation counselors and directors disclose the personal modulation of the probability pattern in each of their counselees or directees. This unique modulation happens outside of the science of formation strictly speaking. Science can be about general patterns only. Counselors and directors not only profit from the general probability patterns disclosed by the science; they also follow a similar style of disclosure and cautious examination of the personalized field of their counselees or directees. In this case, their dialogical articulation becomes empathic. They nourish an atmosphere in which it becomes possible for counselees or directees to participate personally in the articulation of their life.

Formation counselors and directors support their efforts by communicating at the right moment the related probability patterns disclosed by the science. They do so in a language familiar to their counselees or directees. Throughout the session, they maintain empathy with the situated uniqueness and the faith and form traditions to which their counselees or directees may be committed.

Inherent Unique Articulation of the Field

Each specific field is marked by a uniqueness that in some measure affects all its articulations and contributes to their internal coherence. Each field tends to make all past, present, and future events, apprehensions, and directives—which it accepts as formative—congenial with its own unique foundational form. The field as unique confers on its coformants particular properties that they would not have outside this specific field.

For example, the Japanese formation field has been remarkable for its effective integration of foreign Asiatic and Western patterns of production. Yet in the process of integration, these imports have undergone a subtle but unmistakable reformation. The integration dynamic of the Japanese field endowed them with characteristics they would not have in their field of origin. Another example is the formation field of Roman Catholicism. In its two thousand years of turbulent history, it has assimilated within itself countless forms of art, philosophy, science, and cultural traditions. Yet its integration dynamic has somehow reformed them in consonance with its unique foundational form.

The same applies to the personalized field that each one of us is. People aspire not only to transcend the boundaries of their own field but also to integrate within their basic form of life what they assimilate in this process of transcendence. Even the highest religious transformation has to express itself in terms of an existing field, which in turn is basically modulated by the foundational life-form of, respectively, the unique person and the shared field in which he or she expresses religious experience.

Potential Formation Directives

Many events imply directives for formation that may not yet be actually experienced as such. People may be informed about these happenings but not yet realize what they mean for their life. For example, a conservative Islamic country may be invaded by information about the knowledge explosion due to an acceleration of scientific discoveries. This happening carried potential directives that will in due time necessarily reform certain practices of the Islamic community, as it did for Western religious traditions.

Another example would be the directive inherent in the emergence of modern linguistics, archaeology, historical criticism, literary form criticism, and hermeneutics. Sooner or later this rise of new knowledge had to have an influence on the understanding of Holy Scripture in Christian churches and of the practices flowing from this understanding. For many Christians this occurrence carried only potential directives; for others the direction disclosed became gradually actual, offering them much more than interesting information.

We must try to apprehend not only actual but also potential directives. The latter understanding enables us to anticipate and predict certain developments. Such prediction may be helpful in planning for the future and in preparing populations for unavoidable reformations that will challenge them.

In this context we should realize that one of the fruits of our science is the development in many people of the disposition of formative thinking. This enables people to become aware earlier of pending reformations in their field insofar as these may touch their personal lives.

CHAPTER 8

Events and Directives

W e make a distinction between events and the directives they imply. Such directives make events formative. A happening that is merely functional has no influence on our life; a formative event, in contrast, affects it in some way.

For example, a television program can present information about famine in African countries. The impact on viewers cannot be explained by the communication of statistics. They are moved by images of suffering to give generously to the needy out of compassion.

Formation science studies events as more than functional, as ladened with directives. Events disclose themselves as formative when the researcher focuses on this aspect.

Such directives differ in different fields and subfields. In certain South American countries, for instance, one can find various subformation fields of Christianity, two of them being the landowners and the campesinos enslaved to them. The development of the campesinos may be inhibited by a conviction that it would be a betrayal of their Christian principles to protest against abuse by landlords. Through the course of consciousness raising, they may become aware of their duty to assert themselves. This message has to be communicated to them in a language that makes it come alive for them.

The landowners may also be unfaithful to the basics of Christianity. They may feel that providence has put them in privileged positions, exalting them above campesinos laboring in their fields, convincing them to look down on the laborers as inferiors to be used for their enrichment. In this case the raising of consciousness would mean making the landowners aware of the perverse power of this pulsation, of the way in which it forms their way of thinking and leads them to betray their call as Christians. The language to be used with such landowners can be neither that of the science nor that of the campesinos. It must be the parlance customary in their circles, yet enriched by the insights gained through this science or its sources.

Similar examples can be found in certain North American business ventures. In the beginning of this century, successful entrepreneurs were driven by sweeping pulsations falsely derived from a predestination ethic that led to an unjust treatment of laborers. Hence the rise of labor unions.

Common, Segmental, and Personal Ranges of a Field

The common range of a field comprises directives shared by all its segments. For instance, most Americans, regardless of their segments, share certain democratic principles.

The segmental range represents the adaptation of common principles to segmental needs, which implies an addition of directives. American Indians, for instance, live by the democratic maxims of their country but practice them differently in their tribal reservation than people do in cities. Their tribal customs also have an impact on this practice.

The personal range, while interacting with the common and segmental, is marked by the tendency to make such directives congenial with one's uniqueness. For example, an Indian artist may live in compatibility with the traditions of her clan and country. Yet her artistic expression of their vision is relatively unique. How are such personal directives related to the others?

Relations between Institutionalized and Personalized Directives

The science of formation examines the constituted directives of each of the ranges. It explores the system of directives underlying each one of them. It compares the actual directives of people with these directive systems. Examined also is the interaction of these systems themselves. Then the consonance between actual acts of formation and their underlying directive systems can be appraised.

For example, one typical aspect of British tradition was fairness in interaction. This ideal was embodied in customs of politeness, gentle comportment, and fair play in business, competition, and sports. Working-class people implemented this ideal in a system of dos and don'ts different from that of the upper classes. It would find expression, for instance, in the custom of buddies never squealing on each other; of solidarity during strikes; of keeping a "stiff upper lip" in times of need.

In the personal range it would be lived out in a style typical of one's personality. Obviously an introvert will express fairness differently than an extrovert.

To what degree do people live up to established customs? It depends on the situation. An overworked English guide might forget about being polite and show irritation when a visitor bothers him beyond endurance. Like all traditions this one, too, is vulnerable to changing conditions. Today, for instance, the reactions of the public at soccer matches may be less than fair.

Practical Questions

Under what conditions do people deviate from directives that have been established? How do they feel when this happens? How does that feeling affect their life? Can people lose their commitment to such directives if they fail to obey them over and over again? Can this lead to a resentment of the institutions that produced such directives? Or will it lead to healthy reformation? How can people be helped in a crisis of customs? What role does a counselor or director play at such times?

In trying to answer such questions we should recall that the meaning of a directive is coformed by other directives in the same field. For example, the personal directive to be gentle may be coformed by a transcendent directive of reverence for people; by a societal directive to appear compatible in the circle in which one wants to be accepted; by a familial directive to avoid debate and conflict. Usually we find a mixture of directives behind any one action. This explains why articulation of all of them is needed for fuller understanding. Such articulation presupposes that we can distinguish between different directives.

Differentiation of Directives

Formation theory helps us to differentiate directives. For example, we distinguish transcendent, functional, vital, and sociohistorical directives. Each class can be understood only as being marked off from and as related to the other. For example, the transcendent directive to be present to others in love and justice may be embodied in one's functional capacity of serving them by repairing cars or writing inspiring novels, or in one's vital strength in carrying their luggage or spending hours in nursing.

Universal Directives

To examine directives we have to be attentive first of all to the non-verbal and verbal language of people. Directive meanings do not emerge outside of people-in-formation. They have been filtered through their shared and personal experiences and expressed through nonverbal and verbal patterns of language.

The disclosure of directives happens through such nonverbal expressions as posture, facial expressions, gestures, music, sculpture, paintings, cultural manners, dress, makeup. They constitute a primary language familiar to most people who share similar histories. These primal signs are completed by verbal ones we can hear or read.

A comparison of directives as expressed in various cultures points to certain universals. Children seem to be born with a receptive potency to pick up these universals in any culture in which they are reared, if they are exposed to them. Our science postulates, therefore, that children possess a potency for basic human formation.

The underlying identical structure is expressed in countless cultural variations and can be distorted in many ways. Yet the resulting dissonance can be detected in the light of the elementary structure from which they deviate.

Methodological Conclusions

What are some of the implications for our methodology?

First of all, we start out from spoken or written records that report to us directives of which people are focally aware. These are based in part on institutionalized social structures, of whose influence people are not always aware. We must identify them and their influence on focally expressed directives. An examination of both focal and nonfocal directives is possible due to the relationships between them. They coform each other, as it were. Therefore, they cannot be fully understood in isolation. Disclosing the pattern of coformation between them requires a special kind of method, namely, that of dialogical articulation. This method in and of itself is neither inductive nor deductive.

Only after we have disclosed the pattern of articulation can we induce from it certain basic directives and the laws of their dynamics. If our postulate is true—that certain fundamental directives and dynamics can be found as predispositions in all humans—then some of them may have universal validity. Once we have established what these may be, we can deduce from them implications for human formation, thus disclosing a small number of universal patterns. Most patterns of formation, however, have only a restricted generality. This means that they apply only to a certain population. For example, certain directives and dynamics of marital formation differ in various cultures and religions. As such the probability of their appearance can only be generalized to the adherents of the culture or religion concerned.

Taped or written records of directives offer us lasting, objectively comparable sources of access to what may take place in the ongoing formation of people. Gestures, postures, facial expressions, dress, interior decorations, and so on, also communicate such directives. Videotaping can turn these into records available for scientific comparison and discussion. One of our auxiliary sciences helpful in the analysis of such expressions is the science of semiology or semiotics, the study of sign systems in general.

Pluriformity of Common Fields

Not only are the common fields of humanity internally pluriform because of their segments, there is also a pluriformity of the common fields themselves. For example, that of the Chinese differs from that of Eskimo or Bantu.

Research discloses that specific common fields may have certain patterns that are similar. For instance, Western European and American formation fields cultivate rationalistic modes of thought. Asiatic fields are more influenced by intuitive styles of cognition.

Nevertheless, here, too, dynamics are observable that seem operative in all human cultures. For instance, the inclination of adults to care for the newborn and to assist them in their initial formation seems to be a universal predisposition in members of all cultures, if not distorted by opposite pulsations. Probably corresponding to such preformation of our species are certain connections in our neural system.

Such basic patterns are thus not artificially construed by society. It is not so that society first establishes a system of directives arbitrarily, only then inventing some theory of basic human structures and dynamics, propagating them in order to gain support for its arbitrary system. Rather, it is the other way around: a certain preformation of human life precedes the original emergence of any field. The institutionalization of directives in a society is secondary. Insofar as it is not distorted, it is implicitly guided by our human formation potential and its inherent structure and dynamism.

Preformations tend to give rise to the basic patterns that operate fundamentally in each field, no matter how different they may seem in appearance. This appearance may change considerably during our history.

Often it is a distortion of our preformed basic directions or a reaction against them, especially when they have been overemphasized before.

We conclude that human life under favorable conditions tends to generate a relatively open field that takes into account certain preformed patterns, often distorting them in the process. Their expression adapts itself to the events that emerge in our history. Our knowledge about human possibilities and their fields of presence and action is always changing. Over time, information increases, new events happen, apprehensions accumulate, and patterns of response become more differentiated. The articulation of the field becomes increasingly complex.

One source of such complexity are the developments that come with age and experience. For example, the choice of a marriage partner becomes more complex for older persons. Their increasing knowledge of life makes them sensitive to the problems of mutual adaptation of two independently elaborated fields of great complexity.

Further Implications for Methodology

From what we have seen thus far, it follows that the actual appearance of an event can be explained in its concreteness only by dialogical articulation and subsequent elucidation. This articulation does not look for the "cause" of an event in one or the other single aspect. It clarifies each happening by describing how it is *coformed* by the field as a whole.

For example, an event of envy between colleagues cannot be traced exclusively to one's greater success as a business person. It may go back to a preformative influence of rejection by the envious one's family or schoolmates, to intraformative brooding on one's imagined inferiority, to lack of transcendent faith in one's own life call, to the fundamental dynamics of the pride-form leading to excessive competition.

The method of articulation presupposes that our human fields of presence and action are already articulated prefocally, that they are not merely collections of isolated events and facets. The aspects of each field are already connected with each other. Each of them can, of course, be studied by itself. Various sciences research them in this way. They provide us with sufficiently probable, albeit limited, insights. These should be translated and transposed into formation theory. They give a precise account of details that otherwise might escape us. What they gain in accuracy, however, they lose in scope. Their method yields results, but it cannot alone do full justice to the event in its totality. Their method lacks the articulation and elucidation of all the influences of the field's facets on the formative event. Therefore, the formational implications of the findings of already existing sciences need to be integrated and complemented by formation science.

For this we need appropriate scientific methods. Their genesis, structure, and application will be discussed in the following chapters.

CHAPTER 9

Genesis of the Methodology of Formation Science

L ike other sciences, formation science has its own object, language, and methodology.

Scientific methodology can be defined in general as a constellation of systematic operations, which, in mutual collaboration, adapt the theory, formation, and research of a science to the demands of the specific disclosure of its formal object pole.

The methods of formation science differ in many respects from those of other sciences. One way to apprehend their specificity is to reflect on the origin of these methods. In this case the development of the methodology happens to be closely linked with my own history. Aspects of this science's similarity to and difference from other sciences can be clarified by a review of this history.

Beginnings of the Science of Formation

My first specialization was in pedagogy, spiritual formation, and philosophical anthropology. As a professor in the latter field at a Dutch seminary, and as simultaneously involved in the development of a spiritual formation program for the Dutch Life Schools for Young Adults, I began to develop tentatively some of the main principles and methods of what later would become the science of formation.

Interruption and Expansion of the Emergent Science

In 1954 I was asked to interrupt my full-time engagement in this project in order to make myself available for the initiation of a program in psychology at Duquesne University in the United States. The president of the university, who extended the invitation, was a person accomplished in the humanities, art appreciation, and English literature. His sensitivity in these areas made him concerned about the one-sided positivistic approach to psychology prevalent at that time. He feared its peril for the human spirit. Hence he insisted on the creation of a more humane yet still scientifically responsible psychology in this university.

The positivistic approach operated in accordance with the methods of the physical sciences. Important as the offerings of this type of psychology were, I and others shared the opinion that they should be complemented by a distinctively human approach, one which would acknowledge the transcendent dimension and therewith the relative freedom of the human person.

At that time in the United States two circles of psychologists had developed a human approach to the person as free and insightful. One group consisted of existential psychologists and psychiatrists, represented by two circles, one around Victor Frankl and the other around Rollo May. Other psychologists concerned with human freedom, decision, and insight established a humanistic psychology. This movement was represented by Gordon Allport, Carl Rogers, Kurt Goldstein, Andreas Angyal, Rudolf Dreikurs, the Ansbachers, Abraham Maslow, and Sidney Jourard, among others.

Having been assigned to develop one of the first academic programs in psychology as a human science, it was necessary to take into account these important developments. While I shared the basic concerns of the two movements, some reservations remained. In addition to some philosophical reservations in regard to the assumptions of certain existential and humanistic psychologists, I was concerned about their lack of attention to scientific methodology and about their degree of openness to other perspectives in psychology and related fields and traditions.

How could psychology become a fully human or anthropological science without both a rigorous methodology and a critical openness to all findings and insights that could shed light on the typically human, no matter from what source they came? The question would remain unanswered for a while. In the meantime humanistic and existential psychology had already received recognition in the United States, as expressed in the publication of numerous books, articles, and journals. Its metalanguage became familiar to a growing number of psychologists and psychiatrists. Obviously, it would have been irresponsible for a newcomer to initiate a first academic program in psychology as a human science without taking into account the work done by these American scholars and practitioners.

For this reason I saw as a first step the need to engage in critical, creative dialogue with these movements. Attempts were made to reform and broaden these already existing approaches from within, as it were, by using their own metalanguage but giving it a wider scope and a different meaning. If this effort succeeded, then certain findings of these movements could serve the project of establishing a new mode of psychology as an anthropological or human science that would move beyond humanistic and existential psychology without becoming exclusively behavioristic.

To keep this dialogue as open as possible, I took time out to study under Carl Rogers at the University of Chicago, under Rudolf Dreikurs at the Alfred Adler Institute, and under Kurt Goldstein, Andreas Angyal, and Abraham Maslow at Brandeis University. I was also invited to serve on the editorial board of the *Journal of Individual Psychology*, edited by the Ansbachers. To engage in a similar creative and critical dialogue with the existential psychological movement in America I attended for some time the monthly New York meetings of the Association of Existential Psychology and Psychiatry, organized and chaired by Rollo May. I was asked by him to participate for a while also on the editorial board of the *Review of Existential Psychology and Psychiatry*. Similar contacts were established with Victor Frankl, first in the United States and later as his guest in Vienna.

Some followers of the existential and humanistic movements were influenced by Eastern traditions like Zen Buddhism. Valuable insights can be gained from the East. For some psychologists, however, this contact led to loss of concern for the uniqueness of human life as well as for its responsibility for its own acts and dispositions in the social sphere. To explore this on the basis of objective information, I visited the Buddhist University of Tokyo for dialogue, spent time in a Buddhist monastery in Eheie, and consulted during this travel Western experts in Buddhism residing in Japan.

Growing familiarity with these movements did not diminish my basic objections. Deepened were my reservations about their underlying assumptions and selective attitudes. However, firsthand contacts provided me with more solid information. Understanding their terminology also helped me to reform its meaning in a way that would be relevant to psychology as a human science. While I was teaching psychology, I had to use the same terms because they constituted the metalanguage used by psychologists interested in this field. But I tried, when possible and appropriate, to give them a new content.

Personal acquaintance with leaders in the field confirmed the original observation that existential psychology at that time in the United States had restricted itself mainly to philosophical, literary, psychotherapeutic, and psychoanalytic approaches. Important as they were, none of them alone or in combination could be the basis for psychology as an academic science. Thus far, no one had developed a systematic, methodological approach that might be acceptable at least in some circles to meet the standards set by the empirical science of psychology. This absence of a scientific psychological methodology was one of my main objections to existential psychology.

To validate this critique, I wrote a Ph.D. dissertation for the psychology department of Case Western Reserve University titled "The Experience of Really Feeling Understood by a Person." More important than the topic was the methodology developed in the dissertation. Its purpose was to point to the lack of scientific precision in existential psychology. The initiation of this new methodology influenced eventually the development of the articulation method used in formation science, on which I had been working since my early days of research in Europe.

Work on other aspects of the methodology for formation science was inspired paradoxically by the lack of receptivity on the part of many humanistic and existential-phenomenological psychologists to other types of psychology—their relevant contributions tended to be neglected. I was especially concerned about the tendency to ignore the impact of religious, ideological, or syncretic formation traditions on the psychology of people. Last but not least, in many phenomenologists a concentration on the description of focal experiences led to a neglect of the exploration of nonfocal dynamics. In response to this neglect, I eventually developed the method of elucidation of formation dynamics. In addition, my desire to remain reasonably receptive to the findings of other types of psychology, as well as those of other sciences, would give rise to the method of consultation of their formational implications. This development would imply the elaboration of methods of dialogical integration of such contributions by means of translation and transposition. These methods would explicitly include as well the formationally relevant implications of traditions among those auxiliary sources to be consulted by formation science. During my brief period of teaching and research in psychology, I expressed my respect for such traditions in my book *Religion and Personality*.

My ongoing concern with distinctively human formation was sustained during these years by work in formation—both in the United States and abroad, during weekends and academic recesses. This work was a natural continuation of the formation practice and study begun in the Dutch Life Schools for Young Adults. During this nine-year psychology assignment, these formation sessions helped to maintain the link with my original field of academic study, publication, and practice. Some colleagues assisted me in these formation sessions. Assisting also for a brief time was the initiator of the Dutch formation centers for young adults, Ms. M. Schouwenaars, who came over from Belgium to conduct a series of formation courses.

In the following twenty-five years I could again give myself full-time to the study of formation. I was able to elaborate in more detail the methodology, theory, and content of formation science, begun in Holland. My interim participation in the field of psychology had more than ever confirmed my conviction of the necessity to establish such a new science.

Let us pause here to note that formation science is at the same time both wider than and smaller than psychology. It is wider because the issue of distinctively human formation is so varied, rich, and complex that it would be impossible to do justice to it by relying exclusively on the data and insights of only the science of psychology. It is smaller because formation science can utilize only those insights and data of psychology that are formationally relevant. It must bypass numerous other important findings. They may be fascinating and extremely valuable, in their own right and in relation to other purposes, but they have no direct relevance to the praxis of distinctively human formation.

Genesis of the Dialogical Consultation and Integration Methods

Some of the main objections to both humanistic and existential psychology were formulated in university lectures at the time and in my book *Foundations of Existential Psychology* (hereafter referred to as *Foundations*). In the preface to this work, the notion of radical perspectivity set the tone for the critique. Radical perspectivity means in this context that no empirical science as such, by its own methodology, can come to infallible certainty. It may only approximate certainty. One reason is that empirical scientists cannot fully escape their own formation field. Evidently they can and should widen their perspective as much as possible. Some of them may approximate a worldwide transcultural perspective. Yet this amplified field is still limited to the perspective of apprehensions and appraisals available to the scientist at this moment of history.

A science that is truly empirical is thus necessarily restricted by field-bound experience and observation, which can generate only limited points of view. Such perspectives are inescapably restricted by the knowledge available at any given point in the history of humanity.

I am not writing here as a professional philosopher or theologian. Hence I cannot go into the question of how far and in what sense the latter disciplines may claim that they are able to attain truth in a nonperspectival fashion. Nor is this the place to discuss the question of revealed truth as expounded by various religious faith traditions. Functioning as empirical scientists, we can consider the issue of radical perspectivity only *in* the empirical realm as such.

The term *radical* refers to the fact that the perspectival outlook of the empirical scientist is due to the very nature of empirical science. A science can be empirical only when it is rooted in the limited sense-bound experience and observation presently or historically available in spatially and temporally restricted fields.

After this introduction, various chapters of *Foundations* develop in more detail certain implications of the proposition that all schools, methods, and approaches in psychology are perspectival. Each of these perspectives makes available another profile of the psychological reality under consideration. Initially reality cannot be made available to our empirical intelligence in any other way. The profiles thus disclosed increase and enrich our knowledge of psychology. *Foundations* concluded with the notion that psychology as an anthropological or human science should not ignore any serious approach in psychology. On the contrary, it should examine these results carefully and respectfully. In the book, I illustrated this point by discussing at length how certain findings of the behavioristic psychology of Skinner could be integrated via translation and transposition in an anthropological psychology.

The introduction to *Foundations* offered the opinion that existential psychology ought to be defined in a novel and wider sense as a movement of reaction that, in cooperation with similar movements, had made psychologists more conscious of other perspectives in the field of psychology. I cautioned that this movement should not insulate itself as merely another school in psychology. Rather, it should work as a leaven. Once this awareness of radical perpsectivity became common in psychology, the need for a specific existential psychology would vanish. The psychophenomenological approach could then be utilized as a matter of course by researchers, along with various other approaches they deemed to be helpful in scientific exploration.

Psychology as a Human Science

In my ongoing critique of the exclusive tendencies of certain existential psychologists, I proposed in *Foundations* to relinquish the term *existential psychology* and its popular orientations and to replace it by the term *anthropological psychology*. My idea at the time was that this branch of psychology would focus on the integration of the many relevant offerings of various types of psychology in service of practical life formation. The idea was not to develop a kind of superpsychology that would gradually replace perspectival psychologies. On the contrary, all schools should keep on developing their particular perspectives and approaches. In this way experimental scientists would be able to disclose empirically as many profiles of reality as possible.

The perspectival structure of the empirical mind itself, as sense-bound and field-bound, compels initial disclosures of reality by perspectival approaches. Once these are disclosed, anthropological psychology or psychology as a human science could integrate many, if not all, humanly relevant findings of the differential psychologies. Such integration would be performed in the light of a specific consideration. In this case, the practical perspective would be that of the psychological formation of the human person as typically human.

The proposal in *Foundations* for such an anthropological psychology to replace both the existential-phenomenological and the humanistic psychologies was radically new. Gordon Allport wrote an enthusiastic recommendation for this conception. Yet as it turned out the time was not ripe for such a radical critique of two popular psychological movements. As the idea I had could not be followed up by psychologists, given the current state of the field, I was obliged for the time being to keep using for the expression of my thought the limited terminology of existential and humanistic psychologies. Their metalanguage was acceptable to colleagues and students. In the meantime these terms took on an increasingly different, wider, more anthropological meaning. In the end the synonym for *anthropological psychology*, namely, *psychology as a human science*, found acceptance in our psychology department, if not exactly in the receptive, integrative way I had proposed in *Foundations*.*

---

*I would like to pay tribute at this point to the psychology students who sustained my efforts to go beyond popular humanistic and existential psychology. They contributed to the proposed anthropological psychology—and its replacement of existential psychology—by their master's theses and two of them by their doctoral dissertations on this transition.

Worth mentioning are the following master's theses: David Smith's "Anthropological Psychology and Ontology," in 1960; Dorothy Greiner's "Anthropological Psychology and

From Anthropological Psychology to Formation Science

How did my ongoing anthropological critique of existential and humanistic psychologies contribute to the development of certain aspects of the methodology of formation science? This critique was meant to foster, among other things, a reasonable receptivity to all perspectives in psychology. In formation science the kind of receptivity proposed for anthropological psychology widened to a concern with the offerings of all the perspectives represented by auxiliary sciences, disciplines, arts, and formation traditions.

The critique of existential psychology had highlighted the value of all humanly relevant insights and findings of all types of psychologies in the light of a practical, psychological formation perspective. This perspective would function in the proposed anthropological psychology as a unifying criterion of relevance by means of which pertinent selections from the findings of differential psychologies could be made. In time, this practical perspective would generate its own unifying language and theoretical frame of reference in which the various psychological insights could be translated and transposed. A similar practical perspective, but far wider than a merely psychological one, would provide one of the unifying criteria for formation science.

Receptivity of Formation Science

Formation science goes beyond the project of *Foundations*. It integrates not only psychological perspectives, as anthropological psychology proposed to do. Via its methods of systematic consultation and integration, a rich variety of insights and findings of other auxiliary sources is also taken into account. For example, various psychodynamic psychologies, such as the Freudian, Adlerian, Jungian, Rogerian, and the schools of Murray, Horney, and Frankl, have dealt with certain psychological aspects of formation dynamics. Their findings are useful for further elaboration by this science, which provides an open dynamic picture of the formation field as a whole. Each of these dynamic psychologies

Physics," William F. Kraft's "Anthropological Psychology and Phenomenology," Jeanne C. Reeves's "An Introduction to the Methodology of Anthropological Psychology," all written and accepted in 1962; and Larry V. Pacoe's "Anthropological Psychology and Behavioristic Animal Experimentation," in 1963. Two doctoral dissertations, written also under my direction, defended the same transition: Dorothy Greiner's "A Foundational-Theoretical Approach toward a Comprehensive Psychology of Human Emotion," defended and accepted in 1964; and William F. Kraft's "An Existential Anthropological Psychology of the Self," defended and accepted in 1965.

represents one important coloration of the immense spectrum of formation dynamics.

Formation science is concerned with the human life as it unfolds in and through its dynamics. The psychodynamic patterns dealt with by those auxiliary sciences that are psychological represent only one profile of the multifaceted dynamics of human formation. Transposed in the unifying language and vision of formation science, they complement one another. They should also be complemented in formation theory by other types and facets of dynamics. These are examined by such sciences as pedagogy, sociology, cultural anthropology, linguistics, semiotics, political science, economics, journalism, law, nutrition, medicine, and philosophical and theological anthropologies.

The same holds for the dynamics of formation disclosed by the arts and humanities, and by religious, ideological, and syncretic common formation traditions, especially the schools and masters of Eastern and Western spiritualities.

Limitations of Explications of Focal Experiences

Because of the richness of these auxiliary sources, I had already made a plea to psychologists in *Foundations* not to restrict themselves to psychophenomenological explications of experiences as such. Of course, the description of experience does have immense value. Formative thinking starts from experience. Yet descriptions alone provide us with only a limited understanding of human life. They should be the point of departure for more penetrating explorations. This was one of the reasons why I wanted in the title of my book the word *foundations*. This word was meant to emphasize that such descriptions are useful to illumine certain experiential foundations. Foundations are the beginning of a building. By themselves they cannot erect a fully developed psychology as a human science.

A concrete dynamic psychology of human life goes beyond its foundations. This is not to deny, of course, that many humanistic and existential psychologists transcended the realm of phenomenological description of experiences. Some of them excelled also in the study and practice of psychodynamics, albeit often from the one-sided profile of only one or another psychology.

Indispensability of Perspectival Approaches

My critique of existential psychology in *Foundations* confirmed that perspectival approaches are the only way in which we can initially disclose the various profiles of psychological reality. Due to the innate perspectival nature of our empirical intellect, we cannot integrate all such profiles in their totality into one superscience. What we can do is abstract from them certain implications that are similar in that they all refer to the same practical concern or perspective.

To take an example from another field, the science of engineering abstracts certain practical implications for engineering from the sciences of mathematics, metallurgy, chemistry, and computer science. It reformulates their relevant findings in terms of the science of engineering, presenting them to engineers in their own language for use in practical construction projects. Engineering science never aims at integrating into a superscience these diverse sciences, but it draws from them what students in engineering need to know about diverse areas of inquiry pertinent to their profession. There is no need for them to gain a specialist's mastery of these auxiliary sciences. In a similar vein, formation science commends and fosters the development of all scientific perspectives, of the arts and humanities, and of the spiritual wisdom of faith and formation traditions. It uses their results as long as they prove to be potentially compatible with the demand for consonant, distinctively human, life formation.

We have considered the genesis of the methodology of formation science and offered some reflections on the implications of these beginnings in regard to the principles on which this new human science is based. The next chapter will deal specifically with scientific methodology in this field.

CHAPTER 10

Methods of Formation Science

The methodology of formation science comprises two main facets, namely, methods of theory formation and research methods. Because theory formation is the basis of any science, we will expand first on its structure and operation. After that we will briefly introduce the research methods to be discussed more extensively in the following chapters.

Methods of Theory Formation

Theory serves formation by formulating hypothetical propositions about its process and meaning. These are generated by initial apprehensions and appraisals of the formation field; by investigations of multifaceted aspects of this field; and by dialogue with the findings and insights of auxiliary sources.

Hypothetical formulations are arranged in a coherent theory through a two-phase approach. The first phase involves the formulation of assumptions and principles of formation rooted in the view that human life unfolds in a relatively free formation field. These principles and assumptions coform the anthropology of formation science. The second phase of theory formation entails the formulation of propositions that coform the body of specific knowledge of the science. Among them various divisions can be distinguished as relevant to specific facets of the field, namely, the structural, the dynamic, the social, and so on.

Formation science tests its propositions by means of its research methods. It develops coherence between propositions by relating them to basic laws of formation that are rooted in the assumptions of the science as contained in its anthropology.

For example, in our theory of social presence various propositions state that social presence can remain consonant and effective only if it is sufficiently attuned to a person's limits and potencies. These proposi-

89

tions are related to the principle that the disposition of congeniality with one's basic foundational life-form is necessary for consonant formation. This principle is rooted in turn in the assumption of the science that each human form is relatively unique. Of course, application of the research methods may confirm or put into question any one of these theoretical propositions.

Before acting on its research results, the science determines their degree of probability by means of verification criteria. Are these research results reasonably consonant with the validated theory, and with findings and insights, of auxiliary sources? Have the effects of application been validated and has reasonable consensus been reached by members of the research team or by fellow scientists? Are the results obtained by these methods provable as sufficiently probable?

For example, research in social presence led to the proposition that congeniality or personal integrity is conducive to consonant social presence. This proposition was confirmed as highly probable due to its congruence with related findings formulated in the subtheory of social formation. It was in agreement with the opinions of members of the research team who monitored each stage of the process with critical, creative objections and suggestions. This proposition was in accord with a multitude of related findings in auxiliary sources, and its practical-directive effectiveness worked in a variety of different settings.

The formulation of propositions is done in such a way as to avoid confusing connotations with meaning systems in other sciences, in the arts, in formation traditions, or in everyday common language. The scientific formulation must render a proposition not only logically but also lingually coherent with other propositions that coform the formation theory as a whole. For instance, the formulations we used in the example about congeniality and social presence are coherent with others to be found in the body of the science. They do not connote merely a psychoanalytic, Jungian, humanistic, Hindu, Christian, or any other faith and form tradition.

Acceptable scientific formulation does not contradict the related principle that formation scientists and practitioners should be bilingual, that is, capable of translating back into common or segmental language the findings of their science.

Four Characteristics of Formation Knowledge

The methodology of the science must lead to a knowledge that is theoretical, qualitative, directional, and dynamic.

Theoretical Characteristics

The scientific knowledge of formation is *theoretical* in that it transcends, but does not leave out of focus, our prescientific knowledge of the field. The scientists concerned are no longer merely prescientific participants in human life. They know that the acquisition of theoretical knowledge requires a special disposition of focal apprehension and appraisal. One has to be able to distance oneself from prescientific absorption in the field. Relative transcendence of common, segmental, and personal perspectives is also a requirement of theory formation.

Take again the example of research in social presence. As long as we are enthusiastic prescientific participants in social care situations, we may not take sufficient distance from the pressures and pulsations inherent in them to see what is really going on. We may thereby neglect the congeniality needs of self and others. For instance, a mother may subtly induce false guilt feelings that lead her daughter to ignore her responsibility to foster her personal integrity as an independent woman. By distancing ourselves from prefocal involvement, we may be able to appraise our neglect of the congeniality factor and the deformative effect this omission has on our social presence.

The theoretical disposition thus enables us to lift an event out of the flow of life. We can then describe its object and subject poles, and their interaction. The same orientation makes it possible for a scientist to relate the results of such observations to a coherent system. Theoretical distance lets us identify the directives operative in people. Once these directives have been abstracted as general propositions, they can be reordered systematically in the theory of the science.

Qualitative Characteristics

Formation theory demands that knowledge be *qualitative*. The focus of this specific science must be on events in reference to their formational qualities. We abstract these from the event as a whole when we appraise their relevance to human formation.

For instance, the event of a marriage annulment can be looked at from different perspectives. Each brings into prominence one or the other qualifying aspect of the event, such as the law, economic consequences, local customs, technical organization of procedures, and so on. Research in this science focuses on these qualities only insofar as they are formationally relevant to the life of people.

Directional Characteristics

Formation science is *directional.* Theory in this specific science implies, therefore, that research should aim at directives which can proximately guide life in its distinctive humanness. This practical purpose calls for the disclosure of the obstacles and facilitating means or conditions to be taken into account as one pursues and refines directives and their flexible implementation.

Dynamic Characteristics

Formation science seeks a knowledge that is dynamic. It must elucidate for us the manifold dynamics that operate effectively in our field. They affect its spheres, ranges, dimensions, and integrational forms in all regions of consciousness. The human condition is so complex that no science as such has been able to cover these aspects totally, not even the psychodynamic psychologies. Each may disclose one or the other profile of the configuration of human formation while more or less concealing others.

We know, for example, from the life of Sigmund Freud that he was not always capable of seeing through the dynamics of the everyday approaches used by salespersons and other people who tried to take advantage of him. He was at the same time a genius in the disclosure of the dynamics between the infrafocal and focal regions of consciousness, particularly in regard to those of the vital level in its libidinal articulation. He analyzed the interaction between the vital and the functional dimensions. He viewed the impact of these dynamics on the libidinal facet of interformation between people. When his contribution is integrated with the knowledge we have of the other spheres and dimensions of the field, especially the transcendent, it can be of great value for consonant formation. It would be as unwise to neglect his insights as it would be to reduce dynamics only to the basic sets he unveiled so masterfully.

Research Methods

The four main research approaches of the science, besides the methods of theory formation, are dialogical articulation, elucidation, consultation, and application. They are related to one another and to the science by three auxiliary methods: dialogical translation, transposition, and integration.

While each of these methods proceeds according to its own methodological assumptions, all share certain basic *directive* assumptions. Methodological assumptions modulate the methods insofar as their specific facet of research is concerned. Directive assumptions relate all methods to the same basic presuppositions of the science and to its general principles as formulated in formation anthropology.

Each approach enables us to clarify a particular configuration of our field. The science has thus far disclosed four configurations: structural, dynamic, empirical, and practical. The method of articulation makes primarily available the structural; the method of elucidation, the dynamic; of consultation, the empirical; of application, the practical-directive. We say *primarily* because configurations of the field are interwoven. We cannot approach one of them without implicating the others, at least implicitly.

Each method is dialogical-formational. Often these qualifiers are not explicitly mentioned, but they always implicitly affect the research we do.

The Term "Dialogical"

The term *dialogical* refers to the fact that each method implies an implicit or explicit dialogue with:

1. the canons, categories, assumptions, and principles of formation theory;
2. the knowledge of formation science thus far acquired by research in this field;
3. the concrete formation field under investigation;
4. the purposes, functions, and findings of the methods that co-form the methodology;
5. the findings and insights of auxiliary sciences, arts, and traditions;
6. the universal, common, segmental, or subsegmental population to which the disclosed directives have to be applied effectively.

One or the other of these dialogues may prevail in the use of each method. Then, too, the event that is being investigated may favor the choice of one kind of dialogue over another. In such cases the nonprevalent dialogues may become recessive and implicit. Yet while staying in the background, they will never be totally absent.

The Term "Formational"

The methods are also called *formational* to characterize their difference from informational methods used, for instance, by functionally oriented psychologies. The same term emphasizes their distinction from methods that are not primarily guided by questions of the practical formation of people. An example of the latter would be the methods of psychophenomenology. Their primary purpose is the disclosure of the structures of psychological experiences, not necessarily their relevance for the practice of distinctively human formation. The addition of the qualifier *formational* is thus necessary to highlight the identity of the methods of formation science as distinct from those of other sciences. To avoid needless repetition, we will not always explicitly mention the qualifiers dialogical and formational when we speak about these methods, but we do mean them.

Different Research Methods

Selection methods guide researchers in their choice of a topic of attention relevant for the formation of their own life and that of at least a segment of the population. The chapters on the selection and articulation methods will outline these prodecures.

Articulation methods engage us primarily in the identification of the structures of the field, their interconnections with and their ability to point toward underlying dynamics and traditions. This approach could be called architectonic. We draw up, as it were, a blueprint of the apparent features of the field, a description of its more obvious structures. Usually these are described in relation to a specific event that the researcher has made the object of attention. This approach is mainly descriptive. Its genesis and operations will be discussed further on.

Elucidation approaches are analytical-theoretical. We no longer focus mainly on the evident blueprint of the field. What we consider now explicitly are the underlying dynamics between the structures that coform our field. Given the right conditions, the disclosed structures influence the direction of the dynamics. They interact as polar energies in all regions of consciousness, thus playing a modulating role in the unfolding of our life.

For example, the dynamics of a conflict between us and our parents are influenced in their expression by such structures as our preformation; our interformation with them and with our peers; our sociohistorical situation of having more independence than they did in their youth, and so on.

Our field is never static. At times its movement may be slight, almost absent, but movement is there as long as we live. Formation science must deal with these dynamics, their obstructing and facilitating conditions, and their consequences. It must address the issue of how to deal with them in ways that foster consonance and ascendance of our life.

The elucidation approach is mainly analytical-theoretical in that it analyzes the probable interacting movements of formation dynamics in the light of scientific theory and auxiliary sources in other arts, sciences, disciplines, and formation traditions.

Following our discussion of the selection and articulation methods, we will devote some time to elucidation methods, their rationale and their operations.

Consultation widens our search through dialogue with formationally relevant findings offered by auxiliary sources. It accompanies the articulation, elucidation, and application approaches, complementing and correcting their results. For this reason, consultation research will be dealt with in some measure in later chapters.

Something similar can be said of the auxiliary *translation, transposition,* and *integration* approaches. They enable us to assimilate the findings of the auxiliary sources, after consultation, into the science of formation. In the chapters on the language of formation science, we will refer again to these three auxiliary methods in their relation to the scientific language issue.

The methods of *application* engage researchers in general applicative examples and/or in a critical appraisal of the population to which they may want to apply their findings. This research tool is important because researchers in this field are not content with outlining a set of application proposals merely deduced from the results of the former research methods. Thus far they have articulated a more general field and elucidated the dynamics at work there. Now they consult more specifically auxiliary sources that have available validated information about a particular population, statistically or otherwise. They compare these new findings critically with those of their more general research. The result of this comparison may refine, complement, and yet confirm their former findings. It may necessitate a revision of certain probable general propositions they had formulated but that cannot stand up to the new disclosures.

All of these research methods supplement each other in mutual modulation, as may be clear from the following summation.

Selection focuses our attention on the right choice of relevant topics and of formation events that exemplify them. Both topics and events should be amenable to the operations of the subsequent methods.

Articulation provides us with a dialogical description of relevant structures and connections already bringing into relief peripheral manifestations of possible dynamic constellations.

Elucidation penetrates into the underlying dynamic constellations themselves.

Consultation brings into play the formationally relevant findings of auxiliary arts, humanities, sciences, disciplines, and traditions.

Translation, transposition, and *integration* harmonize such findings with the language of the science and with its evolving theory of formation.

Application expands and specifies the findings in dialogue with a specific population. Each dialogical application functions at the same time as a test of the probability of the findings.

The formative intent of the methodology as a whole harmonizes the different methods with one another.

Following this general description of the main methods of the science, we shall in the next chapter deal with the genesis of the first two of them: the selection and articulation methods. The explanation of their historical development will prepare us for a more detailed consideration of these two methods in a subsequent chapter.

CHAPTER 11

Genesis of the Selection and Articulation Methods

I n chapter 9, "Genesis of the Methodology of Formation Science," we traced the historical development of this approach and distinguished its methods from those used in other sciences. The same kind of historical tracing is important in regard to the genesis of the selection and articulation methods and to the part I played in the development of an empirical psychophenomenological method, resulting from a critique of existential psychology. From this critique came the alternative methods, first of all of empirical psychophenomenology, and later of formation science itself.

In this chapter, for the sake of historical clarity, we will compare the selection and articulation methods with the phenomenological. Both have their roots in the formation practice and research I did in Europe. My development of the first empirical psychophenomenological method when I came to the United States did influence somewhat the further development of the selection and articulation methods of the science of formation. While this influence gave rise to certain similarities, a closer look reveals that the methods first inaugurated in psychology and later in formation science are by no means identical, and that the latter went far beyond the former.

The psychophenomenological method itself differs, as the name implies, from phenomenology as used in philosophical or theological circles. As a general rule the methods of philosophy and theology differ from those used in empirical sciences, such as, among others, psychology, pedagogy, sociology, and cultural anthropology. Accordingly, philosophical, theological, and psychophenomenological methods are analogous, not identical. As will be clarified later, the selection and articulation methods of formation science cannot be identified as such with any of the above.

Before developing the methodology of formation more fully, I had been invited by the psychology department of Duquesne University to lay the groundwork for a method of phenomenological research useful for the purpose of establishing a program in psychology as an anthropological or human science.* Some elements of the psychophenomenological method thus developed could be transposed to formation methodology along with elements of methods used in other sciences.

Such transposition is not merely a question of imitation. It is a process through which elements of the method of one science are adapted to the unique purpose of that of another. The resulting transposition actually transforms the elements by their assimilation into a new context. An example would be the way in which hermeneutic methods originally devised for the interpretation of Holy Scripture were later adapted to human sciences like cultural anthropology.

Lingual Considerations

The term *existential* creates some confusion among psychologists unless they can give it a wider meaning than some philosophers and psychologists initially did. It can be used in a basic sense to point to human life experiences. Thinkers like Hans Ur von Balthasar, Karl Rahner, Bernard Lonergan, and Paul Ricoeur seem to use it in this sense.

We prefer in formation science to avoid this term because we disagree with the ideological connotations attached to it by certain existentialists in the field of philosophy. We also want to prevent the mistaken notion that the science of formation represents mainly one perspective or school of its auxiliary sciences, a concern that certainly applies to the existential-phenomenological view. We benefit from all of these theories while identifying with none. Our comprehensive approach transcends these perspectives while integrating the formative implications of their theories and findings.

For similar reasons the terms *experience* and *experiential* are not always used. Often in common parlance these words point to emotional ex-

*Readers who want more information can find my synopsis of this methodology in the *Journal of Individual Psychology*, 15 May 1959: 66–72, and in my books *Existential Foundations of Psychology* and *Foundations of Personality Study: An Adrian van Kaam Reader.* Other discussions regarding my methodology can be found in Hall and Lindzey's *Theories of Personality*, pp. 332–34. The dissertation itself is on loan by the dissertation division of the library of Case Western Reserve University.

periences in their subjectivistic feeling tone. It seems difficult for students to disengage themselves from this connotation. Formation science as comprehensive distances itself from any "-ism." It keeps itself free from emotionalism and subjectivism. The object as well as the subject pole of an event are critically examined. The intellectual as well as the affective facets of form appreciative apprehensions are explored. Therefore, instead of always using the term *experience,* we often prefer the term *form appreciative apprehension. Apprehension* refers to the intellectual, *appreciative* to the affective facet of the experience, while *form* specifies its relation to formation. The methodology of this science implies procedures of elimination of subjectivistic distortions and dissonant accretions that are usually implicit in the act of initial appreciative apprehension, influenced as it is by one's restricted field.

Let us now move to the distinction between the psychophenomenological method and the selection and articulation methods. Since I had a hand in both approaches, the following clarification is necessary.

New Psychophenomenological Method in American Psychology

This new method was developed to describe and analyze scientifically the psychological structures of human experience. In my first attempt, at Case Western Reserve University, the method was illustrated by an examination of the experience of really feeling understood by a person. The challenge was to provide concepts, constructs, and methods that would later enable colleagues and students in the program of anthropological psychology to disclose scientifically the structures of human experiences as they manifested themselves in the framework of the situation in which they were perceived.

For example, the experience of feeling understood had to be described by the 360 subjects who were asked to record the relation between what they were feeling and the corresponding life situation. The instruction to the subjects was so formulated that they would recount only those situations of feeling understood that they perceived as personally meaningful. The new method was concerned with incidences that relate the experience to the formation field of the person. This point was essential. My contention was that the origin of the data for an anthropological psychology had to be the structures of situated experiences as disclosed by an intersubjectively verifiable methodology.

The research started out with the gathering of individual descriptions of a specific experience. From these descriptions there emerged the more general positing of a psychophenomenological structure that would be representative of the experience of the population randomly selected for research.

Psychophenomenological Processing of the Data

After gathering the empirical data in the form of the subjects' written descriptions, the following twelve steps were undertaken.

First, each situational description was read carefully in its entirety to obtain a first general impression of the structure of the experience as it seemed to unfold in the formation field of representatives of this population.

Second, another reading of each description was done with a different mind-set. Instead of focusing on the whole, I now focused on the differentiation of structural elements of the experience. Each time a transition in the description was perceived, it was recorded as a *possible* structural element to be appraised as such later on. The appraisal would determine whether the subject in his or her description was really pointing to the disclosure of a differential element of the experience. The recordings of such possible elements were made in the concrete language of the subjects. They were not yet translated into the metalanguage of empirical phenomenological psychology.

Third, the collections of these records showed many tautologies, redundancies, and other kinds of repetitions, and numerical incidences of the same kinds of statements were noted down. The repetitious statements were eliminated to make the material more suitable for concise empirical analysis.

Fourth, the probable meaning of the structural elements were appraised provisionally by relating them tentatively to each other according to the method of compatibility. Which statements of the subjects seemed implicitly or explicitly compatible with one another, which seemed incompatible? Was the seeming incompatibility real? Did the statement represent a merely accretional private facet of the situation as subjectively apprehended by the subject? In that case, it could not serve the disclosure of the experience of the population represented by the sample. It would be idiosyncratic. Or was it perhaps an essential element of the structure of the experience, which only this subject was able to perceive and express? His or her ability to do so could be the consequence of deeper apprehension, of a greater expressive facility, or of a special situation favoring the disclosure of this specific structural element. Were they still compatible with the descriptions of others at least implicitly?

Fifth, all compatible and incompatible statements were listed in their original concrete formulation by the subjects. They were then subjected to the judgment of three independent psychologists. This operation was introduced into the method to prevent the impact of any bias on my part that could have influenced the selection of relevant statements. Prefocal inclinations to rate statements by the subjects as compatible or incompatible, essential or accretional, on the basis of my own prescientific apprehension of the situation of feeling understood had to be eliminated. Personal apprehension, of course, could in no way be normative for the structure of the experience in relation to the population of representative subjects.

Sixth, once the reported structural components were validated by the three judges as objectively significant facets and as reasonably compatible with one another, implicitly or explicitly, the researcher started the process of methodical phenomenological reflection on these lingual records as pointing potentially to valid coforming elements of the structure of the experience.

Seventh, the records were again related meaningfully to each other as potential elements of an integral structure on the basis of intersubjectively validated criteria of essentiality and compatibility. Then an appraisal was made as to whether and how these tentatively identified elements might point to their belonging essentially to the emergent structure of the experience of the population concerned.

Eighth, I engaged in a psychophenomenological situational reflection on each element of the experiences as still recorded in the language reported by the subjects. Each potential element was examined systematically for what it possibly disclosed about the experience of really feeling understood for that specific subject in that situation. The purpose of this procedure was to capture what the essence of that situation was for the subject who felt understood in it.

Ninth, each element, when found compatible and essentially relevant, was then translated and transposed into the metalanguage of psychology as an anthropological or human science.

Tenth, this translation and transposition were again submitted to three independent psychologists as impartial judges to guarantee as much as possible the fidelity of each procedure to the alleged truth core of the original description.

Eleventh, following validation by the judges and critical discussion of the differences of opinion regarding unclear or ambiguous translations, the final stage of the method was initiated. The results of this empirical data gathering, analysis, phenomenological reflection, and validation by the judges were integrated and synthesized into a probable paradigm of the experience of really feeling understood by a person. This description was submitted to a group of clinical psychologists familiar in their practice with the phenomenon of feeling understood. They were asked if the definition made sense to them on basis of practical application. When they confirmed that it did, the paradigm was accepted as sufficiently probable.

Had the committee raised serious objections, the process of analysis, translation, transposition, and phenomenological reflection would have to have been repeated, with special attention given to the elements possibly lacking or misrepresented according to their judgment. If such a repetition had produced the same results, the conclusion would have been that the descriptive definition could be upheld as a sufficiently probable paradigm of the situated experience of the population represented by this statistically significant sample.

Twelfth, the final task was to state clearly the limitations of the insights gained by this new methodology. I concluded that they would be helpful to approximate with sufficient probability what such an experience means for the population represented by the research sample, within the limits of the questions asked. In this case, my research enabled me to clarify what feeling understood probably means for a city population of American subjects with an above average education.

The statement of limits pertaining to the conclusion reached evoked in me even then questions about the usefulness of this and similar studies. I pointed out that empirical phenomenological analysis could be used as an effective tool for the preparation of questions for interviews and questionnaires. The examination of the structure of a certain experience for people, if it preceded the formulation of questions, would enable one to measure more accurately the extent of their presence in the situation identified by this analysis.

For example, a follow-up study could be done to ascertain the number of people who claim to experience feeling understood. To devise the right questions for such a questionnaire in interview language, one should first know what these words mean for the population concerned. The empirical phenomenological analysis of the structure of feeling understood, as probably experienced by a statistically significant sample of the population to be interviewed, would help researchers to formulate the right questions. Another use of the results could be made by psychotherapists and counselors dealing with such phenomena in their clients, and by writers or speakers referring to them in written or oral treatises.

Substantial but Limited Value of the Psychophenomenological Method

The limitations of the results of the method I had initiated made me aware of the desirability of complementing it with other methods. Later, upon resuming the development of the science of human formation begun in Holland, this awareness gave rise to the mutually complementary methods of dialogical-formational selection, articulation, elucidation, consultation, translation, transposition, integration, and application.

The new psychophenomenological method has proven to be of limited but substantial value in the field of anthropological psychology. It became the basis of one of the main research methodologies developed in the psychology department of Duquesne University. The lines of this method were carefully maintained by some of my colleagues and their doctoral students. Nuances, refinements, elaborations, and philosophical-theoretical justifications of this methodology have been added during the years following its inception, but these did not essentially alter the fundamental research process as laid out originally.

The large number of subjects used in the first study of this kind—360—was decreased in similar studies. This simplification seems justified. The first study was a demonstration of a new methodology in a functionally oriented psychology department at Case Western Reserve University. As such it needed to be bolstered by an impressive array of data. Faculty had to be convinced that they could allow such an innovation without violating their responsibility to the science of psychology as represented by their university. Their openness to grant a Ph.D. for such an original design was widely appreciated.

In the program of psychology as an anthropoplogical or human science at Duquesne University, the sources of the data for phenomenological research remained—both for interested faculty members and students—written descriptions, as I myself had utilized. Others also made use of interviews, observations of human action, and personal imagination. Some used these different sources of data in combination. The method I proposed was intentionally formulated so that it could be expanded in the coming years by colleagues and students in many ways, for example, by such refinements as a qualitative content analysis of the data. Briefly, the methodology had been kept open by me to allow for elaborations without having to violate its essence.

I would like to acknowledge gratefully the work of some of my colleagues in the psychology department. The elaborations they added or approved can assure students and readers unequivocally that the original methodology, while not being essentially altered, could be refined and enhanced by subsequent scholars.

Using this methodology with added enhancements, colleagues and students in the psychology department have investigated effectively topics such as trust, anxiety, decision making, privacy, at-homeness, courage, envy, jealousy, anger, loneliness, disappointment, or the experience of being criminally victimized. Most of them collected lingual statements from a sample of subjects, be it in lesser numbers than 360. They focused in a similar way on their descriptions of the experience they were researching as had been done for the experience of feeling understood. Then they examined the descriptions recorded with the assistance of their faculty. By means of fundamentally the same methodology I had originally employed, they were able to disclose the structure of the experience they had set out to explore.

We needed to go into this explanation of the development of the psychophenomenological method in order to distinguish it more clearly from the dialogical-formational methods of selection and articulation in formation science. Having seen their historical connection, we can now clarify the next stage in the development of the methodology of formation science.

Selection and Articulation

The practical purpose of formation science changes the psychophenomenological method.

The methods of selection and articulation aim at the disclosure of those structures of our field that influence the formation of our life. They pay special attention to the obvious manifestations of dynamics to which they point. From the start they want to facilitate the subsequent methods of the science. Hence the selection and articulation methods—unlike the psychophenomenological—are implicitly modulated by the overall orientation of our methodology toward identification of dynamics, consultation of auxiliary sources, and practical application.

Priority of These Two Methods

To serve the practice of formation we must first of all choose a topic and event that really has something to do with the unfolding of our life. It must be such that we can study it with the methods available to us. After this selection the first thing to find out is how this event is coformed by the structures of the field in which it happens. Without this knowledge the operation of the dynamics could not be fully understood. To articulate such structures and connections of a field a scientific method is needed. For in everyday life we pay no critical and systematic attention to our field of presence and action. Hence we have only a vague and confused idea of the factors that make for a particular event in our life.

The articulation of the field does not have to identify all possible structures and connections. Depending on the nature of a research project, it highlights mainly those structures that seem more directly relevant to the topic of attention and a corresponding topical event.

For example, the occurrence of falling in love would manifest significant connections with especially the pre-, intra-, and interformative spheres in the personal range of one's field as well as with their vital and transcendent dimensions. The same event would manifest less significant connections with outer mondial formation and with the sociohistorical and functional dimensions. Such connections are not totally absent, but they seem less influential in relation to the particular event under study.

Conversely, the event of concern evoked by famine in some parts of the world, as reported by the media, manifests significant connections also with mondial and situational forces and with the universal, common, and segmental ranges of the field. This event is less exclusively linked with the personal range than falling in love is. It also has more connections with the functional dimensions of the spheres and ranges of the field in relation to motivations for practical organization of aid to the hungry and destitute.

Differences between Psychophenomenological and Selection and Articulation Methods

A comparison between these methods is not meant to suggest the superiority of the methods of formation science over those of psychophenomenology. Both types can be valid and effective within their own sphere of competence. They do what they are meant to do within the area of their own scientific concern.

The psychophenomenological method (PPM) describes and analyzes psychological structures of human experience. The selection and articulation methods (SAM) explain the formational meaning of events in reference to a chosen thematic and within the dialogical context of a field as understood in light of the general paradigm outlined by formation theory.

PPM discloses the structures of human experiences as they manifest themselves in the framework of the situation in which they are perceived. SAM discloses the formative meanings and directives of events in reference to a chosen formational theme, not only in the light of their situational context but also in that of the pre-, intra-, inter-, and outer spheres and dimensions of the field of the person who is apprehending and appraising an event as formative.

PPM tends to restrict itself to the focally perceived structure of a human experience. SAM identifies and articulates not only focal but also infra-, trans-, and prefocal connections of an appreciatively apprehended formation event within the limits of its peripheral manifestations in a first tentative description of what actually occurred.

PPM starts out from prescientific descriptions by a number of subjects other than the psychologist. SAM starts out from the prescientific form-appreciative apprehension of a personally significant event experienced by the scientists themselves. Only then may the articulation be extended to descriptions by auxiliary sources and/or by statistically significant samples of populations.

PPM asks subjects to describe the structure of the situation in which they experience a psychological phenomenon. SAM asks researchers to identify and describe the formative meanings and directives disclosed in a personally and form-appreciatively apprehended event. They relate these to the structures of the field as fundamentally outlined thus far in the theory.

PPM relates the psychological experience directly to the life world of the questioned subjects. SAM relates the formation event in the life of the researchers themselves to the formation field as already structured by the general theory of the science and by the thematic chosen as their research topic in accordance with the demands of the science. Only then may they choose to relate to the formation field and to their topic similar descriptions by other subjects.

PPM demands an intersubjectively verifiable methodology based on the plurality of subjects interrogated. They must manifest similar structural elements of the psychological experience that is under investigation. SAM demands an interformatively verifiable methodology based on consensus among the members of a team of researchers regarding the personal selection and articulation of a formation event by one of them; on the congruence of the articulation with previous findings formulated in formation theory and in the body of knowledge of the science; on the compatibility of the tentative articulation with the findings and insights of auxiliary sciences, disciplines, arts, and traditions; and on its applicability to a segment of the population.

PPM aims to produce via its methodology a more general description of the structure of the psychological experience of the subjects. SAM comes first to a provisional selection and subsequent articulation of a formation event, relevant to the research topic. They arrive at such articulation through personal description that is refined in dialogue with participants in the research team. This dialogue may then be extended to a statistically significant sample of other subjects, depending on one's research project.

Formation research proceeds farther via the complementary methods of elucidation, consultation, translation, transposition, integration, and application. The end result is a more generally valid, amplified apprehension of the significance of the event and the formation thematic under consideration. Added to this is insight into the formative effects of these events. The research results point to dissonant form directives and to obstructing and facilitating conditions for the emergence and effective application of those that are consonant. Highlighted by the research scientist is the more general relevance of these findings for a wider population.

Point of Departure: Exemplary Formation Event

We compared the methodology of the science of spiritual formation with that of the science of phenomenological psychology. In accordance with the traditional methodology of the spiritual masters of all traditions, students of spirituality start out from an articulation of their personal experience of a significant formation event. We say *event* not *experience*. Obviously a formation event includes experience. Otherwise it could not be known. Yet the description of an event includes also the objective parameters of the formation field within which the experience emerges. Science in its search for objectivity and highest available probability attaches great importance to such observable parameters of an experience or perception by subjects. We call it a *formation* event to distinguish it from a mere *developmental* one that is the formal object of the branch of psychology called human development. We emphasize that the articulation of the event is only a point of departure. Always and everywhere the articulation of spiritually formative events has been the point of departure for the writings of classical spiritual masters in all religious and spiritual traditions. For example, Teresa of Avila, Catherine of Siena, John of the Cross, Ignatius of Loyola, Francis Libermann, Meister Eckhart, John Wesley, Jakob Boehme, D. T. Susuki, Krishnamurti, Ernest Holmes, the Buddha, and the authors of the Psalms, and Wisdom books start from their spiritual experiences in prayer, direction, labor, leisure, suffering, joy, retreat, spiritual living and meditating. These experiences are a point of departure for their formation directives, always, of course, within the frame of their respective religious or spiritual-ideological traditions. This has been the standard pre-scientific methodology of classical masters for millenia.

The science of spiritual formation neither rejects this ancient and constant methodology nor rashly assails its universal affirmation by religious faith traditions and spiritual ideologies. The science realizes, however, that students of spirituality are inclined to be insufficiently critical of their spiritual experiences. They tend to treat them as an endpoint rather than as a starting point for scientific research. Often they seem insufficiently aware that their experiences—even when not in opposition to the foundations of their own traditions—may be subject to limiting or even malformative influences in regard to practical, everyday formation of the spiritual life. Hence a complementary methodology that evokes and cultivates their sense of critical caution and objectivity seems necessary. This will enable the students to expose in some measure the limitations and prejudices of their own experiential data base.

So far religious and spiritual ideological traditions have developed methods for the assessment of the compatibility of the spiritual directives with their foundational teachings. What they did not develop were methods enabling us to assess the effectiveness of such directives for wholesome everyday spiritual living in specific cultures and communities. An example of the need for such methods would be the "data base of spiritual experience" on which the initiators of the Charismatic movement of spirituality at Duquesne University in the 1960's based their spiritual formation. The experiences of some of their initial followers did not contain patently heretical statements in terms of their traditions. Yet a number of them needed psychological treatment at that time. Some of their directives while not heretical, theologically speaking, seemed less effective from the viewpoint of empirical consequences for the students concerned. All of this points to the desirability of making such experiences a point of departure for a critical review in regard to their impact on the consonant life formation of people.

The science of spiritual formation, therefore, is oriented toward the disclosure of the subjectivistic limitations and possible self-deceptions inherent in private or group experiences. The successive steps of its methodology aim at weaning students away from an exclusive preoccupation with their subjective spiritual experiences. The science submits to examination only those experiences that are potentially open to critical purification and generalization. Then the methodology compels researchers step by step to remove from this first data base all subjectivistic distortions and to take into account objective parameters. The science proposes, moreover, six approaches complementary to the classical spiritual approach. These critical methods operate like successive nets of different sizes. They aim at catching the various subjectivistic distortions that may have crept into the initial descriptions of spiritual formation events. What slips by one net will be caught in one of the following nets. This purification enhances the probability that the students may approximate the objectivity of appropriate questions if they follow up their topic and event selection with interview or questionnaire methods.

This self-critique will enhance also the objectivity of experimental application methods to similar segments. Questionnaires, interviews and applicative experiments are notoriously weak if they are not preceded by critical articulations of the personal events that prefocally stimulated either the questions devised by the interviewer or questionnaire maker or the parameters set up by the organizers of social application experiments.

Human Development and the Science of Spiritual Formation

Our discussion of the distinction between the methodology of phenomenological psychology and that of formative spirituality would not be complete without a comparision of human development and the science of spiritual formation. Human development is a subdivision of psychology; the science of formation is a new transpsychological field of study. The formal object of the latter is the ongoing spiritual formation of people in their response to a mystery communicating itself through its epiphanies as formative in the journey of populations. The formal object of the psychology of human development is the socio-vital-functional and functional-transcendent development of human life insofar as it can be subjected to the methods of the science of psychology. The psychology of human development can include the exploration of psychological phenomena related to certain functional aspects of transcendent experience and their relevance to psychological development, for instance, the structural psychological concomitants of the faith experience.

Results of such human developmental research, as well as those of other branches of psychology and of other positive and human sciences, can be relevant to our understanding of significant concomitants of spiritual formation. They should be taken into account when they touch on the concerns of some related research project of formation science.

Psychological methodology, however, is not primarily devised for research in spiritual formation. This truth became even more obvious to me after I was allowed to return from nine years of work in the psychology department to my original commitment: research, theory, praxis in the area of spiritual formation. The assumptions, arguments, logic and evidence are different in human development and in the science of spiritual formation. One is not per se better than the other. They are simply different because of their difference in formal objects. Each field makes its own contribution to the expansion of the knowledge of humanity about its journey. In mutual appreciation they can profit from each other's insights. Each of these approaches has its relative value. Each can be effective in terms of its own formal object of research.

The formal object of spiritual formation comprises the potential or actual formative relationships initiated by the transcendent mystery as communicating itself to unique persons usually through formation traditions. Changes in this forming relationship itself are *initiated* by the same mystery. They are not the result of psychological development. Hence they are not fully available to the methods of human development. Such changes can never be the result of socio-vital-functional and functional-transcendent stages of human development, examined and structured by developmental psychology. Social and psychological concomitants, however, affect and are affected by the unfolding *expressions* of this transcendent relationship. Such concomitants can be studied by the psychology of human development. Their results should be taken into account by formation scientists, who research such expressions in their relationship to spirituality.

Formation research cannot, like developmental psychology, start out from interviews of samples of a population before its researchers have examined the exemplary experience of unique persons. In them the spiritual formation wisdom of a tradition becomes focally known and reflected. They communicate the spiritual results of the experiment of their own life as nourished by their tradition. The mystery of formation speaks historically in their formation traditions. However, its effect on practical life formation is only expressed well by adherents who know how to articulate their experience of this implementation in their own daily life. This explains why the spiritual heritage of all great faith and form traditions came first to focused awareness and striking expression in the formation journeys of the reflective and articulate representatives of such traditions, honored as their spiritual masters. Not all aspects of their most profound communications can be clarified by the scientific approach of formation science. They are transscientific and hence in need of a corresponding transscientific approach. In Volume V we will show how Formative Spirituality adds to its scientific approach another approach that is partly transscientific. It does so through its articulation of the transscientific communcations of a form tradition in dialogue with the results of its formation science. Suffice it here to emphasize that certain aspects of the communication of spiritual formation events by the masters and others are open to the typical approach of the science of spiritual formation.

The science of spiritual formation is thus concerned with pretranscendent and transcendent changes in formation that are not exclusively caused by developments in the psychological sense. These changes manifest themselves first of all in unique persons who not only let themselves be formed spiritually by the mystery via their form tradition but who are also able to articulate the results of this formation. The concomitant formative expressions of such spiritual changes are secondarily related to socio-vital-functional and functional-transcendent psychological changes in different social and chronological group segments of various populations.

Developmental psychologies have profited from behavioristic, idealistic and related phenomenological-existentialist approaches that for almost two centuries kept emerging in Western cultures in various forms. The theoretical and empirical results of this marriage between psychologies of human development and these approaches have been impressive. Formation science takes these into account while going beyond them. Such methods and results are useful in the area of structural psychological development. They seem appropriate also in relation to psychological concomitants of spiritual development. The formal object of spiritual formation, however, is not primarily structural psychological development. First and foremost we focus on the concrete forming relationship between the mystery and the human life form in and through its spiritual form traditions, as expressed first of all in attentive, reflective and articulate adherents.

The science of spiritual formation assumes a universal transcendent form potency in humanity. This potency can be actualized. It can be implemented in all dimensions of human existence and in formation traditions. Formation science does not consider such form traditions as equivalent species of one and the same generic basic formation tradition. On the contrary the varied actualizations of the universal potency may give rise to essentially different traditions. Spirituality as actually lived is not structurally and contextually the same in every one of them. Not only the content of spirituality but also its actual structure may basically differ in many traditions and cultures. What remains the same is the underlying transcendence potency and its implicit pointing to possible actualizations that are in consonance with the gift of that potency. Everyone is the recipient of this transcendence potency. Under the influence of the formation mystery, many people may actuate this potency is some consonant way. Both the potency and its consonant and dissonant actuations may remain transfocal or prefocal in consciousness. Spirituality, as basically the free gifts of a living formative relationship between the mystery and the human form of life, can thus not be reduced to psychological developmental categories.

The criterion for the relative consonance or dissonance of any spirituality is its congeniality with our transcendence potency. This congeniality is manifested primarily in the content of the gift of an actual forming relationship with the mystery. The primordial norm is the content and depth of this relationship, not the concomitant psychological structure of one's spiritual life. Accordingly, the science of spiritual formation is not about the construction of a psychological developmental theory of the psychic concomitants of spirituality. In this sense it is transpsychological. Its concern is the formation theory of the gift of a transcendent relationship that can be deepened in quality, content and incarnational expression at any moment of life by the mystery. Secondarily it is about the various expressions of this relationship in all dimensions of human life as concretely unfolding within respective formation fields.

Instead of a generic approach to spirituality, the science of spiritual formation takes into account the pluriform approaches of various formation traditions. This enables the science to disclose what elements of formation wisdom they may have in common. This approach starts out from our own and other's explications of formation events. It examines the consonances and dissonances between these various explications.

We can thus not assume that spiritual formation has the same meaning and content for the adherents of various traditions. The science of formative spirituality fosters a dialogue among the spiritualities of diverse traditions. Its students must begin where all sensitive and reflective exponents of spiritual formation began, although in a systematic fashion and usually in regard to everyday formation events. They should not start out from an abstract psychological universal idea of what spiritual life is. Their starting point should be an articulation of what an everyday formation event means to them personally. Only then, after many critical refinements and purifications of this initial explication, can we dialogue with other explications. Otherwise we may lose our form traditional identity and fall into the trap of an absolute relativism of spiritual formation.

Our concrete starting point for a reflective articulation of what a formation event means in our own life is somehow coformed by the formation tradition to which we adhere. That has been the case for all spiritual writings known to us. This predicament is advantageous for it makes clear to others where we come from traditionally speaking. By the same token we expect others to be influenced by their form tradition in their explication of a similar formation event. Such awareness keeps the dialogue in tune with the reality of people's different spiritualities. It enables us to see in our response to a formation event what is the implicit result of our own formation tradition. This insight in turn makes it possible for us to identify elements of our traditional experience that are in some way transtraditional. This means that they can be found also in the spiritual formation of people who adhere to other traditions. We do not have to deny the rootedness of our spirituality in our own traditions. On the contrary, our interaction with others will deepen our committed understanding of our formation tradition. For it will stand out more clearly as unique in the light of our dialogue with other traditions. At the same time we may enrich each other by acknowledging certain existing commonalities and certain commonly advantageous ways of implementing them in our lives. Briefly, by starting out as the masters did from our own spiritual formation, we start implicitly from the perspective of a specific form tradition. The approach of the science of spiritual formation, however, enables us not to restrict all possibilities of spiritual formation to that one perspective alone.

We thus make our own explication of formation, implicitly rooted in our own tradition, point of departure for further reflection. Once we are familiar with the nuances of this experience and the corresponding aspects of its underlying tradition, we can critically dialogue with others whose spiritual formation is differently rooted. They are as committed as we are to traditions that coform their spiritual formation. The frank acknowl-edgment, however, of this basic difference in mutual appreciation will en-able us to tease out a minimum of mutually acceptable general formation principles and directives. These should be basically compatible with the foundations of the various traditions we represent.

Definition of Assumption

We can now define one of the main assumptions underlying this ap-proach to spiritual formation. *Formative spirituality is an intimate parti-cipation in an all pervasive mystery of formation and transformation, in commitment to and congeniality with our own formation tradition, and where and when possible, in compatibility with the varied ways in which the same mystery may speak to adherents of other traditions in their genu-ine striving for intimacy with the mystery.*

Our definition indicates that spiritual formation is rooted in an inti-mate participation in a mystery that forms and transforms us if we affirm its presence and inspiration. Our definition avoids words in which there might linger connotations of autarchic self-actualization, evolution, development, growth. Such terms may be appropriate in sciences that focus on the socio-vital-functional and functional-transcendent facets of human life. The same expressions are inappropriate for the description of the intimate form donation to human life given by the ultimate mystery. Transcendent life formation is dependent on the mystery that as radical we call God; as formative we call it the forming epiphany of God in space and time or briefly the formation mystery. Spiritual formation by the mystery is thus not a facet of self-actualization or human development. Rather it is a way of intimcy with a mystery that forms us. If there is no such mystery then spiritual formation is an illusion. This formation re-sults in typical observable effects that can be identified and researched in their dynamic interaction by formation science. The definition implies that we hold that it is possible for God to give form spiritually to the life of people who are committed to formation traditions other than our own. It is possible for God to form such people also in a consonant response to formative invitations. Some of them, moreover, may have received the gift to articulate competently this spiritual formation of their life by the mystery. This articulation can become their point of departure for finding out whether they may have in common with adherents of other traditions some similar elements of spiritual formation.

Spiritual formation is thus understood as a universal graced possibility of human life. The consonant actualization of this transcendence potency does not happen by necessity. Pseudo-actualizations may take the place of authentic spirituality.

We can affirm or refuse the gift of spiritual formation. Refusal does not mean that we do no longer engage in the psychological acts of human development. We may remain autarchically involved, for instance, in transpersonal psychological acts of functional transcendence, developing our own directives and symbols. Refusal means that we fail to respond obediently to the forming presence of God as speaking in our heart in accordance with our formation tradition insofar as it is consonant. We refuse to make divine formation ultimate in our life and instead substitute human development for it. Conversely to make divine formation ultimate does not imply that we neglect human development. On the contrary human development is elevated and animated by divine formation. Our human development can be examined and integrated in the light of our transcendent formation by the mystery. Divine formation then becomes the superordinate aspect of our life's journey, human development the subordinate. As a matter of fact the science of spiritual formation is mostly about this integration. It helps us to reinterpret our psychological development and to elevate it to the level of spiritual formation. From the viewpoint of our spiritual transcendence psychological development receives a whole new meaning. It is no longer merely psychological. It becomes a preparation for transcendence or pretranscendence.

We conclude that theories of human development can be indirectly helpful for our spiritual formation. By themselves alone, however, they can never provide us with a basis for understanding our divine formation by the mystery. What they can provide is an increase in readiness for competent incarnation of the mystery's transcendent inspirations in all dimensions and regions of our human life form and its formation field. The science of spiritual formation explores this pretranscendent readiness not primarily from the viewpoint of human development but from that of spiritual formation.

On the basis of the general considerations in this chapter of the methods of selection and articulation in comparison with those of psychophenomenology, we are now ready to discuss these methods in more detail in the next chapter.

CHAPTER 12

Methods of Dialogical Selection and Articulation

A s stated earlier, our first concern is to choose a topic of attention and an event that are relevant to the practice as well as to the theory of formation. In this chapter we will consider the scientific criteria for such a selection.

The selected event will be subjected to the articulation method. This method particularizes the general articulation of the field already provided by the science in its basic field paradigm.

We will see later that the mere articulation of the event is not sufficient for application to our life. We need to know more about its dynamics; the knowledge we may gain from auxiliary sources; and the ambience of the people concerned. The event we have selected must, therefore, be amenable to methods that can give one access to such insights.

Process of Selection

The topic and event to be selected cannot be merely a psychological experience in which one may feel interested. Both must be suitable for research in accordance with the following four criteria.

First, the thematic and its manifesting event must refer to some object in the field that has at least potentially a formative influence on our life. This object must be publicly observable. Such a referent can be a natural thing like the weather, a bird, a tree, the sea, the sky, or the stars. It can be an artifact, a cultural creation such as a law, a custom, a rule, a ritual, a symbol, a sculpture, or a painting. The formation referent can be a person—father, mother, child, friend, colleague, neighbor, stranger in need, hero, leader, speaker. It can be an interformative referent, such as an encounter, a love affair, a visit, a lecture, a counseling or direction situation.

It can be a happening; a sickness; a death in the family; a marriage; a demonstration; a local, national, or international calamity or blessing; a war; a segmental conflict; an appointment; or an accident.

Second, the occurrence is suitable for research only if it manifests a subject pole that turns the potentially formative object into an actual formation event. This subject pole is the source of the form appreciative apprehension of the object pole as formative. It is called an *event* precisely because the dialogical movement between the object and the unfolding appreciative apprehension of the subject is not a static piece of information. It is a formative happening, a dynamically unfolding process that affects our life as a decisive event.

Third, the event is suitable for research if it is amenable to articulation and to all the subsequent steps required by the methodology of the science.

Fourth, the event must have the potency to generate directives relevant to the chosen theme. Such directives must be more general than what is given in the personal apprehension of the researcher. They must be applicable to a wider range of the field.

Dialogical Implications of Selection

From the foregoing considerations, it becomes evident that an effective selection of both topic and event implies a dialogue with:

1. the theoretical canons, categories, propositions, and body of knowledge already available in the science: Does anything in these point to a significant thematic and a corresponding event that one would like to research?
2. one's own field in its personal, segmental, subsegmental, common, and universal ranges: Do I apprehend an event in my personal range that manifests in some mode and measure the more general thematic I want to research? Does this event have implications not only for me but also for a wider range of my field or for some or all of them?
3. one's research team: Can I comfortably and effectively, without withholding and without undue attachment to my own prescientific appreciation of the event, submit it to an objective critique by the members of my research team or fellow scientists, also when they are obliged to question opinions in which I may have invested much thought and feeling?
4. one's chosen population for application research: Does my topic

and event carry sufficient significant implications for that population and can these be meaningfully communicated to them in practical-directive application?

5. the purposes, functions, and findings of the elucidation, consultation, translation, transposition, integration, and application methods: Is the chosen event amenable to their operations and can it be related dialogically to former results of these operations?

6. the auxiliary resources of the science: Can I find sufficient information about my topic and event, its dynamics, conditions, and consequences in some of these resources?

7. formation traditions: Can the topic and event be related meaningfully to some of these traditions?

Starting Out from the Personal Range of Our Field

An intimate access to such an event can be found in the *personal* range of our field, hence the requirement to start out from a personal experience. This selected point of departure yields two other benefits.

First of all, starting out in this way and during the study returning to this event continually, keeps the inquiry rooted in reality, which manifests itself first of all in the personal range of people.

Second, the subsequent scientific operations will compel us to acknowledge the accretions of our own apprehensions. This recognition fosters in us a critical stance toward all apprehensions made by ourselves and others. Without this stance, our science and practice cannot avoid distortions by accretions.

Operations of Selection of the Topical Event

In the light of the criteria of selection, we can summarize the researchers' operations of selection in the following ten steps.

First, researchers carefully scrutinize the personal range of their field in its entirety to gain a first general provisional apprehension of events that seem at first glance to concretize the thematic they have chosen as their topic of attention.

Second, they proceed to examine in detail each of these provisional events in the light of each of the selection criteria.

Third, they discount those occurrences that seem redundant of others that have already been listed as possible topical events. They eliminate also occurrences that are not sufficiently compatible with one or more of the criteria of selection or are less relevant to the thematic they have chosen as their topic. Conversely, it is also possible that they have to re-select or redefine their tentative thematic in the light of their search for a topical event.

Fourth, they list the pros and cons for each provisional event that remains on their list after the first cut.

Fifth, they submit this intermediate list with its pros and cons to the critical dialogue of the research team inviting open, objective discussion regarding:

1. their personal identification and formulation of the events from which the final selection may be made;
2. their personal appraisal of the effective researchability of the proposed events from the viewpoint of criteria and of their tentatively chosen thematic;
3. their personal appraisal of the objectivity and accuracy of the formulation of the pros and cons of the provisional selection.

Sixth, if after reasonable dialogue none of the proposed events seems acceptable and the topic seems still promising, they start the operations again from the beginning.

Seventh, if the provisional list is partially or totally accepted by the research team, they incorporate the reasonable improvements suggested by its members.

Eighth, weighing the insights gained by this critical dialogue, the researchers arrive personally at a provisional final selection of their thematic and of one event that seems most in accordance with the criteria of topical event selection.

Ninth, they list their reasons for the provisional final selection of their thematic and its manifesting event. If possible, they identify in a more refined fashion the topic and the occurrence they have provisionally chosen as one of its concrete embodiments in their own life.

Tenth, they submit the tentative final selection, its rationale, and the more refined identification of topic and event to the team for appraisal. If rejected, they start the operations again and proceed until reasonable consensus is reached. If conditionally accepted, they incorporate the valid suggestions of the team, submitting the event once again for critical dialogue. When agreement is attained, they change the provisional selection into a definitive selection.

All team members must keep in mind that this selection is still a *relatively* definitive selection. This means that during the following research operations the team may discover that either the selected topic or its event or both are not sufficiently compatible with the criteria. In that case the selection operations have to be started over again. For example, a researcher may not be able to gain sufficient emotional distance from the selected event to deal with it objectively.

The selection method makes available topics and occurrences that are researchable and that contain potentially significant directives applicable to a wider population. The topics and events thus selected for research must first of all be illumined in their structural connections. This is done by means of the next method, that of articulation of the events within their field in the light of the chosen thematic and of the theory of the science.

According to individual or departmental research designs, researchers may extend their selection of "events to be articulated" to a wider statistically significant number of subjects.

Prescientific Descriptive Articulation

In prescientific descriptive articulation, the researcher first presents a descriptive articulation of the event. This description is submitted to participants in the team. They are invited to examine it critically. Their aim is to obtain, in dialogue with the presenting researcher, a first general sense of the thematic; of its relevant manifestation in a life occurrence; and of the structure of this event, its subject and object poles, its suitability for the methodology and for the practical purposes of formation of a significant group of the population. They examine also the fidelity of this first articulation to the basic meaning of the event and to the thematic it is meant to clarify. Critical-creative comments and questions initiate a dialogue with the presenting researcher that will assist him or her in improvements on all these counts. In case a more extensive research design includes the selection of a statistically significant sample of descriptions of similar events by other subjects, this selection too is subjected to team appraisal.

When the articulation is accepted, the researcher identifies in writing the structural and the possible dynamic coformants of the event. Each time the researcher notices a transition in the articulation, it is recorded as a possible structural coformant. This record of possible coformants is critically studied by all participants in the light of the proposed thematic and the demands of the science. Comments and questions help to continue the scientific dialogue, which is one of the main tools of the presenting researcher for the correction and refinement of the articulation.

At this stage the dialogue serves also as a first movement of purification of merely personal, segmental, or common idiosyncratic accretions. The research starts with the personal in order to rise beyond it toward the general without losing the essential insight born from its first intimate familiarity with the occurrence. The articulation prepares for the moment when some aspects of personal insight in the thematic can be generalized to specific populations. In the case of a more extensive research design, this articulation facilitates the effective formulation of the questions to be posed to the sample in order to obtain their relevant descriptions.

Scientific Articulation

Scientific articulation begins when the tentative identification of the coformants of the event is approved of by the team as reasonably possible and as sufficiently purified from personal, segmental, or subsegmental idiosyncrasies detectable at this state. The researcher relates the identified structural and potential dynamic coformants to the chosen thematic and to the general articulation of the field as already presented in the basic field paradigm of the theory. The researcher relates it also to those aspects of the body of acquired knowledge of the science that are more directly relevant to the articulation at hand. If a wider sample is used, the articulation is also critically related to the essence of their compared descriptions.

In this phase of the process the common language of the initial articulation is translated into the metalanguage of the science. The initial findings are transposed in terms of the canons and categories of formation theory.

Insofar as such transposition does not seem possible, the researcher then refines, deepens, amplifies, or questions the general articulation of the field by the science and those aspects of the body of thus far acquired knowledge that are more directly relevant to the research in question.

Next, the written record of this translation, transposition, and possible proposed expansion of theory and language is again submitted for critical examination by all participants in the team. The subsequent scientific dialogue assists the always necessary correction and reformulation. Such reformulation may be necessary for either the topic or its manifesting event or for both of them.

The objectives of this first scientific phase are increased disclosure of accretions and further progress on the path to either generalization or universalization. This very process compels researchers to compare the more personal form appreciative apprehension of the event with the more general vision of the science and of the more general implications of their chosen topic. In this light, researchers become more and more able to discover and exclude idiosyncratic meanings and directives that have crept into their personal or segmental prescientific descriptions.

The metalanguage and theory of the science (as such, or as nuanced, enriched, or corrected by the translating and transposing person) enable researchers to rise above the exclusively personal, segmental, or subsegmental meanings and directives of the particular event for their own life. They can then open up to the more general and perhaps even universal meanings and directives that analogous occurrences may carry for a wider population.

This first operation of the methodology ends with the integration and synthesis of the final results of the articulation research. A coherent, inwardly consistent descriptive articulation of the event is submitted for critical comment by team participants. After prolonged dialogue, they may confirm the reasonableness and the provisional probability that this description may contain some of the essentials of the event as relevant to the chosen thematic, later to be disclosed in a more precise and probable way by the subsequent operations of the methodology. In case they raise objections and questions, researchers will, after reasonable open discussion, incorporate those that improve this first provisional articulation of the event.

The next task is to delineate the limitations of this articulation. It can only offer suitable material, grounded in personal familiarity with the occurrence, for further exploration by the subsequent methods of the science.

Hence, researchers express their anticipation that these further investigations will disclose underlying dynamics, their modulations by traditions, and their directive implications. The investigations should also shed new light through consultation with auxiliary sources. This latter operation will refine, amplify, deepen, and probably change their first tentative articulation. Researchers also anticipate that the investigations will disclose and remove more idiosyncratic accretions and, therewith, enable them to generalize or in some cases universalize more effectively in terms of their topic the structures, dynamics, meanings, and directives of the event and their obstructing and facilitating conditions.

The acknowledgment of the limits of the provisional articulation may evoke the question of the usefulness of this method. We could respond by making the following seven points.

First, without this starting point, the research as a whole would not be rooted in formative occurrences as they appear in the personal range of people's life. In this personal concrete apprehension, facets are given that might otherwise elude researchers in their attempt to make the study of their chosen thematic applicable to the concrete life of real people.

Second, without any initial explicitation at all of this starting point, there would be no concrete norm to judge if the insights and findings regarding this aspect of formation, both by the science and by its auxiliary sources, would really be about this thematic as it concretely manifests itself in the personal ranges of people's field.

Third, without this initial articulation, it would be difficult to become aware of misapprehensions and misappraisals of researchers as well as other people; we could not caution against such accretions and suggest effective ways of dealing with them.

Fourth, without this initial articulation, it would be difficult to deal with the prejudices of individuals and formation segments rooted in such dissonant accretions; hence it would be difficult to remove these obstacles.

Fifth, without this initial articulation, it would be difficult to surmise in what direction one may begin to search for underlying dynamisms and traditions. This lack of direction would hinder the effectiveness of the elucidation of dynamics; of consultation of auxiliary sources; and of application to populations.

Sixth, without this articulation, it would be difficult to point to essential coformants of the event. These are given together with accretions. They suggest to us where to seek for information in our auxiliary sources.

Seventh, such firsthand articulations can be helpful to psychotherapists, directors, counselors, social workers, teachers, clergy, writers, speakers, preachers. It makes them aware of the limits of the apprehensions and appraisals of directives by their clients and audiences. It may help them to communicate to people the meaning and dynamics of everyday occurrences as disclosed by the researchers at the end of their study. One cannot help people to overcome dissonant dispositions if one does not know about the dissonantly articulated situations in which people may be living.

Insufficiency of the Articulation Method

Dynamics are not as directly available to us as structures are. Much has to be inferred by an analytical reflection on such dynamics. Therefore, the method of descriptive articulation may point to, but cannot sufficiently explain, all the whats, hows, whys and wheretos of dynamics. The articulation method needs to be complemented and even somewhat modulated in its own direction by the other methods of the science.

The first and main of these is the method of elucidation, which enables researchers to draw forth dynamics that might otherwise elude their attention. In the next chapter, we will discuss the genesis of the elucidation method.

The descriptions of the selection and the articulation methods given so far—like the description of all following methods—do not go into detailed instructions. The purpose of this reticence is to keep the methodology open—as I did earlier in my development of the empirical psychophenomenological method—for further adaptation and elaboration by other human sciences as well as by departments and individuals in formation science itself who want a more limited, a more extensive, or a more detailed research design.

CHAPTER 13

Genesis of the Methodology
of Elucidation

Articulation of the field by itself alone does not provide sufficient insight to support the theory and practice of formation. Articulation lets emerge a blueprint of the field without its movements, a skeleton of life without flesh and blood. Knowledge of abstracted structures and their architectonic interconnections is necessary as a point of departure. However, to assist people in the clarification of what is driving them, another method is needed.

Articulation is not silent about the dynamics that operate in a field. It provides a first hint as to where and how dynamics may raise problems. Dialogical elucidation follows up on these hints. Its focus is on dynamics that utilize structures and their interconnections in purposeful ways. For example, a person who applies for a job in public relations may be driven by an ambition to gain notoriety. This striving may make use of the interformational structure of pleasant manners; the preformative structure of good looks; and the intraformative structure of effective appraisal of interview situations so as to impress the interviewer favorably.

The above is an example of an approach to a formative event by the articulation of its field and the elucidation of its dynamics. The science must facilitate such an elucidation by providing the researcher with a set of models of general dynamic constellations that shed light on the particular dynamics involved in a field.

Elucidation

The word *elucidation* comes from the Latin *elucere* (composed of the prefix *e-*, which means "out," and *lucidus*, which means "bright"). Elucidation brings something to light, removes obscurity, renders intelligible

125

what was not clear in its dynamic direction and movement. This method proceeds in the light of specific scientific dispositions of our central and auxiliary intraforming potencies. These are illumined in turn by the dynamic sector of formation theory and by consultation with auxiliary sources. (Explanation of these powers and procedures will be forthcoming in this and several following chapters.)

Genesis of This Approach

The elucidation approach originated prior to that of articulation. During the time I spent in Holland as a teacher, theoretician, and consultant for the Dutch Life Schools for Young Adults, I was faced with concrete formation problems rooted in the dynamics of living. My first concern was to clarify these dynamics so as to be of more immediate assistance to the young people in mills and factories. I soon discovered that no specific mode of psychology, psychiatry, or education, nor any single formation tradition, at least in principle, had sufficient answers to the why and wherefore of these dynamics.

Keeping in close contact with problems as they arose in practice, I tried to elucidate them by utilizing the findings of any source that seemed relevant to the problems at hand. Their insights were adapted insofar as possible to formation. The results of these elucidations were published in a series of articles in *Verbum,* a leading Dutch journal for spiritual formation, and in a popularized version in *Beatrijs*, a Dutch journal for women. Via this attempt at elucidation, I came to see the necessity also to articulate the field within which such dynamics were operative.

Continuing my reflection and research in the United States, I tried to derive an elucidation method that would be distinctive for the emergent science of formation. Experimenting first in a prescientific way with the possibilities of elucidation, I was led to a more or less popular kind of writing where the basic demand of a science for an appropriate metalanguage was less pressing. I applied the nascent method to the segmental ambience most familiar to me, namely, the Christian. During weekly workshops with members of this segment, I utilized the findings of various auxiliary sources.

The dynamics of human and Christian formation, reformation, and transformation—with the directives they engendered—were elucidated and verbalized in common language for audiences and readers who were participants in this segment. The dynamics to which their own tradition gave rise were explicitly related to those emerging in dialogue with the evolving science of formation and its auxiliary sources.

Only after experimenting with this prescientific elucidation approach in more than twenty books and one hundred articles was I ready to formulate it in a scientific-dialogical way—now in dialogue with the faculty and students of the Institute that had been established in the meantime. This method has now become an integral part of the research design of formation science, which is applicable, in principle, to the examination of the dynamics operative in the universal, common, segmental, subsegmental, and personal ranges of all fields. It can also be utilized, with the necessary adaptations, in other human sciences.

Articulation and Elucidation

The distinction between the methods of articulation and elucidation may be clarified by a reflection on the difference between articulation of structures and elucidation of dynamics.

Articulation lays out the field structures and their interconnections. Dynamics pervade the field and its structure in a directive capacity. They are interwoven with, but not identical to, the articulation of the field. Dynamics utilize structures flexibly, adapting them to their directives. Conversely, dynamics and their directives are modulated by the structures in which they are embedded.

For example, power strivings in a female politician may be interwoven with the sociohistorical, vital, functional, and transcendent structures of her field. Sociohistorically, she may be stimulated by women's rights and the opportunities now open to them. Vitally, she may feel a surge of physical energy to engage in a campaign. Functionally, she may have the aptitudes required in the arena of politics. Transcendentally, she may be inspired by a religious or ideological tradition to serve the public welfare as best as she can. It is clear that these structures give a certain direction to her dynamics, yet none of them alone can account for all their nuances. Conversely, the dynamics modulate in some manner and measure the manifestation of the structures concerned. A simple addition of directives cannot fully explain what is going on. We must elucidate the dynamics underlying the political striving of this woman, taking into account as much information as we can gather from the structures of her field.

A dynamic constellation arranges uniquely the structures and interconnections found in our field. It cannot be adequately explained by any of these structural influences. The dynamic arrangement has a life of its own. It develops in its unique way while modulating the directives already peculiar of each structure. This process is for a great part hidden from focal awareness.

Theoretically, if we could attain an exhaustive knowledge of all the structural and dynamic influences in a field at a specific moment in time, it would be possible to explain fully with certainty a dynamic constellation in all its nuances, be it only for this moment.

Factually, such exhaustive knowledge is never available to us. Elucidation can only approximate it. Our practical formation reason and imagination has to fill in the gaps of our actual knowledge. It has to do so responsibly, in accordance with the rules of the elucidation method, which will be outlined in a later chapter. This limitation of knowledge explains why alternative elucidations can be plausible. They force us to make a provisional decision in favor of the demonstrably higher probability of one of them or to maintain the alternatives as equally plausible.

Role of Articulation in Elucidation

The articulation of a field implies also an initial articulation of surface manifestations of its dynamics. It points to them without fully disclosing them. To disclose them in depth, our focus has to shift from primordial structural identification to the elucidation of the dynamics that use these structures and interconnections for purposes that do not directly show up in their totality in our primary articulation.

For example, the articulation of a specific field in terms of a formation event may show that a subject manifests a deformative fixation on compatibility only, with a consequent compatibility compulsion. The person in question may be an anxious people pleaser. Prefocally he may neglect the minimum demands of congeniality and compassion toward himself and toward those who seem displeasing to certain people whom he wants so badly to please. This is a first articulation pointing to underlying dynamics.

Focusing now on the hidden dynamics, we may find out, for instance, that this person had a *biogenetical preformation* that led him to feel inferior in some respects. His *familial preformation* confirmed this feeling. It held out acceptance, love, and protection under the condition of unquestioning compatibility with the family and all it stood for. His *sociohistorical preformation* via the formation tradition of the family confirmed and deepened his emergent compatibility fixation by "ideals" of misappraised excessive humility, detachment, and self-forgetfulness.

In his *intraformation*, he kept strengthening these false ideals by prayers, reflections, and selective readings that seemed to confirm him in his exclusive compatibility striving.

As for *interformation*, he preferred people who would confirm his compatibility compulsion, who would praise him for his selflessness, or show disappointment at the slightest sign of a hesitant awakening of the first experience of congeniality-responsibility. People who suffer from a compatibility fixation may also foster a deformative disposition in others to take advantage of their overavailability.

In terms of *situational formation*, he would prefocally involve himself in situations where excessive compatibility was at a high premium, perhaps even lauded as remarkable or heroic generosity, patriotism, community spirit, or self-effacing sanctity.

This example depicts an underlying dynamic constellation of articulations of the personal range of a formation field. Quite different constellations could have developed, utilizing the same articulation. This procedure applies not only to the case of a compatibility fixation but also to deformations of other dispositions, such as those of congeniality, compassion, justice, peace, or mercy, to name only a few. Each can deteriorate through fixation, compulsion, or exaltation.

Personal Modulations of General Constellation Models

All dynamic constellations show some personal modulation. What is merely personal cannot be validated by formation science as such. Like other human sciences, formation science can only disclose general patterns that can be interformatively validated and applied to wider populations. The director or counselor, however, has the responsibility of helping people to disclose for themselves their unique modulations of general dynamic constellations and the interconnections between these and their personally assimilated form traditions.

Within these limits, the science should identify general dynamic constellations that may emerge in people if and when they are exposed to similar conditions. Formation practitioners should make themselves familiar with these models. They should learn to ask themselves if the people who entrust themselves to their care manifest dynamics which seem to correspond to one or more of these patterns. They should draw on this fund of basic information to explore with their counselees or directees how they have given form uniquely to such constellations and their underlying traditions.

Fourfold Dialogue of Elucidation

Elucidation is a cluster of methods and is called dialogical because it puts formation reason in dialogue with:

1. a specific field as articulated by dialogical articulation;
2. the theory of the science insofar as it offers its own canons, categories, descriptions, and elucidations of dynamics;
3. dynamically relevant offerings of auxiliary sources;
4. the results obtained and to be obtained by the dialogical consultation, integration, and application methods of inquiry.

In the following chapter, we will show the basis for elucidation through an analysis of a number of field dynamics.

CHAPTER 14

Theoretical Basis of Elucidation of Formation Dynamics: Basic Consonance-Dissonance Dynamics

Life is an exchange of polar energies in dynamic interaction. This dynamism is conflicted because our life is always in some degree of dissonance, while its transcendence and integration dynamics tend toward consonance. The transcendence dynamic expands our life outward and upward whereas the dynamic of integration maintains or regains its inner consonance.

This interchange generates our basic consonance-dissonance tension. Prefocal apprehension of this tension may evoke spiritual, functional, or sociohistorical symptoms of stress, anxiety, and despondency; of loss of form potency and its appreciation; of guilt, shame, frustration, suspicion, resentment, hostility, irritability, envy, jealousy. These emotions are likely to be accompanied by vital biophysical responses.

The basic consonance-dissonance polarity is often not recognized in everyday life. People are usually unaware of the dynamism of their own reactions and responses to such tensions. Structural articulation of the field cannot disclose its dynamics in depth. For this kind of analysis to occur, we must employ the method of elucidation.

Dissonance Dynamics

Both of the consonance strivings, namely, those of transcendence and integration, stand in opposition to those of dissonance that are rooted in autarkic pride, which can function as a quasi foundation of human life. Autarky engenders strivings for insulation and exaltation. Insulation is an isolating bent toward complacent self-enclosure. It wrestles with the transcendence dynamic. Exaltation is the human proclivity to exalt some limited form or facet as the ultimately directive theme of life. This tendency goes against the striving of integration. Autarky and its selective exaltation of finite formation themes as ultimate can be individual or the shared autarky of a group.

In service of consonance, the integration dynamic assigns each coformant of the field its limited position. Formative integration aspires after a consonant yet transcendentally open equilibrium of the field as a whole. Any dissonant exaltation interferes with this consonance.

Manifestations of Basic Dynamics

Numerous manifestations of these basic dynamics can be apprehended in the differentiated dynamics of our life. These dynamics are as complex as life itself. The focus of this volume is on the science as such. Thus it is impractical here to examine these dynamics in detail. (A detailed examination of these dynamics appears in the earlier volumes of this series and will be included in Volume 5; see also, the glossaries of the journal *Studies in Formative Spirituality*, the doctoral dissertations and master's theses of the graduates of the Institute of Formative Spirituality, and my own publications and those of my colleagues.) For our purposes here, it will suffice to recall the main structures of the field in relation to their potential or actual expression of basic dynamics.

Field Sphere Dynamics

Basic dynamics manifest themselves first of all in the spheres of a field and in their interconnections. These so-called "field sphere dynamics" maintain a formative or deformative tension between the pre-, intra-, inter-, outer-local, and outer-mondial energies. When equilibrium of tension is lost, dynamic reactions and responses are elicited, initially and usually on nonfocal levels of consciousness.

The same can be said of the *field range dynamics*. They operate in and between the universal, common, segmental, subsegmental, and personal ranges of the field.

Dimensional dynamics express the conflicts, negotiations, and conciliations within and between sociohistorical pulsations, vital pulsions, functional ambitions, and transcendent aspirations and inspirations.

Dimensional articulation dynamics comprise the polar tensions that arise in and between the various articulations of each form dimension, such as, for instance, the dimensional articulations and subarticulations of the vital sphere. Freudian analytical psychology, to use but one example, offers many observations regarding the subarticulations of the sexual expression of the vital dimension that can be translated, transposed, and integrated in formation science.

Integrational form dynamics hold sway in and between the foundational, core, current, apparent, and actual forms of human life. Among them the dynamics of the foundational life-form hold a privileged position.

Foundational dynamics comprise the consonant dynamic directives of our foundational life-form and the dissonant directives of our quasi-foundational autarky-form as they are radiated into the trans- and infra-focal regions of consciousness.

The *form potency dynamics* maintain the tension between form potency and form impotence and the subsequent dynamic polarity between one's potency for appreciation and depreciation.

The *intraformative central dynamics* are the source of balance or imbalance, consonance or dissonance, between the central intraformative formation powers of attention, apprehension, appraisal, affirmation, and application and between them and other dynamics in the personal range of one's life.

Intraformative auxiliary dynamics play within and between the intraformative potencies of memory, imagination, and anticipation.

Dispositional dynamics operate continuously between the various dispositions that constitute together the secondary foundational life-form that expresses itself in and through the personal range of our life.

Object-subject pole dynamics represent the tension between objective apprehension and subjective appreciation that coform each formation event.

Not to be overlooked are the *form reception-donation dynamics*. These strive to maintain the right balance between the extremes of quietism and activism. They, too, permeate the whole of our life in a consonant or dissonant fashion.

All of these dynamics are modulated in accordance with the various *focalization dynamics*, which function in and between the focal, prefocal, infrafocal, and transfocal movements and energies of our formation consciousness. Conflicts, negotiations, compromises, conciliations, repudiations, and refusals take place continually in and between these powers of the ongoing formation of consciousness.

Form direction dynamics are those that underlie the interaction between the various directives of our life that emerge in its spheres, ranges, and dimensions on all levels of focalization.

Guardian directive dynamics refer to the interactions in and between the expanding guardian systems of security, safety, or protection directives. These tend to multiply dynamically around the form directives of the spheres, ranges, and dimensions on all levels of focalization.

Formation-proformation dynamics represent the dynamic polarity between present formation and our constant implicit or explicit tentative proformation of possible occurrences we anticipate in the future.

Personal, inter- and universal consciousness dynamics are the polarities that play consonantly or dissonantly between the dynamics of our personal consciousness; of the interconsciousness we share with people in our formation field in all its ranges; and of the universal consciousness that is the mysterious ground of all form potencies in the universe.

All particular dynamics with their inherent directives, generated in and between all of these structures of human existence, in turn interact with one another, creating an increasingly complex network of formation dynamics.

Dynamic Directives

Human life is dominated by the basic dynamics of consonance and dissonance. Immediately following them are the basic dynamics of integration, on the one hand, and of insulation-exaltation, on the other. These basic dynamics express themselves in the structural dynamics of the field as outlined previously. The universal dynamics are potentially as common to particular fields of life as are the universal articulations.

This commonality leads to the conclusion that basic dynamics express themselves via specific field structures in concrete life directives. Directives are evoked by nonfocal or focal form appreciative apprehensions of the object poles of formation events in dialogue with other structures and dynamics of the field.

For example, the functional directive of cultivating rice in a Hindu culture is evoked by the need for food that can be conveniently developed under the given conditions of soil and climate in that part of the world. A transcendent structure also plays a part. People are influenced by a tradition that forbids the killing of cows, hence there is no abundance of meat. The protein from rice is crucial for survival. Interformative structures of family life lead to population growth. Many children mean more family workers in the rice fields. More rice has to be cultivated to feed large families. The outer mondial structure of the culture is obviously favorable to rice cultivation. Familial preformation instills in everyone a taste for rice and a lasting appreciation of its importance.

This example illustrates the way in which dynamic directives are co-formed by the influence of various structures of their field. No one structure or dynamic by itself alone can explain fully a form appreciative apprehension and its subsequent directives.

Intraformative Sphere and the Origination of Dynamic Directives

A significant role in the origination of directives is attributed to the intraformative sphere. At the center of this sphere, there is a core of central dynamic potencies and dispositions, to be distinguished from the auxiliary intraspheric form potencies of memory, imagination, and anticipation. These assist the central potencies of formative attention, apprehension, appreciation, and affirmation or nonaffirmation. If a dynamic directive is to become focal and intentional, it has to be processed through the central form potencies.

For example, as little children we may be guided in our interformative relationships with adults by the nonfocal directive that adults for the most part can be trusted but we should be wary of strangers. Growing up, we may experience a serious abuse of our trust. It shocks us into focal awareness of this nonfocal directive to trust. An unfortunate overreaction to these threatening consequences may result in the emergence of an opposite nonfocal directive. It says in effect, "In the realm of confidential communication, nobody can ever be fully trusted." Such a directive may give rise to a permanent distrust that insulates us from others.

We can see from this example that each formative directive tends to generate a host of secondary security or protection directives to guarantee the effective operation of the main one. The goal of consonant formation is to make such directives and their secondary implications focal. Often we can do so on our own, though at times counseling is needed.

The directives generated by trust and distrust in the example should be submitted to the process of enlightened attention, apprehension, appraisal, and affirmation or nonaffirmation, followed by tentative application. These processes should be assisted by formative memory, imagination, and anticipation. Memory helps to concretize dissonant directives by recalling their influence in our past. Imagination gives concrete shape to motivations and situations in which the desired consonant directive could be implemented. Anticipation enables us to project situations in which our resolve will be put to the test.

Out of the intraspheric processes in our example may emerge a directive that disposes us to distinguish between trustworthy and less trustworthy people and to give flexible form to our communications with them. The same open-ended directive may initiate through reiteration of its corresponding acts a "form-appreciative-apprehension-disposition" that guides us prefocally in our relationships with people now appraised as either trustworthy, less trustworthy, or untrustworthy.

Ideally the intraspheric formation of such a directive should be assisted by consultation with auxiliary sources insofar as this is reasonably possible. Information gained from them should also be submitted to the central and auxiliary intraspheric form potencies for processing.

In everyday life these processes work fast, without much deliberation. However, when formation scientists or practitioners examine them, they engage in a deliberate systematic procedure. Consequently their results are higher on the probability scale and more likely to be effective.

For practical proximate life formation, dynamic directives must move us from intentions to actions and finally to reiteration. The result will be the development of corresponding dispositions. These give a lasting orientation and facility to our personal form potencies in line with the original directives. Shared dynamic directives may be revealed in actions and dispositions that mark publicly the common and segmental ranges in our field. Dispositions-in-common may also manifest themselves in an institutionalization of form directives according to their various modalities.

Six Modalities of Dynamic Directives

The six modalities of dynamic form directives are: tendential, intentional, actional, effectual, dispositional, and institutional.

Tendential Modalities

A directive is merely tendential if it remains only infra-, trans-, or prefocal in the consciousness or interconsciousness of people. As such, the tendency concerned affects mainly intraformation, with less controllable, unintentional random effects on other spheres and dimensions. Examples are an infrafocal tendency to reject people of another race while focally professing that we accept them; a transfocal tendency to aspire after union with the mystery while focally leaving no room for that mystery in our life; a prefocal tendency to eat sweets that are harmful for us while focally extolling concern for diet.

Intentional Modalities

When a nonfocal tendential directive becomes focal, when it is formatively apprehended, appraised, and affirmed, it becomes intentional. We have made the decision to guide our lives in accordance with this directive. For instance, our infrafocal tendential directive to reject the other sex or people of another race may be made focal through the process of intraformative appraisal. We may replace it by the focal-intentional directive to grow in social presence in justice, peace, and mercy toward the other sex and all races.

Actional Modalities

A tendential or intentional directive, once applied, becomes actional. It now starts to generate a life beyond mere tendencies or intentions. For example, the intentional directive of social justice in regard to the other sex or other races now becomes a directive embedded in such actions as expressing respect and sympathy when meeting with the other sex or people of another race, possibly engaging in protest actions when their rights are violated, and supporting them when they are in dire need of assistance.

Effectual Modalities

Effectual directives refer to the actual effects of a directive. An effect may be different from the original tendencies or intentions that led to our acts. Though we tried to incorporate them at best as we could into our actions, the effect turned out to be different from what we anticipated. This deviation occurs because as soon as a directive is actually inserted into a field, it begins a life of its own. It is influenced by the manifold patterns of the field as a whole. Consequently, we as actors lose control over the possible effects of our actions.

For instance, a woman in a Muslim village may express modesty by wearing a veil over her face when a man passes by. If he lives in another culture, he may take this as a sign of rejection. The woman has no control over this effect of her differently intended directive.

Dispositional Modalities

A directive becomes dispositional when it has engendered, through reiteration, a lasting disposition to act spontaneously and with facility in accordance with the directive when the conditions for such acts are present. For example, the intentional directive to avoid harmful kinds of nourishment leads in some persons to actional avoidance of preservatives. After a certain period of reiteration of this avoidance, the directive becomes a part of one's secondary foundational life-form. It becomes a lasting personal disposition.

Institutional Modalites

A shared directive may not only remain in the tendential or intentional interconsciousness of people. It may lead to collective action. When this action is reiterated by the group, it may become a common disposition expressed in their language habits, customs, artifacts, national symbols, and so on.

For instance, the avoidance of pork as nourishment is a formation directive institutionalized in the customs of people who adhere to the Jewish faith and form tradition. Any institutionalized directive starts to have a life of its own. It may change under historical influences, but it continues to form dynamically the life of people subject to it. For instance, some Jewish people who no longer profess their religion may find it difficult to drop the institutionalized disposition of avoiding pork as nourishment.

Interconnections between Directives and Facets of the Field

We can both articulate and elucidate the links between these directives—in each of their six modalities—with other facets of our life. For example, the directive to participate in an association for spiritual formation can be merely tendential. I am touched or emotionally attracted by this group or community. But there is no real intentional decision on my part to attend regularly their meetings, to commit my own energy, to sacrifice from my own means.

This tendential directive may be linked with a weakness of mine in the area of intraformative stability. I may be debilitated by an exalted imagination arousing ineffective enthusiastic feelings that flit around uncontrollably.

The directive may gain intentional status. I really decide to join, yet my intention is never realized. This procrastination may be linked to an underdevelopment of my potency for commitment to enduring interformative relationships. I remain locked in an insulated mind full of good intentions, often proclaimed to the edification of many, but seldom executed.

The same directive may embody itself in concrete action. But it turns out to be a disjointed, spasmodic outburst of good words and deeds, ineffectual in the long run. This effect may be connected to my failure to develop a well-disciplined functional dimension, enabling me to control resistant feelings and self-centered inclinations to escape what at times is boring, demanding, and uninteresting.

The dynamics of this directive may have been deep and strong enough to give rise to a disposition of regular attendance of the meetings of the association, relieving its material needs, doing the required readings, participating in the discussions, co-creating with others a climate of mutual sustenance, attracting other members. This expression is linked with a mature personality, which makes it possible for me to respond to a call to fidelity to this support group.

Finally I may be able, together with others, to institutionalize this directive in the formation of a solid core of members of the association who are dedicated to its growth and to the unfolding of its ideals, no matter the opposition, tediousness, or material sacrifices the commitment entails.

Distance as a Condition for the Disclosure of Dynamics and Their Directives

When we are fully involved in our field, we cannot at the same time elucidate its dynamics and directives. A certain distance is necessary. In the midst of a quarrel with a person we love, for example, we cannot analyze at the same time what makes us upset with her.

Dynamics of anger are interwoven with many other dynamics. In the midst of this complexity, it is difficult to distinguish one facet from the other. To identify the dynamics that are at the base of our agitation we must lift them out of their context. Was the occasion for our quarrel, for instance, her burning of the toast? What made us so furious? Is there some resentment in us waiting to explode the moment an incident gives us a pretext to turn it from a tendential into an actional directive? Distancing ourselves from the situation in which we are embroiled enables us to appraise its dynamics.

Distance in Dialogue with the Auxiliary and Central Intraformative Potencies

To effect such distance, we use our intraformative potencies, first of all, those of memory, imagination, and anticipation. They help us to create a certain distance between the moment of rage and a later period of reflection on its dynamics. Our imaginative-memorial recall of the event can be submitted to our potencies of attention, apprehension, appraisal, affirmation, and application.

Formative memory provides us with the capacity to bring into focus, to objectify, similar incidences that may have happened in the past. We may disclose a dynamic trend in a remembered chain of events. These acts of memory put us at a distance from dynamics that played a part in our recent or past formation and enable us to deal with them.

Anticipation and Proformation

Formative anticipation serves proformation in that it helps us to proform or project the future by giving form to it mentally in advance of its happening. Proformation enables us to give shape imaginatively to similar situations. Because they are similar, we can expect that they may evoke familiar dynamics.

Proformation is crucial for the implementation of directives. It enables us to appraise possible dissonant consequences of our actions as a result of these dynamics. Reformation is then possible.

Formative imagination serves proformation by enabling us to give some shape to the dynamics we try to elucidate. Imagination plays a formative role in dialogue with memory and anticipation, both of which can be used in service of proformation. Without the potency of formative imagining, we would be incapable of either recalling or proforming situations as they concretely evoke and affect the dynamic constellations that are embedded in our actions. Initially these dynamics manifest themselves only within their interwovenness in a present field. Without imagination, we could not succeed in tentatively reforming the dissonant dynamics that may cramp or dilute our future lifestyle.

Formation experts develop over the years special memorial, imaginative, and anticipatory dispositions in the realms of formation and proformation. By means of these dispositions, they are able to identify with some probability the dynamics that may be evoked by future similar situations. Common and segmental dynamics can also be identified in this way. Because the latter are general dynamics, they can become the object of scientific inquiry.

Formative Attention, Apprehension, Appraisal, Affirmation, and Application

After identifying these dynamics, researchers submit them to the formational powers of attention, apprehension, appraisal, affirmation, and application. Attention directs and sustains our mindful concentration on them. Apprehension penetrates the direction of these constellations, their obstacles and facilitating conditions, in all regions of consciousness. Appraisal evaluates their consonance and dissonance and the directives for reformation they may call forth. The *affirmation* potency says yes to the consonant facets of these dynamics and no to the dissonant ones. *Application* expresses itself first of all in intraspheric proformation. It stimulates us to give form inwardly to what these dynamics would be like if their expressive and tactical functioning became subordinated to formation reason. This step prepares us for the phase of practical application or execution.

We engage in tentative application during a flexible period of trial and error. We try to find out what will work effectively in our everyday functioning. As a result, we may be able to identify the most effective mode of application. This identification is approximated through a process of appraisal and affirmation or nonaffirmation of the effectiveness of the results of these trials.

Only after this identification are we ready for the phase of definite implementation. Then the affirmed or reformed dynamic constellations can be firmly established in our life by reiterated application. Once a disposition is formed, it can sink back in the realm of our prefocal consciousness. There the dynamic regains or acquires for the first time spontaneity.

Intraformative Dispositions of Formation Scientists and Practitioners

Formation scientists and practitioners develop special dispositions of memory, imagination, and anticipation, and of attention, apprehension, appraisal, affirmation or nonaffirmation, and application. Their refined receptivity in this area can be explained by such dispositions as they are generated over years of study, training, and experience.

These dispositions prevent them from taking as their object of research or practice all dynamics under all possible perspectives. Their dispositions of inquiry direct them to those dynamics that can be meaningfully related to distinctively human formation. The findings of other sciences may be relevant to other facets of human life. But the primordial aim of these sciences is not to disclose what is proximately relevant to distinctively human formation. To be sure, their findings can be indirectly valuable for spiritual formation. However, formation scientists and practitioners are disposed to make this implicit relevance explicit by translation into their metalanguage and by its transposition into the theory of the science.

For example, a psychoanalytic approach to dynamics may speculate, on the basis of observation, that there is a specific sexual energy in humans that can be sublimated. Formation theory can integrate this theoretical speculation into its comprehensive approach in the following way. There is a strong overall formation potency, an energy, that can flow into any dimension of our life. The specific sexual energy linked with the vital dimension becomes intensified to the degree that this overall formation energy is invested in it. Because the execution of sexual dynamics implies considerable form reception and donation, this overall energy is powerfully stimulated. In absence of this great force, the relative energy of sexuality can be reasonably managed without the so-called sublimation process. It is a question of strategically redirecting or channeling, the powerful, unspecified formation energy into other dimensions of our life. In this way an insight of psychoanalysis is related in principle to the proximate formation of distinctively human life. In the process, psychoanalytic theory is utilized, complemented, and made compatible with the faith and form traditions that guide many people.

Usually people give and receive form to their life without being distinctly aware of the dynamics behind this process. Only when the flow stagnates or symptoms of malformation emerge is there an incentive to pay attention to the complexity of directives and counterdirectives that move us spontaneously. We may then pause and lift them out of the concrete flow of everydayness. We may consider them in a prescientific reflection or, if that is not sufficient for restoration of consonance, we may turn to formation science for a more probable explanation of their workings in our life. We may engage in the study of this science or consult counselors in the hope that their knowledge and developed skills of appraisal will sustain our own reflection and help us to deal with disturbing dynamics.

Formation Dynamics and Formation History

To elucidate formation dynamics implies the elucidation of formation history. Dynamic constellations are not there all at once. They are formed, reformed, and differentiated over time. So are the directives that flow from them. The same applies to the security directives that develop in the wake of dynamic directives. Their specific function is to protect the constellations that guide our life. They preserve them by such processes as rationalized justifications for, or denial of, their existence, thus protecting their smooth process.

Dynamics make more sense to our formation reason when we bring to light the history of their unfolding. It is helpful to apprehend and appraise the formative and cumulative effects of this history on our style of life.

This historical tracing is true not only of the dynamics that orient us in the personal range of our life. It applies also to the shared dynamics that move us in the segmental, common, and universal ranges.

Elucidation of the Dynamics of Proformation

Proformation is at the heart, so to speak, of the freely directed formation of our life.

In everyday situations, dynamics are indistinct from the flow of our life. To bring them into focus, we have to take them out of this stream. As long as we remain prefocal participants, fully immersed in this flow, we cannot concentrate long enough on only one of its features or profiles.

Imaginative memory helps us to make dynamics stand out as distinct from the background of the field as a whole. Only in looking back reflectively on what transpired can we apprehend and appraise various facets of the formation flow as distinct from one another.

How does this approach apply to proformation? Initially proformation is an intraspheric act. It points our life in the present toward a specific event in the future that we anticipate. We can appraise such an event in advance only if we make it stand out as distinct from the ongoing flow of formation in which it will be embedded. Otherwise we could not submit it to insightful direction; we would allow ourselves to drift without any sense of where we are going, caught in the stream of overwhelming indistinctiveness. Such lack of distinction implies a loss of freedom.

What is needed for liberation from future determinisms is a proformative act of imaginative memory. To appraise future acts of formation, our imagination has to proceed as if the proposed event has already taken place in various possible versions. After this imaginary future accomplishment, the projected memory of that imagined time enables us to look back upon it. It helps us to see the dynamics involved in these versions as standing out distinctly from the flow in which they would have been immersed. In this way we gain in advance some power of direction over our acts of tomorrow. We become less the object and more the subject of our history. Proformation is one of the means by which we grow in freedom.

Imagine a situation in which you are to have a business meeting with a person in authority who is notorious for her enchanting charm, impressive credentials, and unusual powers of persuasion. She wants you to take on new work that you sense is uncongenial. Knowing of her manipulative tendencies from past experience, you fear that she may tempt you to betray your integrity, your fidelity to what you are called to be. You can go into this meeting unprepared, almost directionless, simply flowing with the situation she will structure for you. It will be difficult for you under such circumstances to be distinctly aware of the tactical dynamics operative in her approach. Nor will you be clearly conscious of their impact on the dynamic constellation of directives operating in you nonfocally. Some of these particular constellations may be vulnerable to her manipulative attempts. You may, for instance, suffer from a dependency dynamic or from one of anxious people pleasing. One tactic in her arsenal of manipulation dynamics may be to manifest warm interest in your health, career, and creature comforts. The possibly deforming interaction between her and your dynamics is obvious. Without proformation any of us could be the easy victims of such a strategy.

In this example proformation would imply that you imaginatively preview different versions of what may happen during the meeting. You look back in a projected imaginative-memorial way at these versions of interformation as if they had already occurred. You allow to stand out the interformative dynamics and directives that are operative in each one of these scenes. You then submit these imaginatively recalled future events, as if they had already transpired, to your appraising apprehension. With the help of formation reason, you ask yourself if the end result of each version is congenial, compatible, compassionate, effective, and competent? What were the dynamics that led to the specific results? Which version should you prefer? Are any of them satisfactory? Should you have recourse to still another imaginary scenario? Are all versions the result of a realistic imagination or of an unrealistic fantasy life? If you choose a specific version as most proximate to probable consonance, what can you do to enhance it proformatively?

There is no guarantee that the actual happening will conform to any proformation of it. Yet our freedom of direction will be greater than it would have been without any attempt to proformation. Usually, to be sure, the process of proformation operates with lightning speed, almost totally prefocally. Still it may be useful at times to analyze the dynamics focally. Such may be the case, for instance, if we find out that our prefocal proformation is ineffective or unduly influenced by unappraised intraformative coformants. We may also be called upon to assist counselees or directees who are in such a predicament to start for themselves the process of reflection on the dynamics of their own proformation. The insight they gain in regard to consonant and dissonant directives will affect them for better or worse over a lifetime.

CHAPTER 15

Coformants of Dynamic Constellations

Our considerations so far enable us to point out in a more comprehensive fashion the main coformants of our dynamic constellations. They manifest some or all of the following:

1. expressional and tactical coformants that are peripheral;
2. on a deeper lever, motivational coformants that underlie the expressional and tactical;
3. two motivational coformants that are typical of every dynamic constellation, the personal-historical and sociohistorical;
4. other motivational coformants that can be vital, functional, and transcendent.

Personal-historical and sociohistorical motivations are rooted in the history of our formation as initially propelled by vital pulsions and social pulsations. We say *initially* because these pulsations are later on modulated by other motivational dynamics.

The history of pulsations in the personal range is at least partly the result of the adoption of sociohistorical pulsations from parents, other family members, and the people with whom we interform in the common, segmental, and universal ranges of our life. An example would be the directives that are triggered when we meet the members of a racial segment of the population whom we have learned to appraise as either inferior or superior to our own.

The vital motivational facet of a dynamic constellation is empowered by pulsions; the functional by ambitions; the transcendent by aspirations and inspirations. For example, the dynamics of resistance evoked by a meeting with the other sex when it appraises itself as innately superior may be vitally empowered by an impulse of primordial physical defense against something appraised as threatening to one's biophysical well-being; by the functional ambition to do equally well or better than the self-exalting sex; by the aspiration to be more dignified and magnanimous than such arrogant people are; by the inspiration received in one's religion to insist on the equal dignity of men and women.

Let us now look at each dynamic coformant in particular. The *expressional* coformant of a dynamic constellation comprises the various symptomatic ways in which the constellation is expressed. For example, a functional overambitious dynamic may express itself in symptomatic dynamics of clenching fists, time urgency, muscle tension. An overly strong vital-libidinal dynamic may manifest itself in an excessive receptivity for any sexually evocative stimulus that is immediately elaborated in form appreciative apprehension.

The *tactical* coformant of a dynamic constellation comprises the various implementary ways by means of which a dynamic constellation attempts to realize itself in one's field of presence and action. For example, a functional overambitious dynamic may nourish tactics of overexertion; of family neglect in favor of careerism; of depreciation of recreation because it may take time away from business; of anxious pleasing of superiors who may foster one's career; or of an excessively selective search for acquaintances who can serve one's projects.

The *personal-historical* and *sociohistorical* coformants comprise the various events and corresponding appreciative apprehensions that have given form successively to a constellation during one's formation journey. For example, a boy's excessive drive to excel in football may be traceable to a sociohistorical development of exaltation of football heroes in his country. Added to this may be a personal-historical developmental factor that goes back to interformation with ambitious parents. They instilled their own need to compete and succeed by making their expression of love and appreciation dependent on their boy's sharing in their idolizing of the stars. The power and style of such expressions of football heroism may have further unfolded sociohistorically by adoption of similar dispositions among certain adherents of the sports-fan segment of the population.

The *vital* coformant comprises all of the factors that influence these dynamics vitally. For example, the overambitious football player may try nonfocally to compensate for an inferiority feeling due to some physical handicap in his youth. An overabundance of physical energy may cause him to seek the sport as an exclusive outlet and demonstration of his prowess on the football field.

The *transcendent* coformant of a dynamic constellation comprises the inspirational and aspirational strivings that give form to or significantly modulate the constellation. For example, the dynamics that motivate the football player may be nourished in part by a sense that this is the best way in which he can serve the country, city, or school for which he is playing. He may aspire to help the public to recreate and enjoy itself. He may find inspiration in his sport to develop the distinctively human qualities of fair and disciplined sportsmanship that carry over into his everyday life.

Generalization of Elucidations of Dynamic Constellations

Formation science, like all other sciences, cannot be about what is exclusively personal. It takes its departure from the personal range of form appreciative apprehensions, but it does not stay there. Its objective is to disclose in and through this personal awareness what can be generalized to the segmental, common, or even, in some instances, universal ranges.

This principle applies also to the elucidation of formation dynamics. We start out from an elucidation of what is appreciatively apprehended in the personal range. By abstraction from the merely personal, we try to develop an increasing series of general elucidation models. Each of them, in its fundamental outline, is meant to be applicable to similar situations. One should allow room for universal, common, segmental, and personal modulations that leave the fundamental outline of the model intact. For example, research on the dynamics of congenial living in spite of envy may lead to an insight in general dynamics that are typical of all envious situations, yet leave room for the particular modulations of such dynamics in specific circumstances.

Dynamics of the Foundational Form of Life

In Volume 1 of this series, we developed the concept of the foundational form of life. This unique ground of our existence should be welcomed as a dynamic director of our formation in dialogue with the dynamics described thus far. This basic ideal form of our uniqueness hides the secret of our transcendent identity, of our innermost call to consonance.

The foundational life-form is a source of what we can call congeniality or integrity dynamics. In principle they are not meant to be separated from other dynamics. On the contrary, they should penetrate them, elevating and transforming them. If we enlist these dynamics of inner consonance in our everyday efforts to grow, they will gradually permeate, direct, modulate, reform, and transform our history in dialogue with our field of presence and its underlying traditions.

Our founding form of life, in spite of its latent dynamism, is not directly available to focal apprehension and appraisal. If we do not create the right conditions for its communication, it will remain largely outside our awareness. This gift at the base of our life, when acknowledged and welcomed, endows us with a sense of form potency, of humble and joyous appreciation of the gift we most deeply are. It fills us with a sense of faith, hope, and love.

The founding forming power of our life and its direction transcends all other integrational life-forms and dynamics. When we welcome it, it radiates into our life not only formative but also reformative directives. Its reforming inspiration warns us when we deviate from our inner call and drift off in dissonance.

For example, when human life becomes overly depreciative, the foundational form will attempt to radiate into it the dynamic powers of faith, hope, and love to counteract the dynamics of depreciation and despair. When we are receptive to this warning voice in dialogue with similar voices in our field, the founding form will inspire directives that may lead gradually to a restoration of the consonant unfolding of our life.

In this example we are not speaking of depression that has a biochemical cause to be treated medically, but of the despondency that we all experience from time to time as a result of dissonance. In some instances both ills can go together. In that case medical treatment combined with formation counseling may be helpful.

The dynamic radiation of consonant directives by the foundational form of life manifests itself first of all in our transfocal consciousness, which should be distinguished from the infrafocal region. From the latter emerge the dynamics of drives and instincts. They suggest life directives of their own, many of which may be dissonant.

Life can attain consonance only when it becomes receptive to the dynamics radiated by our founding form into the transfocal region of consciousness. Before these directives can enter our focal awareness, they must pass through the region of prefocal consciousness. There they can be distorted by other influences, such as sociohistorical pulsations, prefocally adopted, or by infrafocal dynamics that have penetrated the boundaries of our prefocal consciousness. Our formation reason has no direct control over the cauldron of the prefocal. Unappraised directives entering from the outside as well as from the other nonfocal regions of consciousness mingle and clash with one another in speedy, multiple, tentative associations. This region is at the same time a source of creativity and a potential source of dissonance.

Certain conditions facilitate our receptivity to the dynamics of unique consonance radiated by the foundational form of our life into our transfocal consciousness. A primordial condition is to create moments of relaxation, gentleness, stillness, and recollection that enable us to step back from the turbulence of pluriform dialogue with the many facets of our formation and from the repercussion of this dialogue in the focal and nonfocal regions of our consciousness.

In the measure that we can establish such pauses of recollection, we become receptive to the communications of our foundational form. Its messages may come to us at such moments in the form of inspirational appreciative apprehensions. They direct us to form or reform our life in dialogue with our field at this moment of our journey. This insight does not diminish the demands of reality; rather it directs our realistic response to be in tune also with our deepest call. Its dynamics are rooted ultimately in the same universal manifestation of the mystery of formation that plays everywhere. Our personal formation consciousness is a unique modulation, like a ripple in a mighty river, of the universal formation of cosmos and humanity. The dynamics of congeniality and compatibility should collaborate in growing mutual consonance. In consonance they should aim at a realistic response to the inner and outer manifestations of this call of the mystery as it slowly discloses itself.

Foundational Dynamics and Intraformative Auxiliary Potencies

Our powers of formative memory, imagination, and anticipation also play a role in our communication with the foundational dynamics. They function as a bridge, a passageway, for the message of our innermost orientation to responsible attention, apprehension, appraisal, and affirmation powers. Our imagination, for instance, may present images and symbols that concretize the dynamics of our transcendent uniqueness. They caution us in tangible ways when we are on the verge of betraying our most intimate direction. Our memory may intellectually or imaginatively recall events that pointed us in the direction of consonant unfolding. It may also remind us of the dissonance we experienced when we were deficient in fidelity to our inner call.

In some people the imagination may give rise to memorial or anticipatory dreams in service of restorative proformation. Our capacity for anticipation may intellectually or imaginatively light up for us the direction to be taken if we want to restore consonance with our foundational dynamics.

Such disclosures of our identity are accompanied by corresponding feelings. They strengthen the impact of the message. A main condition for receptivity to such dynamics is learning to listen more to the inspirations of our innermost life than to historical pulsations. We should be cautious when people who are strangers to our interiority try to compel or seduce us to follow the mandates of their own sensitivity.

We must also be vigilant in regard to exalting fantasies generated by the pride-form and masked as messengers of the life call. Prideful autarky in its manifold subtle dynamics functions, as we have said, is a quasi-foundational form of life. It generates exalted fantasies that estrange us from our calling. The dynamics of exaltation and subsequent insulation from our real field are always ready to spoil genuine inspiration by distortion. To prevent their perversion, we must seek for interformation with the wisdom of traditions. In certain instances, it may be wise to consult friends, counselors, directors, or communities acknowledged for their wisdom in the appraisal of dynamics.

One means to tap the rich dynamics of our intimate direction is to foster the bridge function of our inner auxiliary potencies. We must cherish images, memories, and anticipations that keep us in touch with our inner source of consonant identity. When we allow such concrete pointers to emerge in our intrasphere, they facilitate our access to the dynamics of our deepest self. At the same time we should be careful not to bypass the ongoing pluriform dialogue with other structures and dynamics. Without this dialogue, we may be easily misled by fantasized forms of life and action. In that case our autarky may take over with its exalting and insulating dynamics.

Symbolizing Our Foundational Form

By means of formative imagery, we can symbolize the invisible core of our existence. This imagery can be visual, auditory, tactile, or mental. It can assume myriad forms. What works best for us depends on each one's preformation and ongoing dialogue with other facets of life.

We are not only a dialogue with our foundational form of life but a pluriform dialogue with other structures and dynamics of our field. It is only within a concrete field that our life call can disclose and realize itself. Each disclosure itself is dynamic; it adaptively unfolds our everyday existence in dialogue with the relevant facets of our entire field. Symbols for our foundational dynamics can be disclosed to us in the course of this dialogue.

In the measure that life approximates consonance, the dynamics of its unique call and the dynamics of its pluriform formation field will be coformed by a wisely interwoven dialogue which generates symbols that foster the expression of our unique life call.

Directed Proformation

Another means of creating room for the dynamics of our transcendent identity is directed proformation. It facilitates faithfulness to our life direction. Our life call is not merely a source of information telling us how to unfold here and now congenially, compatibly, compassionately, courageously, and competently. It is also a dynamic power of proformation, an inexhaustible source of wisdom and strength for tomorrow.

We mobilize these dynamics by the imaginative direction of our powers of proformation. Human life is always proforming, always ahead of itself, reaching out to what it might become and is not yet. To be human is to be in proformation. The difficulty is that we are not always in charge of this process. Often we allow it to be determined by unappraised structures, dynamics, and dimensions.

Directed proformation aims at conditions conducive to the responsible, sensitive direction of our life. As already mentioned, a first condition is to allow pauses or periods of relaxation, attentiveness, stillness, detachment, and recollection. Often we are so exclusively involved in the outer dynamics of our field that we do not keep them in dialogue with those of our intimate life orientation. They are allowed to bypass our basic style of being insofar as it is available to our knowledge at this moment of our history. The gentle whisper of the life call is dimmed by the noise of our vital-functional dynamics with their sociohistorical directives. While the latter should be heard and respectfully integrated, they should not dominate exclusively the unfolding of our life.

To come in touch again with our interiority, it is necessary to distance ourselves from these dynamics. We must give the dynamics of inner direction a chance to announce themselves. Otherwise uncongenial elements may invade the appraisal of our identity. These can estrange us from ourselves to the point where our deepest self goes into exile and we risk losing our integrity.

Recollection means literally to collect again the diffused energies and attentions so that we can be present to the message of our interiority. In this silent abiding, images and symbols may emerge that tell us something about our journey, its consonance and dissonance. If we are committed to the wisdom of a tradition, its symbols and images begin to reverberate in our interiority. They are time-honored pathways to the temple of transfocal dynamics. Manifesting a dynamic of their own, these symbols gain a personal relevance, a whole new power in our meditative dwelling on them in silent recollection.

One rich source for our research into the general dynamics of the life call in their interaction with our proformation and with our pluriform field are diaries, biographies, and autobiographies. Preferable are those that can be checked against historical data gathered from other sources. Such data assist formation scientists in their critical appraisal of the biographical accounts of formation dynamics (see my book *A Light to the Gentiles: The Life Story of the Venerable Francis Libermann*). Such biographies illustrate the dialogical interaction between the foundational, pluriform field and proformational dynamics.

The same would apply to similar dynamics in the history of common and segmental populations. The aim of the science is to delineate models of dynamic constellations, including their basic conditions and consequences, that can be generalized in their fundamental features to a wider population.

Aware now of the coformants of dynamic constellations, we are ready for a consideration of the object of elucidation.

CHAPTER 16

The Object of Elucidation

The object of elucidation is the disclosure of dynamics related to distinctively human formation from the viewpoint of the directives they imply. Dynamics and directives can be made available to researchers in lingual and nonlingual expressions. To identify the dynamics that underlie these expressions in a way that is related to distinctively human formation is different from merely identifying them as such.

This specific perspective makes formation science different in its elucidation of dynamics from other approaches to them, such as, for instance, the psychoanalytic or the psychophysiological. Formation science integrates the results of other approaches in its theory of dynamics insofar as they are relevant to proximate, distinctively human formation.

We can also distinguish prescientific and scientific approaches, the latter being a critical elaboration of the former. The prescientific apprehension of formation dynamics is basic. It comes first. The scientific elucidation approaches the same dynamics methodically. Starting out from prescientific apprehension, it penetrates into dynamic facets that may have escaped our initial awareness. It critically purifies prescientific appraisal from merely personal or segmental prejudices.

Pluriform Dynamic Directives

In everyday formation we grasp by spontaneous or reflective form appreciative apprehension the obvious, more or less focal, directives in our field. However, there is more to formation than what immediately strikes the eye.

In any act of formation or proformation, our whole field is involved. Let us say I am in the midst of an act of proformation pertaining to a meeting with my boss. Many dynamic directives are activated in preparation for the session. Some of them may be my earlier meetings with superiors, parents, or principals; my wife's insistence that I should ask for a raise; my ambition for a promotion; my fear of making a less than competent impression. Briefly, all facets of my life that are applicable to this meeting come into play. Formation dynamics and their directives emerge or recede into the background in accordance with their apprehended relevance to my giving and receiving form in this meeting. Dynamics and directives in nonfocal regions of consciousness are involved, too.

It is impossible to disclose such intermingling directives and dynamics by prescientific apprehension and appraisal alone. Scientific elucidation can give us more insight. The questions are: How do we gain access to these dynamics? What conceptual tools do we use to elucidate them?

Pliability of the Dynamic Configuration of the Field

To answer those questions, we should remind ourselves that the dynamic configuration of a field is different from the structural. The latter configuration manifests a certain stability; the dynamic one is always in movement.

Our dynamic life is in principle emergent not static. This pliability is due to two coforming factors. The first is our relative freedom to initiate, negate, or modify motivational dynamics and directives. This freedom is limited by the conditions of our field. Therefore, the second coforming factor leading to pliability of dynamics is dialogical interaction with such changeable conditions. The dynamics adaptively move and unfold in response to the changes of different facets of our life.

Dynamics and directives exercise a modulating influence on our life. Conversely, life in its variability has a formative influence on dynamics and directives. Formation dynamics are thus not static; they are not given once and for all. They remain interactive with our conditioned freedom and with our field. They react and respond to relatively free appraisals, affirmations or nonaffirmations, facilitating conditions or obstacles, confirmations or rejections, and effectiveness or failure.

For example, the dynamics of protest against an oppressive regime may modulate the form this regime gives to its administrative measures. It may, for instance, moderate its tactics or harden them. Both responses have an influence on the dynamics of people. Moderation may encourage open protest to gain more relief. Hardening may move the protest dynamics underground, where they gain in resentment, explosiveness, and plotting tendencies. These may give rise to dynamics of violence. In either case, the field is evidently influenced by the changing dynamics and directives evoked by administrative policies.

Access to Formation Dynamics

We have access to formation dynamics through attention, reflective apprehension, and appraisal sustained by memory and imagination. Our formation reason, thus informed, can then elucidate these dynamics.

Elucidation enhances our control over the dynamics that empower and direct our life. It deepens and illumines our free responsibility for the effects of dynamics on our field.

Not all the directives embedded in the dynamics of different regions of consciousness are directly observable. In ordinary life the apprehension of more obvious, focal directives proceeds spontaneously. They are directly available to us. The same can be said for the obvious, focal directives we discern in the words, gestures, and facial expressions of others. We may have an immediate form appreciative apprehension of what people seem to intend overtly.

Dialogical elucidation goes beyond this ordinary appreciative apprehension. It is a rigorous method of inquiry used first of all to appraise critically some of the obvious, focal form directives and dynamics of people, their movements, and their institutions. Beyond this it discloses also those directives that escape commonplace observation.

Relationship between Scientific Elucidation and Form Appreciative Apprehension

While scientific elucidation can be distinguished from form appreciative apprehension, the two cannot be separated. Form appreciative apprehension refers, as we know, to any spontaneous or reflective appreciative or depreciative comprehension of the dynamic direction implied in a happening. For example, we may comprehend spontaneously or reflectively (not scientifically) the directions implied in a speech, a song, a poem, a celebration, an accident; in an encounter with a parent, friend, counselor, or teacher; in a decision to assist a person in need; in a call to social justice. This commonplace comprehension may be focal or nonfocal, spontaneous or reflective.

When form appreciative apprehension becomes elucidation, it acquires a more circumscribed or specialized meaning. Elucidation refers to a specifically elaborated type of attention. This elaboration initially implies methodical-critical expansion and deepening of what is already germinally present in our initial apprehension. Methodical elucidation is a response to such questions as: How correct are the results of the prescientific awarenesss of dynamics and their directives? Are there perhaps less obvious dynamics at work?

Elucidation corrects, refines, complements, and deepens our common-place apprehension of the formational implications of what is happening.

Dialogical instead of Logical Nature of Elucidation

Neither appreciation nor elucidation can be understood as operations of the functional mind as merely logical. They are not merely inductive or deductive processes guided by logical reasoning alone. This kind of inquiry is not merely logical; it is dialogical. This approach implies the use of our central and auxiliary intraformative powers.

For example, our comprehension of what a classical drama may mean to our life, formationally speaking, implies memorial images and symbols of our formation history that can be related to the images and symbols in the drama. Involved in this dialogical approach is also our power of anticipation. It helps us to appraise the direction that our formation and proformation may assume in light of the impact of the drama on our heart and mind. The dynamics portrayed in the drama and the directives they imply are affirmed or nonaffirmed by our will, acting as a relatively free formation potency. Appraisal and willing are accompanied by corresponding dynamic ideals, desires, passions, and emotions affecting our formation and proformation. These powers also dialogue formatively with all facets of our field that are relevant to the influence the drama may have on our life.

Neither appreciative apprehension nor elucidation are based on the disclosure of one or the other exclusive, insulated facet of the field. We cannot isolate one facet that "causes" in linear fashion the dynamic implications of an event. Both approaches involve a process that moves from formationally relevant facets of the field to the field as a whole and back to these facets again.

Take, for example, the event of racial injustice in the spatial-temporal and mondial spheres of a formation field. We may apprehend the dynamic implications and directions of this injustice if it continues in our life. This apprehension involves a process that touches on various facets of our field, such as our own familial preformation in racial prejudices; the interformative social pressures of our society in regard to minorities; the popular overappreciation of success or failure in terms of material acquisitions and formal education only; the kind of prejudices we ourselves may have sometimes experienced in our own history and what they felt like; the functional discrimination in housing, employment, and education—opportunities we ourselves have been taking for granted; the emergent awareness of thoughts, feelings, words, and deeds of discrimination we have engaged in nonfocally; the unappraised deformative dispositions in ourselves and others that are the dissonant result of such reiterated acts.

The process of apprehension or its scientific elucidation moves from such relevant facets to a comprehensive apprehension of our field as a whole. It appraises this field in its entirety in the light of these apprehended or elucidated facets.

In such elucidation the field appears as deformed by racial discrimination and in need of reformation by acts and dispositions of social justice. Conversely, however, this apprehension or elucidation of the field in its overall dynamic direction throws new light on the various facets we disclosed in the first place. We now see more clearly how these deformative aspects of racial injustice interact dynamically with one another and with the field in its prevalent general direction. We apprehend them as coformants of this socially unjust field.

This example makes us aware of the complexity of the dynamics and directives that operate in our field in relation to any happening. Their pluriformity in various regions of consciousness makes it improbable that they can be disclosed correctly and all at once by ordinary form appreciative apprehensions. Therefore, our common apprehension needs to be complemented and corrected by methodical elucidation.

Theoretical Abstraction and Scientific Elucidation

Formation scientists share the common and segmental apprehensions of people regarding the directives operative in their field of presence and action. These are the starting point of their research. They translate them in terms of the language of the science and transpose them into its theoretical frame of reference. By means of the theoretical distance attained in such translation and transposition, they are able to abstract the dynamics with their directives from what is prescientifically apprehended. Prescientific apprehension, even when it is reflective, does not usually abstract sufficiently from contextual facets that do not belong to the basic constellation of these dynamics.

The researchers give form scientifically to these abstracted dynamics by means of the concepts and constructs of their science. In service of scientific validation by other researchers, they must be able to formulate in distinct concepts what they apprehend as dynamically directive in the occurrences they study. Only then can they submit their tentative scientific elucidations to a rigorous critique by their colleagues. Precise metalingual formulation enables them also to enter into critical dialogue not only with other scientists but also with the elucidations offered by other sciences, disciplines, and by the arts and formation traditions.

The elucidation method, like other methods in formation science, is thus not phenomenological in the strict sense of the word. It approaches the field of inquiry from the viewpoint of a definite formation theory without absolutizing this theory. The theory itself is not merely a derivative from formation experience. It is a construct of formation reason that takes formation experience into account.

Formation reason, constructing this theory, is informed first of all by the research of formation science; second, by formation theories it discovers in auxiliary sources, such as psychodynamic psychologies, personality theories, and formation traditions; third, by anthropological presuppositions. Translating them into its own language, the science manages to create and maintain a unilingual universe of discourse about proximate life formation, thus enabling its scientists to communicate with each other concisely, meaningfully and effectively.

Hypothetical Character of Scientific Elucidations

Research in this regard utilizes the many alternative hypothetical elucidations of dynamics developed by formation scientists and auxiliary sources. In principle, we remain open to any hypothesis about elucidation available to us. We do not wish to deny or diminish the value of phenomenology within its own domain of fundamental inquiry into human experience as such. The valuable, less hypothetical results of such inquiry are impressive in their theoretical and practical impartiality. They are useful but not sufficient for the practice of proximate and immediate life formation.

To elucidate and direct the complex dynamics of human life practically, scientists have to work with theoretical and practical probabilities that cannot be fully explicated by the phenomenological method. Moreover, they must take into account the ontological presuppositions that influence focally or nonfocally the directives of people. To make sense of these dynamics and to assist effectively in the formation process, conceptual hypothetical elucidations are unavoidable, granting that we keep in mind that they are only probable.

Formation is ongoing; it cannot wait until all information is assembled and all dynamics fully disclosed. Formation questions often demand an answer here and now based on the best probabilities available, no matter their limitations. In the very application of this probable knowledge with its generalization power, additional aspects may be disclosed, hypotheses disproved, and new hypotheses initiated. Therefore, our theory is open to revision the moment that the practice of formation demonstrates that hypothetical elucidations do not work effectively as they were presumed to do.

Need for Scientific Elucidation

The prescientific apprehension of formational implications, which precedes elucidation, remains the point of departure for any specific research. It is the primary process through which the formal object of the science is presented to us in each formation event. If this is so, why do we need dialogical-theoretical elucidation? Can we not simply abide by our initial commonplace apprehension? Would it not be suffcient to elaborate the coformants of this apprehension without theoretical interventions?

When we compare the reports of different subjects about the same prescientific apprehension, we realize that they manifest the always present possibility of partial or total misapprehension. This is one reason for significant differences among various popular reports of the same event. The possibility of distortion becomes even more evident if the subjects try to explain the dynamics underlying the incident they describe.

We cannot trust that prescientific descriptions cover the event correctly. Hence our insistence on the development and continual refinement of critical methods of dialogical articulation, elucidation, consultation, and application. Even then our results are not perfect, but their reliability is greater than that of prescientific personal or shared formation intuitions and hunches.

The method of elucidation provides a set of rules that guides our appraising apprehension of the dynamic configuration of the field in the light of formation theory. It safeguards in some measure formation reason from arbitrariness and subjectivism. It keeps this reason in dialogue with contemporary and historical hypotheses, with the results of the judicious use of human reason.

We considered in this chapter the object of elucidation and the requirements it implies for our methods of elucidation. On the basis of these objective requirements we can begin to formulate in the next chapter the principles of methical elucidation.

CHAPTER 17

Principles of
Methodical Elucidation

The process of methodical elucidation is directed by a system of formal steps to be outlined in the next chapter. These procedures are consonant with the principles of methodology of the science.

Two main principles of methodical elucidation are the following:

1. Any dynamic formation directive should be elucidated provisionally in the light of formation theory and in explicit reference to the field in which the directive operates dynamically.
2. The dynamic that manifests itself in a given formation directive should be elucidated first in the light of appropriate propositions in the corresponding dynamic sector of formation theory, and, second, in explicit reference to its coformation by related dynamics that in some mode and measure affect this main dynamic source of the directive under examination.

For example, we may identify and examine the deformative directive that moves some people to engage in what is for them personally an inappropriate operation of social justice. This directive may be popular, but is also happens to be uncongenial to their basic life call. We should elucidate the dynamics of this dissonant directive in reference to the field of the people concerned. Both the dynamics and the field with which they interact dialectically should be elucidated in the light of general structures and dynamics of the field as already established by formation theory.

We may consider, for instance, the personally unappraised sociohistorical pulsations that make only special types of social justice operations popular; the unappraised interformative pressures by authoritarian leaders to engage ourselves only in those specific operations if one wants to gain esteem and promotion; the spatial-temporal and mondial pressure of certain needs that are conspicuously relieved by mainly those types of action and hence gain immediate acclaim, publicity, and popularity.

Having established the dynamics in explicit reference to the structures of the field, we can now seek to disclose those hidden behind the overly coformative, uncongenial response of certain people to these pressures. We may elucidate, for instance, a dynamic of fear in them of what people in authority, respected colleagues, or judgmental acquaintances may feel, think, or say if they refused to become involved in this one type of popular operation. This fear dynamic, in turn, should be elucidated in reference to related coforming dynamics. For instance, it may be intimately interwoven with those of overambitiousness that lead one to compromise in order to be promoted, or with those of unappraised people pleasing, which may be interwoven in turn with the dynamics of indistinct gregariousness as a protection against the demands of one's transcendent uniqueness and of intimate personal encounter.

Many other dynamic constellations, established by formation science or its auxiliary sources, can be critically tested for their applicability to the dissonant directive in the example. Evidently, dialogical elucidation is one of the fundamental methods of a science that aspires to disclose proximate directives for consonant human formation, to unmask their dissonant counterparts, and to unravel the underlying dynamics of both.

Dialogical Elucidation of Universal, Common, and Segmental Ranges

Dialogical elucidation applies also to the disclosure of the dynamics operative in the universal, common, and segmental ranges of the field. Their elucidation can be conducive to an increasing approximation of consonant shared formation, affecting significant groups of people. A continual flow of interaction maintains a certain formative connection between these ranges. This means that the universal and common dynamics of the field are mirrored in some way in the dynamics of the segmental and personal ranges. Conversely, their dynamics influence the emergence of certain commonalities. A fuller apprehension and appraisal of the dynamics operative in each range implies, therefore, an examination of their coformative interaction. This illustrates again how each singular directive has to be elucidated by reference to all related facets.

For example, the competition dynamic operative in individual formation in a capitalistic field must be elucidated not only in reference to the personal modulation of that dynamic but to the common dynamics of free enterprise and meritorious achievement. We have to examine, moreover, the segmental expression of the competition dynamic in companies, clubs, schools, sports, and church organizations. In this research the competition dynamic in the personal range should be related to the dynamics of rewards, high marks, and promotions on basis of competitive performance. Yet the elucidation should extend itself also to the modulations introduced by the personal range into these shared competition dynamics. Finally, all these dynamics can be related to certain universal dynamics of form reception and donation.

The configuration of our field of presence and action is a continuous flux of intermingling dynamics. Certain manifest directives emerge at the surface of this configuration, easily observable by most people. These peripheral directives point back to a high-powered interfusion of propelling forces. Such powers express themselves differently in different regions of consciousness. The peripheral pointers themselves are not sufficent to identify these underlying processes. Hence the necessity of the elucidation method.

The metalanguage tries to convey the interconnectedness of dynamics in a conceptual shorthand. This make dynamics and directives amenable to theoretical procedures that are at once systematic, coherent, and concise.

This scientific language is sometimes tinged with metaphorical allusions. We would not find similar experiential references in the informational languages of the physical sciences or those of social sciences that are functionally oriented. Metaphorical allusions represent the flowing quality of the interfusing dynamics of formation. They point to a certain ambiguity of formative events due to our free interaction with them not found in fields of physical formation.

Introspection versus Dialogical Articulation and Elucidation

Formation science rejects introspection as a basis for research and theory.

Introspection puts a specific experience of ours in relief against the background of the field in its pluriform entirety. The source of this figural emphasis is the momentary subjective relevance of the experience to our personal range. The directives that become available to us in this selected and highlighted experience are usually focal, sometimes prefocal.

Introspection may leave concealed the dynamics of nonfocal regions of consciousness. It lacks the theoretical distance necessary for an objective overview of the dynamics operative in the field beyond and below those that are focal or prefocal.

Another problem is that an introspective exploration might alter the very dynamics one is examining due to the subjective moods and mindsets that attach themselves to memories. The process of introspection also leaves out the objective parameters of the formation experience, which are not available to the subjectivistic self-presence of an individual. In short, introspection cannot produce sufficiently comprehensive, objective knowledge upon which an empirical science can be based.

Danger of Introspective Approaches to Formation

In the history of human formation, people have suffered much deformation because well-meaning practitioners based their generalized directives on introspection of their own experience. Unaware of the objective structures and dynamics coforming their individual experiences, they imposed, for instance, on whole populations safety directives based on their specific sensitivity.

An example would be the battles and demonstrations that occurred in certain Christian European countries against "mixed swimming" in the ocean or in local swimming pools. The presupposition of these crusades was the passionate conviction, introspectively acquired, that the sight of the swimming movement of the other sex, at that time dressed in long bathing suits, in sea or pool would necessarily have a sexually deformative influence on the average swimmer. Such formation directives often emerged from the introspective endeavors of moralists who, never having seen the other sex thus moving, were shocked and somewhat excited when for the first time they were exposed to this view. Not articulating the structures of their own field, influenced by a life of withdrawal from swimming pools, and not elucidating the underlying dynamics of their shock at this first exposure, they generalized it to all people. They did not realize that repeated exposure would make the average swimmer shockproof in this regard. Their correlation between exposure of the average swimmer to the other swimmers of the opposite sex and immoral excitement was based on introspective procedures, not on an examination of the field in its entirety supported by statistical studies from auxiliary sciences regarding the factual relationship between exposure and excitement in average regular swimmers.

Introspective Concentration on the Intrasphere

A related objection of formation science against the introspective approach is its concentration on mainly one sphere of the field. The introspective approach, unlike that of dialogical formation, tends to favor the intrasphere. As the term introspection suggests, it is an inspection of what is experientially *intro-*, or, in the language of the science, the *intrasphere* of the field.

Elucidation, on the contrary, is not an approach to one's intrasphere alone. Its object of inquiry should be the observable lingual and nonlingual expressions of formation events in the field. These are approached critically by means of an articulation and elucidation of the entire field insofar as it modulates a happening as formative. Articulation of the field in all its spheres, ranges, regions, dimensions, and integrational forms, and elucidation of its directives and dynamics are guided by hypothetical propositions of an objective theory. These propositions are maintained as long as they are not contradicted by new findings and insights.

Hence the methods of formation science transcend those of introspection. The science does not restrict the human self to the intrasphere. The self is coformed by one's entire field with its horizons. (See "Introspection and Transcendent Self-Presence" in my book *In Search of Spiritual Identity*.)

Field Conditioned Formation Freedom in Regard to Dynamics and Directives

The distinctively human factor to be taken constantly into account in elucidation is that of conditioned human freedom. One of the objections of the science against existentialism is its conception of the absolute freedom of human life. Radical existentialists like Jean Paul Sartre seem to believe in an arbitrary, limitless freedom. In their view such freedom is not conditioned basically by the structures, directives, and dynamics of the field.

An introspective approach may focus one-sidedly on our intraspheric powers of free attention, apprehension, appraisal, affirmation, and application. Lacking in concrete dialogue with the objective structures and dynamics of the field, introspection may incline us to imagine that we can initiate or reform at will any facet that gives form to our intimate existence. In this case we would fall into the existentialistic illusion of absolute freedom.

The field approach of elucidation avoids the pitfalls both of the illusion of absolute freedom and of its opposite, absolute determinism as fostered by many nineteenth-century scientists. As we have seen, our free intraformative powers function in dialogue with the objective structures, dynamics, and directives of the field. They are neither entirely determined by them nor entirely free in their form donation to them. Our freedom is field-conditioned. Directives and dynamics are not the result of totally independent intraspheric powers acting in isolation. They are the relatively free outcome of a dialogical interaction between the freedom of the spirit and the field in which this freedom is incarnated.

Example of Statistically Significant Conditioning of Formation Freedom

Let us suppose people in a Marxist state are advised that they can have only one child per couple. If they refuse to comply with this demand, they face discrimination and the withdrawal of certain privileges for their children. They are also made the object of public condemnation. When a woman becomes pregnant with a second child, great pressure is exerted to abort the fetus.

Theoretically speaking every couple has the freedom to resist this impingement on their human rights. Some heroic parents may exercise that freedom, no matter the consequences. Practically, however, human freedom is conditioned by the dynamics of public condemnation. Hence it is improbable, although not impossible, that a statistically significant number of parents will have more than one child. This is no argument for absolute determinism—parents *can*, and some *do* freely give form to other dynamics leading to the birth of a second child. It means only that because of the weakness of the human condition under heavy pressures it is improbable that a significant number of average persons will maintain their freedom of procreation.

Even in their intrasphere, the assimilated or adopted pressures may limit the freedom of their attention, apprehension, appraisal, and affirmation in this regard. The fact, however, that some parents initiate dynamics and directives that result in the birth of another child demonstrates that pressures do not have an absolutely determining influence.

Source of Freedom of Formation Dynamics and Directives

The dynamics and directives that give form to our life can be freely attended to, apprehended, appraised, affirmed or unaffirmed by us. We can reform them. They are not *caused* in the way physical dynamics in the universe are irrevocably caused by physical pressures. The right mixture of oxygen and hydrogen under the appropriate conditions always results in water, whether we will it or not.

The dynamics of human life are different in that they are not the automatic outcome of what happens in the field. They are ultimately the result of intraspheric appraisal and affirmation or nonaffirmation of what these facets invite us to do. Motivational dynamics are not causes. We give form to them in relative, never absolute, freedom. We are limited by the actual conditions that coform our motivational dynamics.

A saintly and heroic man, Saint Paul was a champion of human freedom. Yet his freedom was limited by his culture. Being a child of his times and civilization, he was not free to attend to, apprehend, appraise, and affirm the desirability for Christians to free their slaves. Therefore, he advised them only to be kind to their slaves and exhorted the slaves to be obedient to their masters. In this case the limitations of freedom inherent in one's actual cultural condition could not be overcome.

Empirical Studies Not about Freedom as Such, but about Its Limiting Conditions

In many situations we can establish probability rules regarding the exercise of freedom. For example, if adolescents are constantly exposed to pornographic movies, pictures, and literature, it is probable that a statistically significant number of them will experience a diminished freedom in regard to consonant sexual development. It is for this reason that formation researchers value so much statistical data collected by themselves or by the auxiliary sciences. These sciences examine not freedom in itself, but the probable limitations of freedom. They express such limits in probability statements that apply to a significant number of people living under the same conditions.

The power of conditions points to the desirability that specific traditions establish their own subfield of segmental formation. In that subfield their own traditions can be communicated and celebrated. Such practices counterbalance conditions in the common range that threaten the freedom of people to be faithful to their segmental traditions. They enable persons in a pluriform society to confirm each other in their own tradition, thus heightening the probability of the exercise of freedom in regard to their shared principles of consonant living.

Similar conditions limit one's freedom in the personal range. An alcoholic of thirty years is probably not free to abdicate at once this disposition because it is so deeply rooted in all dimensions of his life. Becoming freed from his addiction entails prolonged struggle and a supportive subfield, such as that provided by Alcoholics Anonymous. Field conditions affect thus the freedom of people in regard to the initiation and management of dynamics and directives of formation.

Statistical research of many auxiliary sciences contribute greatly to elucidation research. Formation science as a science is not primarily about freedom in and by itself. It is about the dialectics that concretely condition this freedom. It is interested in predictions of the probable limitations of the concrete freedom of statistically significant numbers of people when exposed to certain field conditions. Only in its formation anthropology, which contains the presuppositions of its theory, does the science speak about the meaning of human freedom as such.

Metalanguage of Formation Dynamics

The configuration of a field is a blend in flux in which various directives manifest themselves as focal points within the field as a whole. The operationally defined metalanguages of the functionally oriented social sciences would be inadequate to capture this flow. A language is needed that is more formational than informational. Informational language enumerates the elements of field dynamics as precisely defined units, separated from one another. Formational language suggests the implicit dialogical relationships between these varied dynamics.

Widening of Personal Form Appreciative Apprehension

To be in touch with our personal experiences, we must start out from the elucidation of the dynamics of a personal event. We try to rise above the bias of introspection by rendering a written account that includes the related objective parameters of the field. It should be subjected to the critique of members of one's research team. Expressing the event in common or segmental language helps us to become aware during critical dialogue that the words we use daily belong to a linguistic usage that may connote feelings, directives, or dynamics that were not part of our initial appreciative apprehension.

For example, the word *primitive* as used in everyday common Western language connotes a certain inferiority of the populations thus designated along with their corresponding dynamics. In fact, however, the dynamics or directives of certain people called primitive could have been apprehended by us as beautifully simple, filled with a rich spontaneity that we have lost.

To have terms available that are not contaminated in this fashion, we must have recourse to a metalanguage. For example, instead of speaking about primitive traditions, we may call them indigenous for this is a more neutral word.

Another way to transcend the accretions of our personal, segmental, or common apprehension of dynamics and directives is the use of the method of dialogical consultation. It expands our elucidation possibilities by dialogue with literature, art, social life, history, laws, spiritual masters, formation traditions, and the observations of other sciences and disciplines.

Yet even under the best of conditions, we must realize that the dynamics of human life as such can never be fully elucidated. The historical character of these dynamics makes human life as such an open realm, always in process. We ourselves, as scientists, are conditioned in some measure by our own history. We have to start out from a field that is limited by its origination in a particular period of the history of human unfolding. Our background makes us aware of certain dynamics and less so, or not at all, of others. This does not mean that we are condemned to repeat what we already know. We can grow by means of scientific elucidation to a more objective approximation of the dynamics of human life, their obstacles and facilitating conditions. The subsequent increase in the probability of our expanding elucidation moves us closer to a more general and objective apprehension and appraisal.

Hypothetical Character of Elucidation

Elucidation is thus a dialogical process between scientists and the events under study insofar as these are directed by dynamics. This process can lead to objective elucidations that provide us in turn with general theoretical propositions. Within the science they function as sufficiently probable hypothetical models. By use of the deductive process, they are applied by researchers to the events they examine for their dynamic precedents, concomitants, and aftereffects.

In this process the hypothetical proposition may be confirmed as still the highest probable elucidation available. As a result of the attempt at application, the elucidation model may also be refined or replaced by a more probable proposition on the basis of newly gained validated insights and information.

At stake ultimately is the right apprehension and appraisal of directives. Consonant formation is dependent upon valid elucidations. Hence this method is crucial for all subsequent formation directives.

The validity of an elucidation is always hypothetical. Within the realm of empirical human science, elucidation cannot present us with absolute certainty. It can only achieve probability. From what we have said about the hypothetical nature of probable propositions in formation theory, it is clear that we can never be absolutely sure that we have developed the best possible models of formation dynamics. Neither can we be sure that we have found the final unalterable methodology that will necessarily lead to the highest probable elucidation. Hence dialogical consultation with fellow researchers and with relevant auxiliary sources, which are themselves in constant development in regard to their discoveries and their methodologies, remains a necessity for the scientist.

Understanding the principles of methodical elucidation, we can now consider the process of elucidation in the following chapter.

CHAPTER 18

Process of Elucidation

C ertain directives may be immediately obvious to all observers. There is no need for elucidation. Others are less manifest. We may only sense that something else underlies a formative incident. It may be a motivation that keeps eluding our apprehension, something without which we cannot fully appraise what is happening. Here scientific clarification may be desirable.

In such a case, formation scientists first engage themselves in a preliminary elucidation based on:

1. their own form appreciative apprehension of its dynamics and directives;
2. the pointers to dynamics contained in their structural articulation of the event;
3. the dynamic models provided by the formation theory and by previously validated research projects.

An initial elucidation usually provides only low probability. The elucidation at this stage may still depend too much on the conditioning of researchers by their own experience, on their own articulation of the field, and on the dynamic models of the theory developed thus far. This does not necessarily mean that the low probability may not in fact turn out to be a high one. It means only that a higher degree cannot be bestowed on the results of an initial elucidation without complementary research.

One complementary method is that of consultation (to be dealt with in detail in a later chapter). Here it suffices to indicate that consultation takes two main forms: regular critical dialogue with fellow researchers and interaction with the dynamic insights, facts, and theories constantly developed by auxiliary sources. As more evidence is gathered by means of consultation, the initial elucidations are critically reconsidered in light of the added evidence and, if necessary, refined or expanded. Each successive tentative elucidation has a higher probability of being correct.

Formation science offers compatibility criteria for the appraisal of the reliability of each elucidation. They are:

1. the precision of the consultation procedures in their exact rendering of the information;
2. the faithful translation of the information into the metalanguage and its enlightening transposition in formation theory;
3. the compatibility of the new insights with those tenets of the theory that so far have not been disproved;
4. the evident compatibility of various findings and insights of the auxiliary sources with one another, manifested when their different metalanguages are translated into the comprehensive metalanguage of the science, making comparisons possible;
5. the compatibility of the new elucidation with the validated insights already gained during the selection, articulation, and previous elucidation of the event under study;
6. the reasonable consensus of the members of the research team when the new elucidation is submitted to their critical appraisal.

For example, the leader of an organization may insist on the retention of a vice-president in spite of critical remarks by other vice-presidents. The dynamics underlying his decision may at first seem like stubbornness born from pride concealing insecurity. Next it may be elucidated as an inordinate fear of the vice-president, who may remind him of his father. Finally it may become evident after more study and consultation that the main dynamics at work are unusual perspicacity, enabling the leader to see important qualities in the criticized vice-president. His administrative talents benefit the effective running of the organization in spite of rough edges that exasperate other people on the team. If the latter elucidation corresponds more than the former with the criteria of compatibility outlined above, it has, for the time being, the highest available probability.

This shows that conflicting elucidations should be appraised according to which one most adequately takes account of the results of dialogical consultation. The one most probably compatible is the one that the weight of confirmation supports.

Spiraling Movement toward Enhanced Probability

Which elucidation is most probable? This question turns elucidation into a spiraling movement. A first elucidation may be questioned by newly gained information from auxiliary sources. This may lead to a change in the elucidation. Subsequent consultations may give rise to further changes, and so on. In this way the process of elucidation becomes a spiraling movement toward enhanced probability.

The analysis of a formative incident thus follows a spiral pattern. It starts out from our own personal apprehension. Then it goes beyond our personal range, but cannot approach it from outside our common field. In some sense we are our field. Hence, we cannot avoid certain limitations in our attention, apprehension, and appraisal. Once we acknowledge the boundaries of our point of departure, we can attempt to widen our vision by transcultural consultation. Even then we must realize that there are limits to how far we can eliminate any remaining influence of our own culture.

If consultation and integration are done in consonance with the principles of the science it does not end in an eclectic collection. On the contrary, translation and transposition correct and expand our theory and methodology, which are basically unified by the unique demands of distinctively human formation. It harmonizes all findings in light of the underlying unity of distinctively human life. Awareness of this unity is easily lost in the pluriform dialogue of the multiple structures of the human formation field. Regaining this original consonance is a homecoming, a return to what we most deeply are.

Continual Reference of Elucidation to Original Apprehension

Elucidation must keep in touch with one's original apprehension of the event that was the critically chosen object of one's selection and articulation. Experience cannot be replaced by theory. Models of dynamics should function only as exemplary possibilities of elucidation, not as straitjackets in which to force our experience. After every methodical approach, the researcher returns to this first apprehension, purifying it increasingly from merely personal accretions, discovering increasingly the essence of its personally apprehended core.

Furthermore, the dialogical movement of elucidation should not be lost. This is essential to the field approach of the science. The elucidation of an event moves dialectically between the field as a whole and its structures, dimensions, dynamics, and directives. The formative influence of each of them on the event should be taken into account continually.

Formation science must provide consonant directives for the present and future. Elucidation extends itself, therefore, to relevant implications of both the here and now and the future effectiveness of the disclosed dynamics and directives.

Ambivalence of Dynamics and Pluriformity of Elucidation

Due to the character of the human subject, elucidation may lead at times to ambiguous statements. Formation science must allow for these provisional probabilities. Functionally oriented psychologies strive for mathematical precision in their experiments and analyses. For certain types of data this is a necessary methodology, yielding important findings. If these methods were applied indiscriminately to distinctively human formation, they could eliminate ambivalent outcomes, but only at the risk of eliminating the richness of the dynamics conveyed in the original experience.

The ambivalence of human dynamics may render diagnosis difficult and uncertain. This factor could hinder the attainment of consensus among the members of a research team. What may be attainable in such cases is an agreement that different elucidations seem equally possible. They should be recorded as alternative elucidations, with a listing of the pros and cons of each. They can be provisionally maintained as equal possibilities until further research and dialogical consultation succeeds in demonstrating that one elucidation is for the moment more probable than others.

One reason for such pluriform elucidation is the above-mentioned fact that the process of elucidation remains always a spiral dialectical movement that is never completed. Another reason can be found in the field approach of the science. No event can be apprehended and appraised dynamically in isolation from the field and its structures.

The elucidation of the dynamics of the event presupposes dialectic apprehension of the dynamic configuration that gives sense to each facet of formation. Such apprehension cannot be the outcome of exact measurement of each element of the configuration in isolation. It is precisely the ongoing dialectical movement that bestows meaning on each facet of the flow—a meaning that emerges not from itself but from its position in the total dynamic configuration.

Dialectical apprehension leads to probable insight supported by evidence. This evidence is often ambiguous. The dialogue, elaborated further in elucidation, is an operation of formation reason, which reconstructs the dynamic patterns of the field. Such patterns, as given to our observation, do not fully and unambiguously manifest all the dynamic connections of the actual configuration. Formation reason has to supply the missing links. Because the connections cannot be shown directly, the proposed elucidation may not be fully convincing or compelling. Other researchers may propose missing links that make equal sense in the elucidation of the configuration.

For similar reasons prediction of future dynamics and their formational consequences, on the basis of such elucidations, cannot be absolute either. Formation science can only provide us with conditional predictions. Under the condition that the elucidation is fundamentally correct and that the same dynamic configuration will repeat itself, we can predict relatively similar formation results, which still will leave sufficient room for personal and situational modulations.

Summary of Selection, Articulation, and Elucidation Methods Thus Far Disclosed

Selection, articulation, and elucidation methods aim at the description and clarification of events which people live through in ways that give form to directives and to their implementation in actions and dispositions operative within their life.

The human field in its many facets is available to these methods through attention to direct interformation of people with one another, to written and other symbolic expressions, and to institutionalized ideological, religious, syncretic and common cultural form traditions.

Such attention teaches us that the formation fields of people are structured and dynamically moved by relatively free dialogical relationships rather than by relationships that are a priori deduced and ordered by means of formal logic.

The methods give us access to these dialectical relationships, made available in the aforementioned expressions. They make us aware of the various structures, dynamics, and directives in which a field organizes itself. They keep refining the approaches that make the field increasingly accessible to formation reason. The methodology is especially attuned to the dialectical and spiral nature of our apprehension and appraisal of distinctively human formation.

Preceding the later methods is the dialogical selection method. It guarantees that human formation is examined from within itself by starting out from a written account of a critically selected personal form appreciative apprehension of a relevant event. This approach facilitates intimate familiarity with such a decisive happening in human life.

The nature of an unfolding pluriform field, experienced as an ongoing formation flow, makes it difficult to provide exact statements about its dynamics and directives. It is a distinctively human field. Generated in relative freedom, it is at the same time subject to already existing conditions. This conditioned or preformed field expresses itself in continuously interacting structures and dynamics.

For all these reasons this field cannot be captured in well-defined unchangeable delineations, as material appearances can. Therefore, it is not always possible to reach full consensus on proposed elucidations of the dynamics involved. In spite of this limitation, or perhaps because of it, dialogical elucidation grants us a more direct access to the realities and ambiguities of human formation than functionally oriented approaches can ever hope to attain.

We have stated some of the main aspects of elucidation. The question to be dealt with in the next chapter is, How do we make this process concrete in methods of elucidation?

CHAPTER 19

Methods of Elucidation

Interaction of All Methods of Formation Science
in All Phases of Research

The methods of formation science are determined by its formal object, namely, the proximate formation, reformation, and transformation of human life in service of consonant ascendance. The approximation of this goal implies the disclosure of formation directives and, if necessary, of more consonant ones that may replace those that are dissonant.

To identify ways of facilitating transitions upward from a current form to a higher one, the science has developed the methodical categories we have been considering. Each type or category represents a cluster of methods that share the same basic function. Researchers can choose from these clusters those that best fit the purpose of their particular research.

As we have seen, the methods of articulation enable us to structure a formation topic and its illustrative event in terms of the overall blueprint of the field in which the event transpires and the topical problem emerges. Interacting with these methods of articulation are those of elucidation of the dynamic directives at play in the event and the topic. These are indirectly articulated through the structural method, which in effect elucidates dynamic directives in their explicit obvious appearance. The elucidation method proper, however, draws forth also their implicit focal, prefocal, intrafocal, transfocal, and other qualifiying factors. Methods of consultation of formation science and its auxiliary sources, and of translation and integration of the results of such consultation, are used in some measure in all phases of the research. The same can be said of the methods of general and specific application of the outcomes. Application can be made, for example, to unadhered-to form traditions, adhered-to form traditions, and sociohistorical segments of populations.

176

Preliminary, Referent, and Prominent Use of Categorical Methods

All of these procedures can in some way be interwoven within actual research exercises. Working on a concrete project, it is practically impossible to separate them always and absolutely from one another. All of them can be involved in various phases of inquiry. Not all of them, however, can be involved in the same measure. Hence we distinguish a preliminary, a referent, and a prominent use of these categorical methods.

Preliminary means that each cluster may be used in a preparatory way in an earlier phase of the research in which another cluster happens to be prominent. This preliminary use prepares for a more *prominent* use of the same methods in a later phase of the research.

The process of elucidation of directives is central in a practical human science. Through it the researcher can disclose the directives that proximately guide the everyday formation of people. Knowledge of these dynamics enables scientists and practitioners to propose effective and consonant directives. The probability of their effectiveness is greater than that obtained by hunches, feelings, intuitions, personal or group experiences, or customs that are not sufficiently appraised scientifically. Attainment of the objectives of the science presupposes such elucidation. Such elucidation methods will be prominent in the elucidation phase of research.

Nevertheless preliminary elucidations may appear in the process of structural articulation. The reason is that one cannot structure a human field without becoming aware in some way of the dynamics operative within these structures and influencing their emergence. Researchers in this field are sensitive to any appearance of dynamic directives already within this preliminary phase.

Similarly, in later phases of the research, *references* may have to be made to former articulations, elucidations, and consultations so that they may serve adaptatively the later disclosure of practical form directives that are distinctively human.

The interwoveness of methodical procedures does not take away from the fact that in a specific phase one procedure may be more prominent than others. For example, researchers must necessarily start out with some structural articulation of the theme and event whose formation dynamics they propose to explore. This method will then naturally be more prominent than that of elucidation, without excluding the latter. In this initial stage of research, methods of elucidation cannot yet be prominent.

Our conclusion is that as far as the practice of research is concerned all methods of formation science may be used in some measure and modulation in any phase of this research. It is up to individual researchers, research teams, departments, and institutes to decide which one of these categorical clusters and their particular methods could be selected and used effectively in what phase of their particular design of study. They should decide how these selected ways of research should be adapted to the limited aims and means they want to establish for their specific projects.

Elucidation: Central Methods of Formation Research

The methods of elucidation can be considered central in formation research. As such they can be used in various forms in any phase of this inquiry.

A brief reflection on the essence of a human science can clarify why elucidation is central. Human sciences are essentially distinguished from the humanities and from speculative and speculative-practical sciences by their radical orientation toward practical change.

Political science, for instance, differs from history as taught in the humanities by its purpose to facilitate effective change in the course of history. Similarly formation science is marked by its orientation towards change in human life. Methods of elucidation are more relevant to such change than others are. They provide us with the insights necessary for practical formation, reformation, and transformation as may be clear from the following considerations.

Primordial, Remote, Proximate, and Immediate Formation Dynamics

Primordial dynamics represent the basic type of energy that lies at the root of a formation event. Remote dynamics specify the expression of this energy in a certain general direction. Proximate dynamics implement this general direction in concrete acts and dispositions that apply, at least potentially, to a significant number of people. Immediate dynamics represent the individual modulation of the proximate directives.

For example, the dynamics of anxiety may generate a tendency to avoid any risk in life. In this example anxiety is a primordial dynamic; avoidance of risk is a remote dynamic. Concrete proximate directives have to do with how to avoid risks effectively, such as never to argue, never to compete or complain, never to appear different. The immediate particular way in which a person manages to avoid such argument, competition, complaint, or conspicuousness is guided by the dynamics of their implementation within the personal range of that person's life.

Methods of elucidation direct us not only to identify such dynamics but also to look at the obstacles and to consider facilitating conditions to replace dissonant dynamics with those that are more consonant. Any change in the right direction presupposes that we have gained some insight in regard to primordial and remote dynamics and their subsequent proximate and immediate directives. This bent toward practicality is one of the factors that makes formation science one of the human sciences.

Take as a point of illustration the elucidation of the primordial dynamics of guilt. Let us say that we study guilt as it operates in a subsegmental range of a field. What are some of the remote and proximate dynamic directives that guide the living of guilt in this group? Exploring this experience, we may discover among other things that the group fosters proximate directives of deformative apprehension, appraisal, and affirmation of their guilt feelings. These directives are of such a nature that they tend to proliferate experiences and expressions of despondent negativity, depreciation of one's life, and incompetence in the art of relieving tension and promoting healthy recreation. To appraise the consonance or dissonance of these directives, we may apply the criteria of faith, hope, and consonance as embedded in congeniality, compatibility, compassion, courage, competence, and social presence in justice, peace, and mercy. In the light of these criteria, their way of dealing with the primordial dynamic of guilt appears less effective than it could be.

In accordance with the same criteria, researchers may disclose during various phases of their study more consonant corrective or complementary directives. These should be in tune with the basic faith and form traditions of the subsegmental group concerned. They should take into account the findings of the science in regard to dealing more consonantly and effectively with the primordial guilt dynamics operative in all human forms of life. The outcome of this research may be prudently communicated in the language of the subsegmental population by its own leaders. The proximate directives and practices of this segment may improve significantly as a result. Such practical purposes stand behind all of the research methods. An intrinsic orientation toward effective change of people or world distinguishes the human sciences from the humanities.

Possible Ways to Identify Primordial, Remote, Proximate, and Immediate Dynamics

Structural articulation makes us aware of the pre-, intra-, inter-, and outer manifestations of the topical event. What may stand out first in our experience are probably the immediate personal manifestations of the more general dynamics which lend themselves to general scientific statements. It is difficult, if not impossible, to articulate an experience without becoming aware also of some of the general dynamics that play a *primordial* role in these events, such as the overall dynamics of anxiety, love, guilt, despair, resentment, pride, envy, or insecurity. Nor can we escape during this procedure of articulation some impressions of the actual *remote* and *proximate* dynamic directives that seem to influence the unfolding of the event significantly.

We have thus already, during the first phase of our research, an opportunity for some preliminary elucidation of certain more obvious and explicit primordial, remote, proximate, and immediate dynamics. In view of the formal object of the science, this preliminary elucidation is essential.

Let us consider again the primordial dynamic of anxiety operative in a formational event. We may spontaneously identify some of the more obvious subsequent remote dynamics that flow from anxiety, such as the directive to withdraw in the presence of authorities. This remote directive gives rise to proximate directives in the various spheres of the field—directives that coform this event. The event has been articulated structurally in terms of the spheres of the field. In the course of this articulation, we have become aware of how this anxiety dynamic influences concretely the remote and proximate directives that are the coformants of anxious form reception and donation.

In this case, for instance, we may discover a *preformative* transcendent appraisal of the divine as a wrathful, punishing authority mirrored in all those who hold office. An *intraformative* directive to interiorize this threatening divine authority in the functional conscience of our intrasphere may also be operative. Our anxiety and its proximate dynamic directives may be reinforced by *interformative* selective experiences with certain authoritarian figures we had to face in our own formation history. It may be deepened by *situational outer* experiences in certain authoritarian institutions and by a selective attention to *world* news about the ways in which authorities oppress people under their rule with whose experiences we identify uncritically. We also try to think of consonant directives that may overcome dissonant ones in these various spheres.

Some of these insights may come to us while we structure the event in terms of these spheres. Thus we list the dynamic coformants of events along with the sturctural as a first step in the elucidation process. In subsequent phases we may decide that we would like to continue this elucidation process. For instance, we may try to penetrate the trans-, infra-, pre-, and focal facets of primordial, remote, and proximate dynamics at play in this experience.

A Description of How to Identify Proximate Dynamic Directives

Remote dynamics foster the proximate directives crucial to a praxis-oriented science. They concretely direct the everyday form we give and receive in our life and its field. Hence it is necessary to identify and elucidate those that are dissonant and consonant. They form the bridge between the primordial and remote dynamics, on the one hand, and our immediate actual form reception and donation, on the other.

As we know, structural coformants shape an event; dynamic coformants identify what really occurs. A main rule of disclosure is to eliminate the distorting influence of unchecked subjective opinions on the part of researchers and to treat their appraisal of the dynamics as hypothetical. To serve this goal of objectivity, it is advisable to list and identify each hypothetical directive. Such a listing, accompanied by a rationale, is to be submitted to critical discussion by a research team or fellow scientists. The aim here is to remove as far as possible from this formulation personal and sociohistorical accretions that obscure the fundamental structure of both the remote and proximate dynamics at work in an event. This purification of accretions enables researchers to expand the significance of their findings from the topical event to the wider formative theme itself. The application of the results of their research to a wider population is thus more likely.

Let us return to the primordial dynamic of anxiety. In this example, it generates, let us say, the remote dynamic of anxious withdrawal from authorities. This dynamic gives rise to such proximate directives as the following: avoid contact with all authority as much as possible; if contact becomes unavoidable, be subdued; always pretend to agree no matter how you really feel; take on any task or style they seem to suggest without reflecting on how it may fit into your life of effective service; always flatter those in authority despite their oppression of people; always distrust them —no matter how just, compassionate, and competent they may appear, they always try to get you.

Of course, elucidation of such hypothetical dynamics can always go deeper. It can seek directives that would be more effective and consonant. It is never exhaustive. The more we delve into the infra- and transfocal coformants of dynamics, the more we may be able to establish what is really formational in the event and in the general topic we are exploring. Our aim is in the end to help people in their consonant transition upward from one current life-form to another. How deep we go into the elucidation process depends also on the nature of our particular research project, its limitations of aims and means, and the extent of its application to an unadhered-to or an adhered-to form tradition or sociohistorical segment of the population. The process may also be restricted by the limits of the research projects to which a team or department has committed its members or students.

Qualifications of Proximate Dynamic Directives

Some researchers, teams or departments may choose to add to the cluster of elucidation approaches the examination of certain specific qualities of proximate dynamic directives. The following suggestions may be helpful for the expansion of a research design in that direction.

Qualifications of the directives may be disclosed by paying attention to aspects of the field other than its spheres. The directives associated with the spheres of the field are revealed for the most part through structural articulation.

In addition to the procedure described above, we can ask ourselves several questions. In which of the ranges of the field—personal, segmental, common, or universal—does a directive manifest itself in some way? Does it appear in all of them, in some of them, in one of them? If so, how does the range affect the directive dynamically? In which region of consciousness—infra-, trans-, pre-, or focal—is the directive operational? Does it appear in all or some of them predominantly or exclusively? Is it mainly in one of them? Does this region or regions significantly alter the directive? In regard to the modalities of a directive, is it dynamically speaking, tendential, intentional, actional, effectual, dispositional, or institutional? If it involves all or some of these modalities, what is their dynamic interaction?

In our example, some researchers may begin to surmise, on the basis of such questions, that the intentional directive always to flatter any authority is mainly operative in the intraformative sphere and in situations that mark the formal appearance of authority. They may furthermore find that it is probably a prefocal directive. Finally they may discover that it is influenced in its particular dynamism by the fact that bowing to authority is institutionalized in the subject's segment of the population. Here again, as in the other phases of research, it is imperative to submit the qualifications to critical discussion by a research team or by fellow scientists.

Modes of Extended Appraisal of Proximate Dynamic Directives

Appraisal is always involved in the investigation of directives, no matter how limited the elucidation of dynamics may be. Some researchers, teams, or departments may want to extend this appraisal for the sake of clarification of their topic.

In our most recent example, the selected topic could have been "Consonant Interaction with Authority." To relate this to our own experience, we selected a personal event profiling an implicit remote dynamic that inclined us to anxious withdrawal from authority. We identified as primordial the underlying dynamic of anxiety. We then pinpointed in the event the remote dynamic of anxious withdrawal. Subsequently we observed how this remote dynamic initiated proximate directives such as avoidance of contacts with authorities. All of this was done not merely for the sake of clarifying this particular event for fellow academics. What we were ultimately committed to do was to shed some light on the dissonant and consonant dynamics of any person's interaction with authority and on the hindering and facilitating conditions of this encounter.

We must also appraise our findings from the perspective of the overall research topic. First of all, we ask ourselves in general about the dissonance or consonance dynamics of our topic in relation to what has been elucidated. To what degree can human formation, generally speaking, be enhanced or hindered in its consonance by the dynamics we have disclosed? To enhance this evaluation, we may consult the hypothetical criteria for consonance suggested by the science of formation, namely, faith, hope, consonance as embodied in congeniality, compatibility, compassion, courage, competence, and social presence in justice, peace, and mercy.

To return to our example, we may find that the proximate directive of false flattery of authority under all circumstances betrays our congeniality with who we are most deeply called to be; it leads to incompatibility with fellow subjects who resent our flattery of authority as well as the potential promotions and positions that may accrue to us because of this deceitful disposition. This proximate directive would also be incompassionate toward people who suffer discrimination because of our uncritical support, let us say, of a repressive government. This lack of compassion might tend to increase the deformative impact of the autarkic pride-form of people in authority and to hinder their liberation from its encapsulation. The directive of excessive flattery paralyzes the courage of right form donation and renders one incompetent in regard to realistic productivity in society. For effectiveness in this respect is partly based on the courage of dialogue between subjects and authorities about what objectively is to be done, whether or not it is flattering for their image.

A researcher might also decide to investigate in more depth and precision the primordial, remote, and proximate directives that could correct the wrong course set by these dissonant dynamics. In our example, one could search for new proximate directives of respectful yet courageous dialogue with authority that could foster more consonant interformation and therewith give way to the possibility of enhanced social presence in justice, peace, and mercy.

One can go even farther and ask whether it is possible to disclose the dynamics operative in the past history of a group or an individual. These may now be infrafocal. Yet they may still prevent a change from occurring in the direction of more consonant directives.

To illustrate this possibility in our chosen event, we may discover that both the remote and proximate directives are modulated and nourished by sociohistorical experiences of traumatic encounters in childhood with authoritarian parents, teachers, or clergypersons. This historical fact may nourish infrafocally the anxious withdrawal and overly submissive patterns of interaction previously detected.

These and similar approaches to elucidation enable us to discover how far we can generalize what we have found to similar events of formation. In this respect, guiding questions for research may be: What role does excessive flattery play in the relationships of a significant number of people to authority? How does it deform both them and the authority concerned? How may this directive affect society as a whole? How can these dissonant dynamics be replaced by ones that are more consonant? Would this research be of help to people who live under totalitarian regimes?

As a result of elucidation of these more general dynamics, researchers may come up with possible conditions of diminishing dissonant directives. They may propose ways to introduce to a population dynamics that are more consonant. In the case used for illustration, we could ask: How can formation in family, school, or church foster dynamics of respectful, appreciative, yet courageous interaction with authority? How can such formation help people to overcome the opposite deformative effects?

As we shall see in the next chapter, this elucidation is made more effective by its essential interaction with other methods of the science.

CHAPTER 20

Interaction of Elucidation and
Other Methods

In formation science all methods of research are interwoven. That of
elucidation does not exclude the methodical categories of structural
articulation, of consultation, translation, integration, and application.
In this chapter we will consider how the methodical categories of dialogical consultation, integration, and application interact with dialogical elucidation.

Consultation in Service of Elucidation of Dynamics

Researchers in formation science have developed hypothetical models
directly useful to new students of the science who are guided by the same
perspectives, assumptions, formal object, and metalanguage. Researchers in auxiliary sciences, arts, and formation traditions, too, offer hypothetical models useful to our topic of research and to the event that is its
point of departure. We should compare the models of both with our own
initial hypothetical findings insofar as possible. There are so many
sources of consultation that no one researcher can explore them all.
One's choice in this matter depends on the nature of the particular theme
to be researched, on the limits of the aims and means of a project, and on
the restricted objectives of the team or department to which one is committed.

The various ideological, religious, syncretic and common cultural
form traditions of humanity also contain models of dynamics that can be
relevant to one's research topic. Within the restrictions of a practical research design, one may decide to examine these traditions. As always one
must adhere to the principles of restriction or economy of research enun-
ciated previously.

Applications of Consultation Research to Elucidation Research

Once the potentially relevant hypothetical models have been identified and formulated, consultation research in relation to elucidation can be conducted as follows.

One can choose to pair the borrowed models with corresponding areas disclosed by means of one's earlier elucidation of dynamics. Similarities and divergences need to be critically appraised. On the basis of this comparison, researchers may formulate as clearly and concisely as possible how certain hypothetical models of formation science and those borrowed from auxiliary sources may in some way complement, correct, expand, or deepen the tentative findings of their initial research. These borrowed models need to be reformulated in the language of formation science and transposed into its theoretical frame of reference. If more than one hypothetical elucidation seems equally possible, scientific ethos demands that one formulate them as equally probable for the time being. The outcomes of these operations should then be submitted to a research team or to fellow scientists for critical discussion leading to a provisional decision in favor of the probability of one of these alternatives or their equal plausibility at this moment of knowledge.

Dialogical Integration of Elucidation Results

Dialogical integration methods comprehend another set of research procedures. How do they interact with the methods of elucidation?

Elucidation may yield probable dynamic coformants of the field in relation to the topic under investigation. An exhaustive elucidation of all dynamics is not possible; absolute certainty is not attainable in empirical sciences, only probability about the restricted areas of knowledge presently available to our cognition. What we should strive for is the highest probable approximation of the dynamics of a field as available to the limited potency of focal cognition at this moment of history.

Integration of these dynamics aims at a coherent, internally consistent paradigm of the dynamics that underlie a topic and its illustrating event. This paradigm should summarize the most probable explanations currently available of the consonant dynamic formation of life and presence in the area of a selected research topic.

The process of integration may proceed as follows. Researchers scrutinize their elucidations and focus on potential coformants that can help them to devise an integrational paradigm of consonant dynamics that does not contradict their research findings. Once these potential coformants are identified, they try to define them as precisely as possible in terms of the science. If necessary, they correct, complement, or differentiate its metalanguage. In the light of formation logic, they reflect on these identified coformants, seeking to find out how they may be logically related to one another and to the totality of a potential integrational paradigm. They may explore the formation theory to apprehend possible insights pertaining to this paradigmatic integration. Such an exploration enables them also to situate the resulting paradigm within the totality of the theory.

During this additional research, they may discover that the existing theory cannot totally cover their own probable elucidations. In that case, they may be interested in proposing and precisely formulating possible expansions, differentiations, completions, or corrections of the theory as it now stands.

Formation logic alone may not enable researchers to find the needed integrative connections between the disclosed coformants themselves or between them and the emerging paradigm as a whole. In that case they may choose to use scientific symbolic imagination to complement logic. The missing connections in the integrational paradigm may be supplied by meaningful symbolic links that neither contradict the probable results of elucidation research nor the reasoned conclusions of formation logic. These links are inserted hypothetically into the paradigm. They are thus open to revision when new factual or logical insights into more probable connections become available.

Application of Hypothetical Paradigms

What is the interaction of methods of application and those of elucidation?

One criterion by which to judge the probability status of a hypothetical paradigm is its demonstrated competence to be applied effectively to a variety of formation situations or traditions. Application competence rates high in a human science because of the radical practical intent of its research and theory formation. The enduring probability of a paradigm depends on this competence.

The degree of probability of a paradigm is intimately connected with the focal knowledge about proximate formation available to us. The history of formation unfolds on the basis of our increasing knowledge of the consonant effectiveness of proposed hypothetical directives. The updating of such knowledge depends in turn on a continual checking of the implementation competence of a probability paradigm in the situations and traditions in which it is implicitly or explicitly applied. The moment it becomes evident that it does not work, that it fails to foster consonant formation, its probability status is in question. Renewed research becomes necessary to discover the probable reasons for such failures. A rejection or an amelioration of the integrational paradigm may be needed.

In a human science applicative competence is not merely an interesting external implementation of research results. Practical application is not extrinsic to the research and to theory formation that preceded it. It is essential to fulfill the radical practical orientation of human sciences. Researchers need to run a repeated test of the provisional results of their past and present methods.

There is always the possibility of competition between alternative dynamic paradigms in formation science and its auxiliary sources, when they provide equally probable elucidations. This ambiguity may be solved in the course of time when tests of the competency of application demonstrate for the time being that one of these paradigms is most competent or consonantly effective in the greatest number of actual formation situations and traditions.

Two Kinds of Application Competence Research

The first kind of application competence research is an initial, general test of application competence. Researchers who choose to add this type of research to their project concentrate on a limited variety of situations that they subject to a general application of the paradigm. The second kind of testing refers to specific traditions and/or particular populations that researchers select at their own discretion as their preferred segment for application. For the moment we shall only consider the first kind of testing.

In general the outcome of the first kind of test not only determines whether a paradigm as a whole can maintain its highest available probability status; it also indicates the necessity of total or partial reform of the paradigm, its presuppositions, its borrowings from auxiliary sources, its directives, or its implementations for actual formation. For instance, the results of this added test may compel researchers to repeat critically some of their earlier attempts. They may still need to identify and remove any merely personal, form traditional, or situational accretions that may have slipped through any of the earlier processes of research.

General Initial Test of Application Competence

To perform the initial application competence test, researchers may tentatively list and define some of the practical implications of their dynamic paradigm for procedures of actual formation within concrete fields. They illustrate the application of these implementations first of all in the topical event in which they have grounded their research topic in their own practical experience. After this, they may try to establish whether the implications of the paradigm are general enough to transcend the particularity of their selected topical event. To find out, they may collect descriptions of a variety of situations different from their original event and from one another. All should represent the issue that is the chosen topic of the research project.

To identify and describe such analogous situations, researchers may utilize the auxiliary powers of formational memory, imagination, and anticipation. The results of these potencies, when actualized, may be found in the arts—plays, paintings, films, novels, diaries, biographies—or in descriptions by spiritual masters or psychologists. The potencies may also enable researchers to find such analogous situations among their own or others' remembered, imagined, or anticipated significant life incidents. This process of imaginative variation can be helpful in the creation of analogous situations for initial application competence tests in this additional phase of the research.

They may now attempt to demonstrate how their hypothetical paradigm can effectively facilitate consonant formation in various situations. If successful, this test will raise the probability status of their paradigm. If not it will enable them to improve the paradigm by being attentive to new implementations. Such indications prompt a critical review of the integrational paradigm, its presuppositions, its borrowings from auxiliary sources, and its directives and applications. This method, too, in its procedures and hypothetical results should be submitted to the critical considerations of a research team or of fellow scientists.

Elucidation research in this phase can be concluded with a tentative formulation of the highest probable paradigm presently available of the dynamics pertinent to a selected research topic, taking into account any new findings that may have shown up during the added application competence research. A caution to researchers at this point would be that their initial, limited testing of application competence can only be considered a provisional measure. In fact, all future applications will be implicit or explicit tests of the effectiveness of the probable paradigm. At any moment the results of such continual tests may necessitate critical questioning of what has been developed and lead to renewed research.

The ultimate rationale for elucidation research remains the scientific probability to be attained. It is to be higher than that resulting from mere prescientific intuitions, hunches, or insufficiently appraised group or personal experiences and customs.

We have considered the methods of elucidation. We have related them to the methods of dialogical consultation, integration, and application. These latter methodical categories will be discussed in their own right in the following chapters.

CHAPTER 21

Dialogical Consultation and Formation Reason

Overview

The preceding chapters reviewed the first three methodological approaches: selection, structural articulation, and elucidation. We showed how they were interwoven with and supported by the methodological categories of dialogical consultation, translation, transposition, integration, and application. We must still discuss these remaining clusters of methods, their purpose and position. In this chapter we shall consider them mainly in the light of dialogical consultation. The next chapter will focus on dialogical integration.

Before going into the topics of formation reason and consultation we will use this overview for some general remarks.

Formation science—in tune with recent developments in other human sciences—fosters in all its methodological categories the addition of new designs and alternative modes of inquiry. These are called alternative because in contrast to traditional methods they are more qualitative than quantitative, more experiential than numerical, more empirical-experiential than empirical-experimental.

Yet at the same time a holistic view of a topic under investigation must take into account relevant numerical data offered either by its own methods or those of its auxiliary sciences. This is one area where dialogical consultation can serve the integration of numerical findings within the total picture the science tries to provide for each topic it examines. In case the limits of a research project do not allow the researchers themselves to execute all possible statistical and interview methodologies, such consultation is crucial.

191

The methods of research, traditional or alternative, presently available under our categorical methodologies are not meant to be exhaustive. Researchers in this field and in related sciences may add to each cluster compatible methods to enhance the probability degree of their results. They may also adapt to each category methods developed in auxiliary sciences. An example would be the many interview, questionnaire, statistical and test techniques that can be adapted to the object pole of formation research and subsumed under one or the other of its methodical categories. One researcher in this field, Dr. Carolyn Gratton, published scientific interview techniques in her book *Trusting*, a study of the role of trust in distinctively human formation.

The methodology of the science continually expands and refines itself. As a result it is increasingly used by other human sciences that want to expand their research arsenal with methods that grant them new perspectives.

This general overview has prepared us for a consideration of dialogical consultation, the main topic of this chapter. A clarification of this methodological category and its intrinsic relationship to our power of appraisal presupposes an understanding of the concept of formation reason and its relationship to both appraisal and elucidation.

Formation Reason

Given the variety of approaches we have discussed, a first question of dialogical consultation is: Which approach will be most effective in a specific kind of research?

A first answer to this question involves what we have called formation reason. This specific disposition of reason is one of the sources of our knowledge of formation.

To explain what formation reason means, we must first consider human reason in general. We can distinguish transcendent from functional reason. The former operates by a type of higher affinity and intuition. The latter works by means of concept formation and conceptual argumentation. Both kinds of predispositions are endowed with special types of reasoning. Both may become dispositions that can be more or less cultivated. For example, functional reason carries as part of its character a predisposition for numerical accounting that can become a scientific numerical disposition useful in statistical studies of formation segments of a population.

Prescientific and Scientific Formation Reason

Human reason under both its transcendent and functional aspects is endowed with the predisposition to attend to, apprehend, appraise, and argue meaningfully about the form reception and donation to be given in life. Without this predisposition it would be difficult to explain why humans have been engaged from the beginning of recorded history in attempts to give direction to the reception and donation of form within their field. Often in history these attempts led to effective and consonant projects of formation, albeit after much trial and error. The innate capacity to find one's way is attributed to formation reason. It is always at work in any endeavor and study of human formation.

Formation reason enables us, at least in principle, to attend to and to apprehend, among other things, the dynamic formation directives operative in our field and to appraise in some measure their probable consonance and effectiveness. Subjectivistic factors and sociohistorical pulsations can and do interfere with the prescientific disposition of formation reason on both its prefocal and focal levels. Hence, we need to cultivate the scientific development of formation reason. We must enhance by the proper methods the probability of our knowledge about the consonance and effectiveness of formation directives. Universal formation reason enables us to induce from our attentions, apprehensions, appraisals, and argumentations hypothetical probability statements that lend themselves to further scientific investigation.

Admittedly prescientific formation reason is used effectively by countless parents and representatives of traditions who never studied this science. Their use of this reason cannot always sufficiently eliminate dissonant interferences of the common, segmental, and personal ranges of the field. But it can transcend these influences to some degree.

Formation reason is, therefore, a predisposition of transcendent and functional reason. As transcendent, it can enable people in principle, under the right conditions, to rise above ranges of life that are less than universal. As functional, it enhances our ability to communicate, under favorable conditions, with people of all ranges and fields about a certain minimum of basic probabilities of consonant formation rooted in the universality of human reason.

The reliance of the science on dialogical consultation and integration is similarly based on the notion of universal formation reason. Universality makes it probable that certain consonant effects of formative reasoning can be detected in the auxiliary sources of the science.

In summary, we can describe formation reason as a universal predisposition of transcendent and functional reason that enables people, focally or prefocally, to attend to, apprehend, and appraise distinctively human formation directives that foster the consonance of their existence.

Probability Knowledge of Formation Reason

Human formation reason in its prefocal and prescientific stages often gives people sufficient probability knowledge to carry out effectively their responsibilities, to consult wisely with others, to integrate and apply spontaneously what they have learned by their efforts. Not only for them but also for scientists and practitioners, it remains true that a relative uncertainty always accompanies any probability statement about empirical formation. We can never be absolutely sure that we have so exhaustively expressed in concepts and contructs a directive that it cannot be improved upon in any way in any of its coformants. The contrary seems more plausible.

Dynamic directives are first known in lived experiences of people as involved in a dynamic field. The richness of such lived experiences can never be exhaustively captured in a set of abstract concepts or constructs. They can only be approximated. The full mysterious dynamism of the human life-form within its varied field spheres is never conceptually captured in all its possible depth and complexity. Hence at any moment new knowledge may emerge that will compel a modulation of the probability statements of our knowledge.

Affirmation of Probability Statements

To reach probability, it is not enough for reason, enlightened by research and consultation, to attend to, apprehend, appraise, and argue to the point of highest available probability. It must also *affirm*.

The affirmation of a probability proposed by reason should be based on evidence. It should take into account all probabilities to which evidence seems to point. Initially our reason may affirm these probabilities as equally rooted in evidence. In this phase consultation of fellow researchers and auxiliary sources may be helpful.

Which one of these probabilities is in fact most probable? We examine the evidence again. More consultation of the science and its auxiliary sources, in dialogue with fellow researchers, may throw new light on the meaning of the available probabilities. One of them may prove to be more probable than the others. On the basis of this newly illumined evidence, researchers may reach a consensual affirmation of one or the other directive and its implementation as probably more effective and consonant than others.

The ground of our affirmation of one probability over another is thus the evidence offered by articulation and elucidation as illumined by consultation. Through a process of formation reasoning or scientific argumentation, we may find more support for a higher probability of one statement over another. There may also be a case in which we definitely prove directly or by means of consultation that one or more of the hypothetical statements is false to begin with. In that event we can choose only from among those that are not demonstrably false in content or expression.

As long as the science moves in the realm of the examination of lingual expressions of people about their formation experiences it is closer to the logic of formational argumentation than to the logic of empirical demonstration. This relation changes when its procedures of investigation move into the realm of empirical application competence testing. In that phase one goes beyond articulation and elucidation of the lingual data that express experience, to observation of the effectiveness of applied hypothetical directives in concrete past or present formation situations.

Forms of Dialogical Consultation

Dialogical consultation takes two main forms: with the participants in a research team or fellow scientists; with formation science and its auxiliary sources.

Dialogical consultation of the research team is a main means of objectifying and expanding the inner process of formational argumentation in which we are involved prefocally or focally, prescientifically or scientifically. By means of a shared argumentation process, directives that have been hypothetically articulated and elucidated by one's research are appraised and subsequently discarded, revised, or affirmed as most probable or insufficiently probable. Argumentation is a mode of appraisal. For appraisal can assume three main forms: affinity appraisal, affective appraisal, and argumentative appraisal.

Formational affinity in the realm of appraisal refers to the process of making focal in our consciousness an implicitly apprehended, potential, or incipient conformity between one's field and a formation possibility appearing within it. For example, people whose intrasphere is endowed with an aesthetic sensitivity may experience a prefocal affinity to poetic or artistic creation. This felt affinity may be made focal by them and appraised as a congenial possibility for the particular formation of their life.

Affective appraisal represents the focal deepening of one's felt appreciation implied in attraction, liking, fondness, and enthusiasm for a formation possibility that appears to be congenial and compatible with one's field. In our example, the focal awareness of aesthetic affinity may imply some incipient attraction to the reading and writing of poetry or the practice of other art forms. This affective appreciation can be deepened, refined, and enhanced by selective attention to various kinds of art. As this affectivity is cultivated, one grows in the ability to appraise what style of poetry or art seems to be most congenial with one's life.

Argumentative appraisal comprehends intra- and interformative processes of formation reasoning. It conceptually and critically evaluates the content and direction of affinity and affective appraisals. In the example, people who feel an affinity to, and a nuanced affective appreciation for, poetry and art may argue with themselves or with teachers of aesthetics about how solidly this affinity and affection is rooted in their real talents. How competent can they really be in the area of artistic formation? How compatible will a career in this field be with the realistic demands of their responsibilities? Such argumentation may result in personal probability statements in regard to the form people want to give to their life. These probability statements—to the degree that they are affirmed—will generate directives that can give unique form to an artist's life.

Of the three modes of appraisal, argumentation is decisive. The appreciative identification of modes of affinity and affectivity is not necessarily decisive for one's projects of life. Such identification does not imply that we should indiscriminately cultivate all such affinities and affects.

Argumentative appraisal takes into account critically and creatively not only such affinity and affective appraisals but also other significant coformants of the field, together with the relevant findings of the science, inclusive of its auxiliary sources and the cogent arguments of consultants.

This is not to say that we can dismiss formational affinity and affectivity appraisals. They remain indispensable. They provide us with an inventory of congenial potencies that can help us to devise or reform our projects of life after due argumentation.

Mutual Dialogical Consultation through Argumentative Appraisal

The process of consultation within a research team is an externalization of our private process of argumentative appraisal. The methods and results of research must be submitted to the community of scientists represented, for instance, by a research team. This team can appraise the process and its outcome not only in the end result but in its various stages. Their work makes it possible to redirect an ineffective process before it ends in probability statements that prove to be untenable in application competence testing.

The purpose of shared argumentative appraisal is to evaluate the claim of the appropriateness, precision, and effectiveness of the methods used. Is the probability status ascribed to the results obtained by these methods credible? What of the correctness and clarity of the formulation of these results in either the metalingual or common language of the science?

We assume that it is possible to attain a level of cogent argumentation that can effectively improve the research methodology and its results—an assumption based on the fact that the universal formation reason is in principle shared by all participants because they are human. It has been cultivated moreover in a special direction by their increasing learning and expertise in the field of foundational formation.

The objective of this type of consultation is not the attainment of metaphysical truth, as might be the case in philosophical or theological discourse. Formation science is an empirical discipline. It is mainly concerned with the probable and convincing approximation of the truth of effective and consonant formation to be attained by empirical research. The hoped for result of this kind of consultation is reasonable consensus.

Argumentative appraisal is formational. The arguments used are not merely the result of formal logic, as in philosophy or systematic theology. Their convincing quality depends on both functional and transcendent reason, sustained, nourished, and cultivated by a person's increasing learning and experience in this field. Formation reason is stimulated by the mutual communication of expertise, experience, and information, expanding and refining the argumentative appraisal potency of the team members. Simultaneously the reflective dimension deepens considerably. It enables participants, if necessary, to call into question a research project or to propose a restructuring of its processes and coformants.

Effective dialogical consultation by argumentative appraisal implies a concomitant growth in scientific asceticism, involving humble identification of subjectivistic pride-form motivations, such as one-upmanship in debate; emotional attachment to one's own opinion; indolence; inertia; or laziness in the hard labor of research. Researchers grow together in their search for reasonable agreement of what can serve best distinctively human formation. They realize that their being set free for science imposes on them a duty of social justice to serve zealously by honest argument those for whose service they have been freed by society for a shorter or longer period of time.

Dialogical Consultation of Incarnational Sciences

The incarnational sciences are another source for dialogical consultation. We utilize their findings and methods to incarnate distinctively human directives in the sociohistorical, vital, and functional dimensions of a field. We are faced with an increasing need to dialogue with the sciences that disclose these dimensions more fully. To appreciate this urgency, let us briefly consider the present historical phase of human formation.

One of the main characteristics of human life in the present era and in the near future is the historically unparalleled growth of the capacity for sociohistorical, vital, and functional reform. This age of reformation has already begun, and we are part of it. The socio-vital-functional formation of life is for the first time in history coming under our free control. We are increasingly free to change the design of our own socio-vital-functional life and its field of presence and action.

Our amplified potency of form donation in the realm of socio-vital-functioning is one of the remarkable effects of such sciences as biology, biochemistry, sociology, medicine, pharmacology, technology, economy, and political science. All such sciences and their specialties affect in some way the form the human race is able to give to its vital-functional life and its sociohistorical field. What people choose to reform in this realm will also affect their overall lifestyle. Hence the science must raise the question of the relationship between these interrelated kinds of formation. It must enter into dialogue with such incarnational sciences. What are the implications of these socio-vital-functional sciences for distinctively human formation as a whole?

Some proponents propose projects of reformation that go beyond the data provided by their special expertise. They extend by extrapolation their partial findings to the reformation of humanity and its field as a whole. This attempt usually fails because no speciality as such can address human life in its transcendent wholeness. Still, we can never ignore or bypass the information these sciences dispense. Our present and future formation cannot be thought of as insulated from the scientific-technological developments by which we are influenced daily in countless focal and nonfocal ways from infancy on. Without dialogical consultation of these sciences, we cannot realistically answer the question of how our life in its empirical concreteness can be transformed, safeguarded, and enhanced in a distinctively human way.

The reformation of the vital and functional dimensions is today becoming an object of scientific experimentation, which may or may not be compatible with the requirements of distinctively human formation. Basically the human striving for this kind of experimentation is an extension of our essential freedom and obligation to give form to life and its field in more effective ways. Yet certain modes of experimental reformation can be incompatible with what is distinctively human or transcendent. Hence it is necessary to initiate in humanity as formative a disposition of consultative dialogue with the scientific-technological modes of vital-functional reformation. Only by means of such dialogue can we begin to appraise what in these approaches and their results is conducive to a formation that is congenial with our transcendent distinctiveness.

Topical Projects of Consultation and Integration

One problem faced by dialogical consultation is the pluralism of scientific-technical approaches combined with the rapid acceleration of their expansion and diversification. Their methodologies, theories, and metalanguages, their stores of highly specialized information, have grown in immeasurable complexity, specificity, and quantity. No one is able to absorb everything in a comprehensive fashion.

Dialogical consultation and subsequent integration, therefore, can take place only on a limited scale through a succession of specific research projects. Realistically speaking, consultation and integration are possible only if they are restricted to a succession of topical, practical, selective projects.

Topical restriction refers to the fact that researchers must limit themselves to only one finely delineated topic at a time. They should not extend their consultation to anything in an incarnational science that is not directly relevant to that topic as strictly defined. This restriction is facilitated by the first categorical approach of formation science: that of cautious selection and sharp delineation of a topic accompanied by a provisional appraisal of the availability of sources of consultation relevant to it.

Practical restriction implies that researchers limit their consultation and integration to only those implications of selected incarnational sciences that are directly relevant to the concrete practical direction of distinctly human formation. One purpose of the choice and exploration of a topical event within the life experience of researchers is to promote and sustain this practical outlook with its inherent realistic limitations during their research and especially in their consultation and integration efforts.

Selective restriction of consultation and integration refers to the necessity to restrict this process to only a limited number of auxiliary sources. The criteria of such restrictive selection can be many. A few possibilities are: selection of only those sources that are relevant to one's topic and event; selection of sources in which one has already acquired some expertise through earlier study, experience, or practice; selection of only those sources that are most relevant to one's topic. A subselection within selected sources can be made of some of the relevant findings, methods, and theories.

Intimately connected with and dependent on the methodical category of consultation is the category of integration, as will be discussed in the following chapter.

CHAPTER 22

Integration, Translation, Transposition

The purpose of the science cannot be the integration of all knowledge of formation presently available. Such a project would not only be grandiose; it would be impossible. The accelerating explosion of specialized knowledge is of such magnitude that even generations of scientists could not catch up with the formational implications.

The project of the science is far more modest and practical than this utopian dream. Its main purpose is to enable researchers and practitioners to develop a disposition of integrative apprehension and appraisal of distinctively human life directives. This disposition should be marked by a critical openness to any relevant information from any source of formation knowledge within reasonable reach.

Researchers and practitioners in turn can promote the development of similar dispositions in the people they reach by their communications. They should also develop a hypothetical, integrational theory of distinctive humanness based on their own research and on the consultations conducted so far by them and their colleagues. One purpose of such a tentative theory is to cultivate, sustain, and enlighten the integrative disposition in people.

Full integration can thus never be achieved. To accomplish such an impossible feat would require a kind of superscience that would have to bring together for our consideration the findings and insights of every existing sociohistorical, vital, and functional science and their numerous proliferations. Neither our most advanced computers, nor the integrational projects of hundreds of researchers, nor any worldwide academic organization would be able to perform such a mammoth integration. Even if such a goal were to be momentarily realized, it would already be

201

behind the ongoing proliferations of newly emerging scientific specializations developing with ever increasing speed.

Disposition of Praxis-oriented Integration

What can be achieved is the cultivation of a disposition of formation-oriented integration of the principles, practices, and findings of the science of formation with those vital-functional scientific insights that seem relevant to the practical events and problems with which people are faced in their everyday existence.

Without this disposition humanity would be overwhelmed in the near future, if not already, by an endless stream of scientific information about how to form and reform one's life vitally and functionally speaking. There would be no way for people to relate what is happening to them to their need for transformation. Hence transcendent directives should permeate and integrate vital-functional reformations.

This ongoing disposition of practical integration is precisely meant to be dialogical not confrontational. It looks first of all for what can be affirmed in the findings and hypothetical propositions of the incarnational sciences. It helps to establish by affinity and affective appraisal the potentially fruitful relationship between certain findings of these sciences and corresponding directives from the science of formation.

Subsequently this preparation for integration moves toward argumentative appraisal. This disposition enables the researcher to discern what modulating corrections, complements, and reformations may be necessary in order to integrate the implications of the incarnational sciences within the framework of transcendent human formation.

Technological Change and Dialogical Integration

It belongs to the formation potency of human life to seek for functional reformation by means of techniques. Initially such techniques were simple and obvious. Early in our history of formation, people began to use herbs to improve their health and stamina, to cure disease. They tried to enhance their corporeal form by means of skin carvings, paint from tree barks and plants, ornamentation of shells and feathers. To increase their muscular powers of attack and defense in tribal warfare, they invented martial arts and arms. All of these technical reformations were of a rather limited scope. Sufficient insight into technical means of change and their consonant service of human life formation could be easily gained by living in a simple society and being exposed to its common education. A sophisticated systematic way of dialogical integration was not necessary.

Today a radically new phase of formation and reformation in the domain of vital-functional living is upon us. A new technological preoccupation with reformation of the human race is fast emerging. Unlike the science of distinctively human formation, this approach is not primarily concerned with the transcendent foundational form of life and its gradual consonant expression in the empirical realm. Hence the need to integrate the findings of scientific-technical research in service of transcendent wholeness.

Dialogical Integration and Proformation in Relation to the Incarnational Sciences

We recall that proformation comprehends the anticipatory tendencies toward future formation that are already operative in the present. The rationale for our concern for proformation is threefold. First of all, if anticipatory tendencies are already in some way active in present-day formation, this formation cannot be understood—nor, if necessary, corrected —without taking these active proformative tendencies into account. Second, a timely appraisal of such tendencies promotes the readiness of people for their own future form reception and donation in case such tendencies develop into directives. Third, we are responsible for the formation of future generations. An appraising apprehension of present-day proformative tendencies will enable us to become experts of tentative integration of the approaching future. Through mutual dialogue the science of distinctively human formation can become a unique participant in the wider scientific efforts that prepare for the formation processes of tomorrow and their integration.

The spheres of the human formation field point to a few of the proformative tendencies that seem to emerge in the exclusively sociohistorical, vital, and functional sciences whose formational implications we are called to integrate in a wider framework.

At the center of this framework is the dynamic movement of ongoing preformation. This preformative center is coformed by various dynamic powers, such as the transcendent, genetic, biochemical, and familial-cultural powers. In relation to genetic and biochemical preformation, the sciences of biology, biochemistry, genetics, medicine, and pharmacology are devising experiments and theoretical models whose results may to a high degree affect the ongoing preformation of humanity. Already many preformative implications are extrapolated from their scientific findings and theories. Far-reaching proposals are formulated for the technical reformation of the biochemical facet of this preformed base of human life.

The sphere of intraformation represents the area of life where we give form to our personal directives, thoughts, feelings, modes, and decisions. Here psychopharmacology is developing potent drugs and other means to facilitate form reception and donation by relieving tensions, depressions, and anxieties that interfere with skillful, relaxed functioning. Psychology is developing modes of conditioning, brainwashing, electrical brain stimulation, and systematic indoctrination that can instill in the intrasphere certain dispositions a society may want to foster.

The sphere of ongoing interformation, too, is affected by scientific-technical approaches. Many researchers in the fields of andragogy, pedagogy, education, sociology, social work, psychotherapy, counseling, and group dynamics experiment with techniques that promise to expand the possibilities of effective interformation in the vital-functional dimension of human encounter and collaboration.

Moreover, the sphere of local, situational, space-time formation is altered by vital-functional sciences. They enable people increasingly to change their life situation as dependent on their natural environment by manufacturing synthetic products and surroundings, by using new sources of energy such as atomic power, by replacing natural environments with environments that are technically controlled human creations.

Finally, the sphere of the outer world of our formation field is expanded by the increasing power and outreach of the media that bring the world into one's living room, by exploration of outer space, by projects of space travel and of the colonization of other planets. Political science and the discipline of international law tend to project the formative possibility of a worldwide government. Economical sciences do the same in the realm of world economy.

Most of these tendencies are still far from becoming concrete practical directives. Nobody can predict with certainty whether or how they will come true. But it cannot be denied that simultaneously in many sciences the building blocks are fashioned for a potential integral reformation of the whole human field as we know it. Someday all these blocks may be assembled into an integrative master plan of human reformation. Then our life-form will have attained the possibility to control its formation by an integrative control of its field.

This integrative control, to which human life-as-formative is called, can be consonant or dissonant. It can lead to a nightmare of dissonance or a dream of consonance. The chances of consonance for the newly emerging formation field of humanity are for a great part dependent on the dialogical interaction of the science of distinctively human formation and the sciences of exclusively sociohistorical-vital-functional formation. In some way this reformation has already begun. We should start the dialogue before it is too late. It is our task to remind these sciences of their incarnational function in regard to the integrative mission of our distinctive humanness.

Dialogical Integration in Relation to Other Formation Systems

Simultaneously with the sciences today, and millennia before their emergence, numerous communities of people developed their own integrative systems of formation. Often these systems were implicit, embedded in past or present streams of tradition. At times they were focally known and interpreted; mostly they were lived nonfocally. They were the basic sources of claims to formation wisdom in humanity. As such, they represent treasures of insight and experience in the art and discipline of formative living that can be mined by scientists in this field.

Cultural formation systems are typical of such populations as the African, Asian, European, Russian, and South and North American. They may be a mixture of form directives and symbols of forgotten or active religious traditions and directives that provided integrative answers to cultural needs and demands.

For example, an agricultural population may develop directives that are different from those of a hunting, fishing, or manufacturing culture. These directives may be mixed in a variety of ways with streams of religious traditions, such as Hinduism, Buddhism, Judaism, Islam, and Christianity. They may be commingled with ideological traditions, such as humanism, Marxism, fascism, scientism, socialism, or capitalism. Later on, the system thus formed may continue in some fashion, even though its origins, initial cultural demands, and streams of tradition are forgotten or dismissed.

The history of formation is in fact, the history of many communities, each with their own integral formation system. These communities have their own formation contexts and hence their own limited wisdom. All use in various ways the universal formation reason and formation imagination we as human hold in common. What has been disclosed by this reason varies from community to community. Formation directives that are more or less systematized were put to some kind of application test. What was affirmed by individuals in their intrasphere and confirmed interformatively by the community depended on certain existing standards. What becomes acceptable as a formation system is usually rooted in underlying religious or ideological belief systems. Hence the integrational approach to formation systems often includes a probe into supporting belief systems that clarify the original meaning and power of the accepted directives. The pluralism of formation systems survives only if it is nourished by a pluralism of belief systems.

Dialogical integration in formation theory of relevant contributions of formation systems is rooted in the assumption that a fuller knowledge of the inexhaustible richness of human unfolding can be reached only by a critical-creative appraisal of the manifold approaches to formation tried out in the pluralistic laboratories that are the past and present formation communities of humanity.

Another assumption underlying this integrative approach is the conviction that the universality of truth is approximated empirically by a wide variety of practices leading to a bewildering pluralism of fields. Critical scientific appraisal is necessary to distinguish the more general formation values from the underlying belief systems and historical accretions that may have obscured the original intuitions of formation reason.

The same applies to the more recent psychological faith and form traditions initiated by such psychological schools as the Freudian, Jungian, Adlerian, Rogerian, and Maslowian. They go beyond mere scientific fact in the development of their own underlying integrative belief and subsequent formation systems. Here, too, strange syncretic systems may develop through an indiscriminate intermingling of psychological faith systems with Christian, socialist, capitalist, or other formation traditions.

Dialogical integration must take into account the faith and form traditions in which particular perspectives of the sciences are embedded. Such consultation treats seriously the perspectival appraisal of formation through the cultural, ideological, and religious expressions of the human community. We can reach the universal range of our field only through the exploration of the insights and practices of its segmental and subsegmental ranges.

For example, the formation wisdom of Christianity reveals certain commonalities among a wide diversity of schools of formation within various Christian religious communities. Each of these subsegmental communities has something different to offer to an integrational formation knowledge of humanity.

Dialogical integration of this sort generates an understanding that is wider and deeper than that of any one perspective of formation by itself alone or by any community of people in formation. When formation scientists are confronted with directives that are different yet consonant, their formation reason and imagination as integrative is stimulated in a new way. The affirmation of possible alternative modes of consonant formation pushes them beyond the limits of their own systems, whose integrations seem now partial. The naive prescientific assumption that the way of formation in their particular field is *the* way for all is replaced by the scientific awareness that it is *one* way for some because of the ever present limits of a formational context.

Out of the integration of various formation positions that are partially integrative a fuller understanding arises. Scientific formation knowledge is not the outcome of direct experience. It is a human construct, coformed intellectually by increasing sets of interrelated constructs. The application of these integrative constructs to the concepts, customs, and expressions of alternative formation systems can lead to an increase in the depth of understanding of these constructs and their correction, amplification, or addition. Here again the economy of research demands that researchers practically limit the formation systems to be consulted in compatibility with the restrictions set by their research project, team, or department.

Dialogical Integration of Prescientific and Prefocal Understanding

To make this kind of integration possible we must realize that the articulation of the prescientific experience of others resembles the prescientific articulation done by researchers in reference to their topical event. It is the point of departure for their entire research project. Something similar can be done in regard to the prescientific apprehensions of other people. I did so in analyzing in my doctoral dissertation the formative event of *really feeling understood by a person.* Dr. Carolyn Gratton, using a variation of this method, analyzed *trusting.*

Depending on the limits of one's research topic, team, or department, this kind of consultation in service of integration can be added to the articulation of one's own experience. What is the rationale for consulting the prescientific formation knowledge of people? Focal expressions of awareness can never fully comprehend the nuanced richness of original events and our spontaneous preconceptual apprehension of them. Scientific articulation and elucidation is necessarily done by abstracting from this original wealth of spontaneous appreciative presence. This lived knowledge is the matrix of all subsequent conceptual understanding. It cannot be observed directly nor can it be captured fully by any scientific method.

Formation science is ultimately based on this prescientific knowledge that it tries to describe, articulate, and elucidate. In this sense original apprehension is the ultimate standard against which we measure our scientific understanding.

As we have seen, formation reason and knowledge can be both functional and transcendent. Direct transcendent knowledge is intuitive in regard to formation agents and their influence on human lives. If later scientific findings are in conformity with the fundamental intuition we have about the basics of our everyday formation, the probability status of any hypothetical description of this process will be greatly enhanced.

Dialogical Integration

From what we have seen so far, it is evident that integration is more than a collection of information. While such an accumulation of recordings may have its own usefulness, it would not give us an insight that is more profound and comprehensive than what could be obtained by means of any of the methods or sources of information utilized thus far during our research.

Dialogical integration is really a research tool. The term dialogical refers to the process of comparison between the results of the methods used in former phases. Integration is guided by formation reason and by creative scientific imagination. This comparative research aims at an integrating paradigm that produces a coherent, more profound appreciative apprehension of the topic under consideration.

Integrative apprehension is expressed in a comprehensive paradigm coformed by carefully interrelated constructs and concepts. All the methods used up to this point enabled us to disclose, articulate, and elucidate certain facets of our topic and of its remote and proximate dynamic directives in their consonant or dissonant impact on our lives. However, each of them alone misses significant facets of the total event. Utilizing the integrational comparative reflection powers of formation reason and sustained by creative imagination, we can disclose the event in its totality. This cannot be done by any one approach alone or via a mere mechanical addition of the results of all such approaches.

Translation and Transposition of Borrowed Data,
Methods, and Theories

Integration should take into account that methods, data, and theories borrowed from auxiliary sources may be one-sidedly slanted in the direction of the purposes of such sources. For example, the knowledge of formation accumulated by a Buddhist scholar about relaxation in service of meditation will highlight other aspects of leisure than the knowledge gathered by a medical stress therapist to help patients who suffer from hypertension. Nevertheless both sources of information and some of their methodologies may be relevant to a study of the role of relaxation in the everyday formation of people and its relation to their distinctively human formation.

A first task of integrational research is to translate and transpose such formulations in a way that makes them relevant to a selected topic and to formation science as a whole.

All methodical categories of our science may be used in some measure in each phase of research. Applied to the categorical methodology of integration it means that some integrational direction will be present from the beginning in the other research phases because they are guided by the same selected topic and by the formal object of the science. In the end phase of integration, however, we pay more full and explicit attention to the translation and transposition of borrowed data and methods in relation to the topic we have chosen and to the boundaries established by formation science.

This phase of research implies an awareness of both the common and metalanguages of auxiliary sources. Language is ladened with theory. We cannot blindly adopt lingual expressions of another science or source whose language has been coformed in its open or hidden meaning by the specific purpose of the science or tradition concerned. We study similar topics. However, we look at them from the particular perspective of everyday, distinctively human formation. The specific connotations of other terminologies resulting from different ways of viewing would make integration impossible or confusing. Hence it is necessary to translate these results into the metalingual and/or common language of formation science, transposing them in the framework of its theory. Because lingual expression and study is central in formation science, we will devote the final chapters of this book to the issue of scientific and common languages and their uses.

Integrational Paradigm of Formation Science

Effective dialogical integration presupposes that researchers have at hand some tentative, basic, coherent paradigm of the human formation field in its main differentiations. Such a fundamental paradigm can guide them in the coherent yet differentiated structuring of the specific facets disclosed in their topical research project.

The science of formation has developed such a basic paradigm as the fruit of research that began several years ago. Gradually we were able to define carefully the constructs pertaining in some way to this paradigm. Its basic shape or structure has been tested and enriched by the particular research projects of many people. At this point it seems the best available paradigm to guide the integration phase of our research. This does not mean that it is sacrosanct. On the contrary, like all scientific paradigms, this one remains in principle tentative, provisional, and hypothetical. It is open to revision whenever statements made by a legitimate source or researcher are demonstrably more probable and have won reasonable consensus of fellow scientists after due argumentative appraisal.

Researchers should submit their tentative integration to a community of fellow scientists. A research team that from the beginning has argued critically over the phases of the research project would seem best prepared to judge also the probability status of the integrational result. In their critical appraisal of the proposed dialogical integration, they should be attentive to the following questions.

Is the integration proposed by the researcher really in tune with the outcomes of the various methods used under the methodological categories? Has the researcher in a forced or hasty attempt at integration not only translated and transposed their contributions but perhaps falsified them?

Was the researcher able to go beyond the surface data and insights gathered in the former stages to identify underlying structural articulations and dynamics that gave rise to such apparent data? Did he or she base the integration of these underlying articulations and dynamics on the similarity of their fundamental patterns?

Were the articulated structures and elucidated dynamics as identified and used in the integration phase really the outcome of scientifically valid investigations within formation science or its auxiliary sources?

Did the integration avoid the temptation of facile addition? Did it really transpose the separate data and insights sufficiently to relate them in a new way to the integrated whole of the particular paradigm without falsifying them fundamentally?

Does the researcher remain clearly aware that this paradigmatic integration must remain open to revision the moment a more probable insight, agreed upon by a community of scientists, has to be taken into account?

The purposes and questions posed in this chapter on integration, translation, and transposition point to the crucial role of language. Like all sciences, this science cannot escape the inevitable formation of a theoretical idiom. But unlike some other sciences this science is especially concerned about training its students from the beginning in a common language in which to present the science's findings to various segments of the populations entrusted to their care. Therefore, the final chapters in this volume will deal with the issues of meta- and common language.

CHAPTER 23

Prescientific, Scientific, and Postscientific Language

A distinguishing feature of formation science is its precise scientific language combined with its commitment to develop simultaneously a more common language to popularize its findings. The latter is designated postscientific language.

No science can exist, nor has one ever existed, without its own theoretical idiom. Formation science is no exception to this rule, rooted in the very notion of science itself. In spite of its sharing in this primary commitment of any science to the development of an appropriate language, formation science adheres to the principle that human sciences can and should, because of their proximate-practical intent, develop a corresponding popular postscientific idiom.

There have always been attempts to popularize science, to make its insights amenable to public consumption. Usually such efforts were not initiated by the main researchers involved in the development of a discipline. They were attempted by a few scientists among them. Some considered these efforts marginal to the scientific enterprise, removed from the burden of research and the tediousness of exact theory construction leading to the formulation of a precise scientific language. However, there are other legitimate reasons for scientists to translate their findings into common parlance.

The problem is that certain popularizers, not acknowledged as experts in the field concerned, may try to translate a specific science into common language without being sufficiently familiar with the fine nuances of the language they want to simplify for average readers. Subsequent deficiencies have given popularization a bad name among some scientists.

Compare, for example, in the medical field *Prevention* magazine and the *New England Journal of Medicine*. A significant number of physicians read with trust the *New England Journal* while feeling doubtful about articles, advice, and letters that may appear in *Prevention*. Conversely, laypersons not acquainted with the language of medicine may feel unable to read the *New England Journal*.

Unfortunate instances exist where practitioners of a science turn against its theoretical communications. They refuse to keep in touch with its continually new disclosures that are expressed initially and tentatively in the scientific idiom. Clergypersons, for example, may become so preoccupied with their practical tasks that they neglect to study theology after finishing their courses in graduate school. Their sermons, articles, or other publications may attract wide audiences, their words may be inspiring, clear, and down to earth, but they fail to check, complement, and correct this popularizing by theological insights expressed in the metalanguage of this discipline. The same can be said for medical doctors or psychologists who neglect to update their scientific knowledge.

What we are faced with here is the problematic of scientific truth and its accurate, up-to-date popularization in a postscientific language. Formation science must face this issue, inherent in the scientific enterprise and its need for communication to a wider public. In our case this common problem may be more acute. For the findings of our science can be crucial for the correction of harmful formational practices among significant segments of the population. It is for this reason that formation science has chosen to confront this problem head-on from its inception. It does not hesitate to foster in its scientists and aspirants a bilingual skill and disposition, already at the beginning of their training. In this way we strive to prevent encapsulation in a scientific idiom while at the same time fostering proper formation in the metalanguage of this field. Only formation in scientific language can prevent faulty popularizations of its insights and findings. This new type of bilingual preparation on the part of a formation scientist may stimulate similar attempts in other human sciences.

Formative spirituality facilitates bilingual formation through its research and publications. Its scientific journal, *Studies in Formative Spirituality*, is complemented by a popular magazine, *Envoy*. Students are as well-trained in the use of common, postscientific language with uninitiated audiences as in the scientific idiom of their field. Doctoral candidates are obliged to begin their dissertation with an extensive description in ordinary language of a concrete formation event. Faculty members, current students, and graduates publish bilingually in one or the other journal of the science and in other periodicals.

This commitment to popular postscientific language training, concomitant with one's preparation in scientific language, calls for an explanation. What is the subtle, complex relationship between prescientific, scientific, and postscientific language?

Prescientific Lingual Articulation

The methods of the science, outlined in preceding chapters, start out with prescientific articulation, which may be in part personal, segmental, common, and popular. For example, the prescientific description of lingual data, provided by researchers at the onset of their project, is about personally apprehended events. Because these take place in a pluriform field, the lingual records manifest a mixture of expressions. In fact, appreciative apprehension of a formative event should first be described in personal ordinary language, with its inevitable segmental and common patterns, in order to present as well as possible its intimacy and immediacy. Theoretical language should be avoided in this first phase of investigation.

An event gains its immediate formative meaning through the persons who experience it firsthand. Consider, for example, falling in love. Lover and beloved enjoy spontaneous moments of awareness that form their love life uniquely. Social customs of dating, the influence of parental interformation, sexual mores—all of these perspectives can be enlightening from a theoretical viewpoint, but none of them make this event directly formative for two lovers. They can best recount what happened to them in the prescientific or common language most familiar to them.

Any event is necessarily located in a specific field. This is the indispensable matrix in and through which its features and textures are specified. Hence its description in prescientific language will manifest implicit references to various spheres of the field insofar as they are involved in the event *as formative.*

The description should *present* rather than *represent* what actually took place. Researchers who labor to perfect such prescientific descriptions are in search of an articulating language adequate to their appreciative apprehension of the event as it really occurred. They strive to approximate as nearly as possible its original givenness. Prescientific language as formative does more than report; it gives birth again to the event itself. It does so through a language resonant with it in its forming dynamism.

In this prescientific preparatory phase of research, one must attend with full patience and care to the texture of the event as it appears in its field. One must try to get at the immediacy of what happened through the kind of language that embodies one's intimate form receiving and giving relationship to the event. In short, prescientific language as formative attempts to present in lingual form the intimate relationship between a researcher and an original event that has had a significant impact on his or her ongoing formation.

A research team can be of great help in this labor of prescientific verbalization. Its appraisal of attempted descriptions can draw researchers out, enabling them to give a more accurate literary form to what really happened to them. Researchers may choose to add to the personal articulation of their own event, prescientific articulations from reports of similar experiences or from other auxiliary sources. Among these we would include videotapes or films that portray in verbal or nonverbal language one's response to an event. A great deal is said through gestures or facial expressions, such as a glance, a slight smile, or a long silent touch. Posture and movement constitute a rich and complex source of direct appreciative apprehension of the forming influence of a happening. Much of what goes on between us and our world at such times cannot be easily transposed into articulate speech.

Formative and Informative Language

From infancy on, we learn at home and in our neighborhood, school, and church the words and rules of informational language. By means of language signs, we are able to inform one another about what transpires in the common and segmental ranges of our field. A living language, however, is not restricted to this informational capacity. It also has the potency to give and receive new form, either by coining original expressions, by rearranging familiar words in fresh contexts, or by speaking with an animation that goes beyond information to bestow a formative impact. Lacking such changes in verbal use, a language would be numbered among those that are "dead."

In certain situations, we may actually be forced to give form to words in a new fashion. What we want to express seems so different that the common informational lingual system and its routine diction cannot relate adequately our original appreciative apprehension of what happened to us. Take, for instance, a mother who loses her child. The full impact of this event on her emotional and mental life cannot be conveyed adequately in the lingually correct phrase, "Our beloved son died after a prolonged illness." To her, this information fails to express what she is going through.

Ordinary language in its routine correctness cannot communicate in words or diction what she feels. Nor does this informational system offer her the means to approximate what she needs to say.

Imagine that she is a poet who can write about a mother's loss of her child. Now the elements of a familiar lingual system come together in a new way, enhanced by striking rhythms, images, and pauses. Common words light up in an original fashion. In a different context, they point to shades of meaning and potential connotations that were known less explicitly before this usage. The poet does not invent a strange language as a schizophrenic might do, but she gives new form to what is familiar. She remains faithful to grammatical rules while transcending boundaries of meaning. Hence anyone who has had a similar experience is likely to be touched by her message.

This example demonstrates how ordinary language is open to reformation. Poetry is one form that especially releases the receptive possibilities of our language. Rhythmic, melodious constellations of words, sentences, and images enrich expression and enhance appreciative apprehension.

Not only in poetry does language move from the informative to the formative realm. The same happens the moment people use existing informational language in an original fashion. We do this more than we realize. If our choice of our words is right, what we say or write may be taken up by others. Through subsequent repeated use, new expressions slip into a common or segmental language. In this way language remains alive. Together we are always forming and reforming our ordinary language by utilizing a variety of lingual forms in an original way.

Formation Fields and New Language Formation

Living languages are always in a process of rapid reformation. They are continuously amplified by new words and connotations. How does this happen? The answer may have something to do with the concept of the formation field.

Each sphere of the field with its dimensions and articulations gives form to new disclosures of pre-, intra-, inter-, and outer formation. Reality is increasingly disclosed by various apprehensions—the academic, medical, scientific, religious, practical, poetic, and aesthetic, to name only a few. Specialists in such fields must form new words or use existing expressions in unfamiliar ways to convey what could not have been known and communicated before such disclosures. Language cannot be restricted merely to the current use of informational words in their customary contexts. In fact, common informational language is itself form receptive and form productive. Specialists utilize this potency, teasing out, as it were, the dormant possibilities in every living language to disclose new meanings.

Intrasphere and Language Formation

Lingual formative power resides in the intrasphere of any formation field. Dialogue with the dimensions of its own sphere as well as with the other spheres of the field and their dimensions can probe the formative potencies of existing informative languages to see whether they stil express adequately new disclosures.

All language, formational as well as informational, is an expression of dynamic existence. It develops in dialogue with the changes that are typical of a free human presence in a formation field. Language, like life itself, grows from current form to current form. In times of transition, living language abandons old forms and adopts new ones. The language of Thomas Aquinas is not Karl Rahner's nor is the language of John Calvin that of Paul Tillich. Any reformation of human life leads to the process of creatively reforming a language. The English of present-day American poets is different from the English of Chaucer. Writers, scientists, and thinkers contribute more than most to this constant process of language reformation.

Formative speech or composition shapes and fashions new words for the first time, or it uses old words with a different meaning or connotation. These words may be spoken with an original animation that lifts them beyond mere information even as it re-creates their meaning.

Unavoidability of Scientific Language in Formation Science

Formation science examines, among other things, the descriptions of distinctively human formation offered by people in the present and by masters of the past who represent the ideological, religious and common traditions that emerge in different times, societies, and segments of the population. Many expressed themselves in the prescientific idiom of their common and segmental field.

The question is: How can the knowledge of formation be advanced by the translation and expansion of their original prescientific languaging into the idiom of a science? Do we have the right to introduce such changes into their verbalization? How can we justify a new lingual system that differs from that used by people in formation themselves or the classical masters? It is evident that our language, like the theoretical idiom of any science, differs from their common language.

First of all, we must emphasize that the descriptions and appraisals communicated in their own prescientific language are a primary source of our knowledge of distinctively human formation. Nothing can replace this indispensable ground. In my study of the event of *really feeling understood by a person*, I made clear that a first necessary step in such an investigation is an empathic sharing in the intuitive apprehension and prescientific appraisal of this event by the subjects themselves as expressed in their common language. Their language will convey, at least implicitly, the main relations between this event and the field in which it emerged. These relations exist only in and through the directives or verbal symbols that are current in their specific fields in time and space. To tap this primary source of knowledge presupposes an intimate appreciative apprehension of the prescientific symbols alive in a dynamic field. This intuitive knowledge of people in formation and of their popular masters can be a *primary* source of formation cognition, but by no means its *exclusive* or *ultimate* source.

While taking intuitive apprehension and its prescientific basis into account as a primary source, formation knowledge is more than mere intuition and its spontaneous appraisal. No matter how basic and indispensable intuition is, it is not enough. An approximation of probable empirical knowledge of practical formation demands more.

For example, in the past certain traditions in the West held the belief (as certain powerful Middle Eastern traditions hold today) that coeducation of young men and women is always and necessarily ethically, spiritually, and psychologically deformative. This conviction was based on prescientific appraisal of an intuitive apprehension of relations between the sexes. A critical investigation made in the light of scientific theories of formation and supporting statistical evidence would contest the probability of this appraisal. We do not deny that the original intuition may contain some wisdom regarding ideal conditions for coeducation. Intuitions are rich in experiential content. Their lingual expressions are practically inexhaustible, but by the same token they are most vulnerable to mistaken appraisals.

The formative language of a significant number of Shiite Muslims in Iran, for instance, is part of the common idiom of a fundamentalistic Islamic formation field. Among other things, it forms people to believe that infidels who reject the message of the Koran are to be considered beyond salvation. Is such an appraisal unchangeable? Or can we begin to develop a new, postscientific language in the light of the findings of formation science regarding the necessity of global interformative cooperation and mutual appreciation?

We cannot at once translate these new formation directives postscientifically into an Islamic idiom that has not yet words for them. First we have to help them formulate for their own clarification such findings in a scientific language different from their own—a language that makes known to their intellectuals for the first time the possibility of a transcultural formation and its benefit for humanity. Their Islamic idiom is lacking descriptions of this ideal. Hence it is impossible for their intellectuals to assist people in the proper translation of new ideas into their customary postscientific idioms of formation before they themselves learn the exact meaning of such concepts in a scientific language.

Example of Formation Direction or Counseling

To illustrate the unavoidability of a scientific language different from the ordinary self-expression used by people, let us take as an example formation direction or counseling.

Formation directors reflect upon the ultimate directives of a specific religious tradition shared with directees who come to them for guidance in the light of this tradition and in accordance with compatible principles of formation science. Formation counselors represent distinctively human formation in general. They give counsel in accordance with what they have learned in the study of the science of formation.

Suppose a young woman complains in her own words that despite her best efforts she cannot be at ease with the God in whom she believes. She feels that this condition is the result of her own bad will. How else can she explain her strange, guilt-ridden reluctance to pray.

A formation counselor will try first of all to apprehend empathically what she is trying to communicate in her own prescientific idiom. It is enough for the moment to be with her in appreciative apprehension of what this predicament may feel like in her life. She is encouraged to articulate once again in her own words what she is going through. To enter into the personal range of her field, it may be helpful to repeat thoughtfully words that seem to capture most poignantly what she is thinking and feeling without yet penetrating into the unspoken hidden directives behind her problem. During the sessions, there may come a moment in which counselor and counselee are ready for a deeper kind of reflection into her painful state of fear of God and guilt. Now is the time to draw upon the knowledge available in the theories of formation, its auxiliary sciences and traditions. Such theoretical knowledge is formulated in a language other than the prescientific idiom of this counselee. It contains insights into her situation she herself does not yet have. Therefore, she cannot yet express them in her own language.

In the light of this scientific knowledge, she may be advised to expand and deepen her communications by asking more questions related to tentative theoretical insights. Gradually, in tune with what she conveys in her own language, her prescientific emotional appraisal is complemented in the mind of the counselor by a kind of argumentative appraisal to sort through the many possible assessments of this case proposed by the science and its auxiliary sources.

Counselors may ask themselves: Is this a problem of the "dark night" that certain masters of formation speak about in their own language? Is it perhaps the result of nonfocal anger and passive hostility hidden behind her compliant apparent form of life? Does the problem stem from a residue of repudiated or refused guilt feelings she does not want to acknowledge? Is the source of her unease a disposition of antagonism against any authority instilled in her early in life during interformation with harsh or inconsistent parents or their substitutes?

These are a few of the many possible appraisals, verbalized in various theoretical metalanguages unknown to the client. In such argumentative appraisal, one seeks a theory that can be adapted uniquely to her problem and its consequences. In tune with her response, this theory is then translated into a language she can understand.

The translation of such a theory, if it happens to be the appropriate one, may correct, complement, or expand her own apprehension of her predicament and offer a possible solution to her depression. At the same time her language will be enriched. It is no longer merely prescientific. Nor is it couched only in the idiom of scientific theory. She may return to the common or segmental language familiar to her; but now, because of her lingual form receptivity, what she says has been expanded, by the translation of pertinent scientific insights into her problem and its solution. This new addition makes her language postscientific.

Consonant Scientific Theory and Metalanguage

Scientific theory and its metalingual expression has to be consonant with certain conditions. It should be based first of all on critical reflection upon prescientific apprehension and appraisal. This reflection should not be forced, artificial, or merely speculative. It should be grounded both in empirical evidence and in the logic of formation reasons.

Second, it should find confirmation by other experts in this field. They should be able to acknowledge it as the most probable empirical theory available at this moment. They should also confirm the scientific idiom in which the theory is expressed as adequate to its essential insights.

In the case of formation science, it must be a theory that gives rise to appreciative apprehensions of certain concrete facets of distinctively human formation apprehensions that go beyond the prescientific intuitive and reflective language of people.

Affinitive, Affective, and Argumentative Appraisal

Returning to the example of direction and counseling, we can disclose further uses of formative language.

We may start out in the initial sessions with appraisals based on our methodological affinity with the questions, thoughts, and feelings presented by the counselees. In this phase we may engage mainly in an empathic affinitive appraisal of their situation. We enter into their field as if it is our own. By means of empathic imagination, we try to step into their shoes, as it were. We pay full attention to all the implications and nuances of their prescientific communications.

From this affinity flows naturally an affective appraisal. Our empathy and subsequent affinity with the counselees' overall predicament extends itself to the various affects or feelings evoked by the problems with which they cope. It brings us in touch also with directives behind their acts and dispositions.

All of this is still in the realm of prescientific languaging. These appraisals make us ready for the argumentative phase of appraisal. To argue scientifically, we must deepen the distance between prescientific appraisal and our appraisal-disposition formed by the study of the science and its auxiliary sources. Argumentative appraisal about the formation event is perspectival. We first argue in our own mind or in consultation with other experts about the theoretical perspectives that may be available to us in the scientific language of formation or its auxiliaries.

The next phase is that of reflecting on such possible interpretations with the persons themselves who seek our care to find which perspective applies best and how it can be uniquely adapted to their situation via translation into their language.

These phases, together with their language variations, do not necessarily follow one another in rigid succession. While one approach usually prevails in one phase, all approaches, with their respective language uses, may intermingle to some degree at various moments of the process. Moreover, an earlier phase may need to be repeated in later sessions, when new material is brought up for discussion.

Transition from Prescientific to Scientific Language

We gave the foregoing example to clarify the diversity of language use. Essential in the example is the transition from prescientific to scientific language, at least in the mind of the formation counselor or director. Without this transition there would be no science at all, only prescientific apprehensions and appraisals of primary intuitions.

Physicians can better apprehend and appraise their cases thanks to a medical metalanguage that delineates the ailments of their patients beyond what can be expressed in their own prescientific idiom. Anthropologists appraise the meaning and function of certain cultural customs of a primitive tribe better than the members of the tribe do. They express this appraisal in a scientific idiom different from the tribal idiom. Their language at this level enables them to explain tribal customs beyond the limited horizon of the tribe itself. The very expression *primitive* is a linguistic invention of the science of anthropology. This construct within a community of scientists has a precise meaning. Members of the tribe do not know themselves as "primitive." They cannot realize the way in which this construct clarifies a main characteristic of their culture. Similarly, economists apprehend and appraise the fluctuations of a national economy in a language above that of the prescientific apprehensions and appraisals of average buyers and sellers in neighborhood stores. The science of economy crafts its own language to better express its scientific findings and insights.

Something similar can be observed in the disciplines of philosophy and theology. For example, many clergypersons may recall that their first sermons during or immediately after graduate studies in theology were not sufficiently translated into postscientific language to be effective in their congregations. Yet they usually admit that the metalanguage of philosophy and theology, while foreign to the faithful, gave the clergypersons themselves access to new insights and perspectives. This insight enables them to enrich the prescientific faith apprehensions of their listeners, when such theoretical reflections are translated into their common idiom. Lacking this formation in a theological metalanguage, they would have little to translate.

Reason for the Necessity of Scientific Language

Why is it necessary for the human sciences to reach for scientific apprehension, appraisal, and expression that goes beyond prescientific knowledge? In the case of formation science, it is necessary to appraise distinctively human formation as a field of presence and action, disclosing a vast array of ranges, regions, spheres, dimensions, and integrational forms, with their dynamics and their facilitating and hindering conditions. It is impossible to accomplish this task merely on the basis of the prescientific approach of people in everyday life. Scientists must articulate these facets with more accuracy and penetration than people in ordinary conversation are able to do.

Consider these examples. Many people in Christian formation, especially in the eighteenth century in Western Europe, were convinced that spiritual formation implied a rejection of the body and its needs. Today we can identify an implicit ideology promoting a spirit-body split as the source of this dissonant formation. Some constructs of formation science and its underlying anthropology can be applied to the problem of dualism incurred by this segment of the population. The construct "spirit-body split giving rise to dissonant formation" gives us a more accurate appraisal of the deformation occurring during this period of Christian formation.

In a related example considered earlier, the counselor assumes that the counselee expresses what she really believes to be happening. She complains about her uneasiness with the divine and ascribes this feeling to her sinful will. Yet the counselor may know similar cases and theories from the science and its auxiliary sources that convince him that being ill at ease with God is not necessarily a sign of bad will.

Prescientific appraisals in their common expression must be taken seriously, but they must also be transcended. One does so by integrating them into a wider scientific appraisal with its own lingual expression beyond that used by the persons with whom the scientist interacts. Scientific appraisal is then uniquely adapted to these persons and segments with their ordinary languages.

Such application and adaptation of a metalingual theory is only admissable if it produces an appreciative apprehension that has a higher probability to approximate what is actually happening, formatively speaking, or what has to be done from the viewpoint of restoring consonant formation. If the theory does not work, either the theory, its expression, or its unique application is defective. One main reason for such a failure may be a neglect of the prescientific empathic phase of appreciative apprehension and articulation of the field as communicated in common language. This empathic approach is a necessary condition for accurate scientific appraisal and a subsequent postscientific expession.

Similarities and Dissimilarities among
Prescientific, Scientific, and Postscientific Languaging

One striking way in which lingual differences manifest themselves is found in the distinct formative impact each type of language may have on people. For example, theories of distinctively human or spiritual formation are communicated in an idiom of abstract concepts and constructs. This scientific language engages more the mind than the heart of the reader or listener. In and by itself it will generally not evoke immediate and spontaneous sentiments of edification, devotion, inspiration. The same applies to the metalanguages of other sciences. For example, a psychophysiological theory of sexuality rendered in its peculiar idiom will, in and by itself, not be sexually arousing or evoke romantic feelings in the average person.

There is thus an intrinsic dissimilarity between the original intuitive apprehension and subsequent pretheoretical appraisal of a formative incident as expressed in prescientific language, and its scientific appraisal as expressed in an appropriate idiom. This dissimilarity is due to the scientific viewpoint of the researchers. Ordinary points of view, in contrast, are rooted in spontaneous appreciations. These initial apprehensions and appraisals are blindly borrowed or personalized by people via current popular language.

However, this dissimilarity can never be total. There must always remain a basic similarity among prescientific, scientific, and postscientific modes of presence and their corresponding languages. This fundamental similarity is indispensable for a consonant scientific approach.

This principle of the science can be illustrated by some examples. Someone who has never experienced in any way the forming influence of a transcendent life call cannot really develop an appreciative apprehension and a consequent argumentative appraisal of what it means to be inspired by such a call. To be sure, scholars who never had this experience may, on the basis of publications by others, write a treatise about the consequences of discovering and assenting to a life call. But their work will be helpful only to the degree that the others whom they quote or paraphrase have had some experience of this theme and have been able to reflect seriously on it in some measure.

In the realm of prayer life, conceptual reflections based on the intuitive experience of contemplation have been developed, for instance, by Saint John of the Cross. As a result, his analytical language differs considerably from everyday remarks about prayer. Yet his poetry testifies to his primordial intuitive presence to the life of intimacy with the mystery.

Our conclusion is that we can never forego the initial apprehensions expressed in common language. Every theoretical appraisal in our science, as in all other human sciences, presupposes some primordial presence of people in real life to the events about which they theorize. Researchers who engage in scientific appraisal must be familiar in a prescientific way with what they are going to appraise scientifically. For example, a student who wants to write about the tensions people may experience between congeniality with their own uniqueness and compatibility with other people must know this problem in some personal way for the research to succeed.

These examples demonstrate that the differences among prescientific, scientific, and postscientific apprehensions and appraisals, with their corresponding languages, should never become an unbridgeable gap. There is similarity as well as dissimilarity among them on all levels. In short, there is operative between these levels the principle of cognitive and lingual interformation.

Formation Directives Implicit in Prescientific Languages

Any investigation of prescientific languaging from the perspective of distinctively human formation discloses that it is permeated by directives. They invite some kind of commitment from the people who are formed by this language from infancy on. For many persons the measure of their fidelity to such commitments implicit in this language may be the yardstick by which they judge their appreciation of self and others as people in consonant formation. This prefocal measure of consonance points to a kind of formation conscience whose development is fostered also by prescientific language.

Certain Islamic populations, for instance, may consider the state of holy war with infidels a blessed event guaranteeing their immediate entrance into paradise if they fall as martyrs for their sacred cause. This apprehension gives rise to lingual formation directives that ready them for war.

These in turn foster warlike dispositions and create a bellicose facet of their conscience. These factors will be inextricably interwoven with the verbal and nonverbal expressions permeating their formation field.

It is impossible to understand such populations if we do not consider the prescientific common language out of which emerges their thinking about war, martyrdom, paradise, and the centrality of certain culture-bound interpretations of the Koran. Empathic participation in the prescientific language and directives of unfamiliar populations is an essential starting point for researchers. They must adopt an initial, methodological disposition of tentative affinity with their lingually expressed apprehensions and appraisals. For reasons of research, they should put the directives of their own culture or subculture momentarily into brackets. This affinitive appraisal will gradually enable them to sense also the prescientific affective appraisals flowing from such directives and their immense formation power.

To apprehend and appraise the intimate formative meaning of the prescientific language of a people is thus a precondition for any subsequent correct scientific argumentative appraisal. Empathy does not mean that scientists are committed to assume these alien directives as their own. It is only a phase of their research to be followed by the next step of translating what they have learned into the language of formation, and appraising it in the light of theoretical insight.

During their research they neither deny nor blindly confirm the lingual directives with which they become familiar during the phase of empathic apprehension and appraisal. They see this reformative transition from prescientific to scientific and later to postscientific appraisal and languaging as a bridging function between the three idioms of formation.

Focal and Nonfocal Language

Focal and nonfocal language are related, respectively, to the focal and nonfocal regions of consciousness. This distinction has practical implications for the proximate and immediate formation, reformation, and transformation of people.

An essential condition for reformation is the awakening of formation reason to facets of our field over which our free will seems either to have lost or never to have gained control. Often we are unaware of the unspoken apprehensions and appraisals that guide our life via the implicit directives they disclose. These are couched in a language of which we are no longer conscious. This nonfocal language tends to flash automatically through that region of consciousness the moment a seemingly similar situation elicits an identical lingual reaction. This process takes only seconds. Before we can become aware of this hidden idiom and move to reform it by argumentative appraisal, it has already given form to our moods, feelings, and sensitivities. We may be conscious of these consequent emotional states, but we are no longer able to trace their roots in the instantaneous flashing language game that evokes them. Our moods and feelings in turn have a forming impact on acts and dispositions.

To gain insight into this nonfocal language and its reasonableness or unreasonableness in our present situation, we have to make it focal. In this way the directives, implied in our prefocal language reaction become available to the critical appraisal of formation reason and the free exercise of our will as enlightened by it.

Certain modes of counseling and therapy are rooted in anthropologies that underestimate the role of reason and will in human life. As a result, their followers may focus mainly on feelings and their conscious release instead of concentrating also on getting in touch with the hidden language game that evokes depreciative, envious, depressive, manic, anxious, compulsive, or hostile feelings, acts, and dispositions. Consequently, they are less apt to reestablish the power of formation reason and free will, at least explicitly. Implicitly, of course, any effective lasting change they actually effect in the life of their counselees is necessarily due also to a subtle change in the hidden language game that secretly deformed their life. This lingual change implies a liberation of both reason and will.

Application to Larger Populations

The principle just discussed applies not only to individuals but also to the hidden language games of populations or their segments. Take, for example, the anti-Semitic feelings and actions prevalent in certain people and places. At the root of this emotional violence may be an unexamined collection of lingual directives spawned by past depreciative appraisals communicated by fellow citizens. These may have been assimilated prefocally early in life or learned focally in interformation with other anti-Semitic types. They become part of one's nonfocal speech dispositions. As long as these underlying assumptions and appraisals are not brought into the light of focal speech, it will be difficult, if not impossible, to reform the prejudicial moods and feelings they engender. Only an open confrontation of this hidden speech pattern with formation reason can initiate a reformation of disposition and action.

What is the genesis of such secret, deformative language games? To the degree that our initial intuitions are not tainted by the pride-form, they have a certain innocence about them. For example, children tend to appreciate spontaneously their beloved companions regardless of their ethnic background or socioeconomic status. The relative innocence of some of these intuitive appraisals may be lost when focal prejudiced appraisals of the family or of their formation segment affect the children. These prejudices are couched in denigrating words about other races, creeds, or social conditions. Soon they slip into children's nonfocal idiom, to distort, perhaps lastingly, the good feelings that may have been engendered by intuitive appreciative apprehensions. Popular or segmental deformation through language often announces a loss of original innocence.

Summary Conclusions Regarding the Language of Formation

We can now summarize our conclusions regarding the language of formation.

1. Scientific language presupposes for its correctness an empathic appreciation of the prescientific language in which people originally expressed the event that is the subject matter of investigation.
2. This scientific idiom will be basically related to the prescientific language but will also be essentially different because of the varied perspectives assumed by the scientist.
3. The scientific language will be a necessary means to widen our horizon of insight into a formation topic or event by letting it light up under different general perspectives.
4. This widening of insight can bring about an apprehension and appraisal of possible flaws in the original appraisal of our field and its dynamics.
5. Such new insight may facilitate a change in focal and nonfocal language dispositions and their implied directives. This change in turn will facilitate a desirable reformation or transformation in service of the ascent of human life as fostered by its transcendence dynamic.
6. Unlike positivistic approaches, the approach of formation science takes seriously into account the directives and affects of the people under study. The theoretical appraisal of these directives

presupposes critical attentiveness to the pulsations, pulsions, ambitions, aspirations or inspirations implied in them.

7. Formation scientists, and especially practitioners and communicators of the science, should give equal attention to the development of a postscientific language that can clearly and attractively convey the findings of the science in an idiom familiar to individuals or to the segments of the population they try to assist in their journey.

8. The test of the correctness of the findings of the science, as expressed in its scientific idiom, is that it can better clarify and effect formation, reformation, and transformation than did prescientific understanding as expressed in pretheoretical language.

9. The implicit fundamental unity between prescientific, scientific, and postscientific appraisal of formation will become more obvious if the basic concerns of formation scientists and practitioners are the same as those they personally cultivate in their own ongoing ascending life formation.

10. Formation science assumes that human life is called to a formative ascent inspired by an inherent transcendence dynamic. This same dynamic is operative in the prescientific, scientific, and postscientific modes of presence and action and in their corresponding languages. Each higher and more general mode of apprehension and appraisal enables humans to attain a deeper and richer understanding of their life. This comprehension can facilitate the ascent of consonant formation and its expansion into the whole field.

11. Different modes of apprehension and language can be steps toward transcendence. Whenever new perspectives of the science or its auxiliary sources penetrate the various facets of a formative incident, the possibilities for human life to foster consonance are expanded. These new perspectives, without detracting from the basic event as such, throw new lights on it that might otherwise have gone unnoticed.

12. There is no essential difference between the ascending knowledge expansion in the natural sciences and that in the human sciences. Both foster our comprehension of the human condition by approaching phenomena in the light of different general theoretical perspectives. Hence we should not assume an absolute dichotomy between these branches of science.

This chapter gave us an overall insight into the general meanings, roles, and mutual relationships of prescientific, scientific, and postscientific language. We referred obliquely to various types of lingual systems. Formation science has to take them into account without confusing them. Hence, the next chapter will discuss the appropriate use of these lingual systems.

CHAPTER 24

Common, Segmental, Traditional, and Metalingual Systems

Among the language systems developed by humanity, formation science distinguishes four types: common, segmental, traditional, and metalingual.

Common language is shared in the national or cultural field of a people. For example, American English is common to all Americans who have assimilated this parlance.

Segmental language is formed by a special branch of the population, such as farmers or city dwellers, soldiers or sailors, marines or monks, career women or homemakers, adolescents or adults, blacks or whites. Segmental language adds to the common language typical modulations. They represent the specific apprehensions and appraisals of a branch of the population.

Traditional language develops among those who adhere to the same ideological, religious, or syncretic faith and form traditions, such as Protestants, Jews, Catholics, Muslims, Marxists, or humanists. They modulate the common language to express apprehensions and appraisals typical of their tradition.

Common, segmental, and traditional languages have their own dynamics. They keep forming themselves along definite lines. One principle is the demand for consonance of each new lingual form with those already in use. Lingual forms can be understood only in the context of related verbal forms. (We shall return to this principle in our section on jargon and metalanguage.)

Metalanguage is any type of parlance that goes beyond the common, segmental, or traditional language of people. Most conspicuous is the metalanguage of science. However, while all scientific language is metalingual, not all metalanguage is scientific. There are many prescientific metalanguages. Examples are professional and occupational languages, such as those devised by the armed forces. There are metalingual expressions in poetry and literature; in families, clubs, or street gangs; in religious communities. Some of these, for example, in professions, may be partly taken over from related scientific languages, but this is not true in all cases.

Scientific Metalanguage

In this chapter we are mainly concerned with the language of science. Hence, if we use the term metalanguage without any qualification we mean *scientific language.*

The prefix *meta-* means "beyond." In the case of scientific language it refers to a system of words and phrases that goes beyond the common, segmental, traditional, and prescientific metalingual systems of populations at large. Philosophers and theorists of science agree that each science needs its own language. It reaches maturity and distinction from other sciences only when it has developed this language sufficiently. Historically, no science or scholarly discipline is known that does not have its own idiom. Philosophy, theology, medicine, physics, psychology, psychiatry, biology, chemistry, and engineering all have their own terminology. To learn a science or scholarly discipline is to learn a new language of which significant parts are not used in familiar, common, segmental, or traditional languages. Nor are its expressions used in the same way by any other mature science or scholarly discipline.

Three Factors in the Formation of a Scientific Language

Scientists specialize in new, precise apprehensions and appraisals. These result from the use of scientific methods. Scientists construe and apply such methods in the light of a rigorously maintained viewpoint. That viewpoint binds the science and its language to a specific object pole. The newness and specificity of such concentrated apprehensions and appraisals make their adequate expression different from the expressions of the familiar apprehensions and appraisals of people who communicate with each other in ordinary common, segmental, and traditional languages about what is already more widely known or intimated by their culture. Hence, there are no precise words to cover new insights in everyday parlance. A new language has to be formed to give expression to such highly specialized apprehensions and appraisals.

A second factor is the need for scientific precision in interforming communication between scientists. The living common, segmental, or traditional language is constantly changing its connotations. The popular term *gay*, for instance, has new connotations that diminish the exactness necessary for uniform scientific communication in communities of scholars and scientists who specialize in the study of this lifestyle. This example may help to explain the recourse most sciences have to so-called dead languages, such as classical Greek or Latin: for example, the terms *myocardial infarction*, in medicine; *schizoid, introvert,* and *neurotic,* in psychology; *transubstantiation,* in theology; *pre-, intra-, inter-, extra-,* and *proformation,* in formation science.

A third factor in metalanguage is the necessity of consonance of each new metalingual form with the already existing forms of the same language of a particular science. This demand is even more strict in scientific than in common, segmental, or traditional lingual formation.

The language of a science serves the communication of coherent scientific theories in effective abbreviated expresssions that are defined precisely. Any dissonance in the terminology may affect the consonance of the theory itself. This accounts for the importance of the definition of terms in each science. Formation science, for instance, has already defined descriptively over two thousand terms that coform its language. Most of these definitions have been published as glossaries in its journal, *Studies in Formative Spirituality.*

Metalanguage and Jargon

Language deformation takes place when the requirement of internal consonance is resisted. This applies to scientific language as well as to the other types of languages discussed so far. A language is deformed to the degree that lingual forms are introduced, without sufficient assimilation, that are incompatible with the characteristic forms of a particular language. Formation science calls this "jargon formation."

Jargon jars; it breaks through the consonant flow of an existing language without enhancing significantly its meaningfulness, coherence, clarity, or precision. Jargon is thus the introduction of a dissonant term into a coherent language process. Such a jarring introjection is more deformative in a scientific idiom than in a common, segmental, or traditional idiom. Often jargon in scientific language takes the form of arbitrarily inserting terms of an auxiliary science or of ordinary language systems without sufficient translation and transposition.

For example, insertion of Jungian, Freudian, existentialist, behaviorist, Maslowian, Rogerian, Buddhist, Hindu, Islamic, or theological terms, or terms from ordinary talk, into the language of formation science without critical validation and, if necessary, translation and transposition, would lead to dissonant jargon formation. Hence part of the bilingual training of formation scientists and practitioners comprehends the art and discipline of preventing jargon in either the scientific or postscientific language they use.

The touchstone of maturity of a science is advanced development of its own language with a corresponding elimination of jargon due to blindly borrowing from other sciences and ordinary parlance. Conversely, when we use the terms of the language of a science outside its own context, they may sound like jargon too. For instance, the theological term *transubstantiation* can be understood in the context of the metalanguage of Roman Catholic theology. Used loosely, outside this context, without explanation in ordinary parlance, it sounds like jargon.

Our common awareness of human experience is expressed in language forms we can all understand. The penetration of human experience, however, by systematic, scientific reflection will disclose structures, dynamics, directives, and motivations not yet expressed in everyday wordings in a precise fashion. Hence it is necessary for the sciences to develop their own languages to express the as yet unexpressed.

Sometimes we find more resistance to the languages of the human sciences than to those of the natural sciences. One reason may be that physical sciences do not challenge common and personal views of life in the same way human sciences do. The latter disclose the deeper grounds of experience, the directives and dispositions people may unwittingly have made their own. Many feel threatened by such disclosures.

Another source of resistance is the challenge to admit that there is more to life than people may have suspected. Their cherished control is less than they imagined. This "more than" may imply new demands in regard to their ongoing formation.

A third reason may be a lack of translation of relevant parts of scientific languages into ordinary language; such a translation would allow people to profit from new findings. A solution to this problem could be facilitated by clarifying the differences between metalanguage, common and popular language, and jargon.

Conclusions Pertaining to Scientific Metalanguages

We can draw several conclusions that pertain to scientific metalanguage.

1. A scientific language is a consistent lingual system appropriate to the special object and approach that constitute the science in question.
2. A scientific metalanguage consists of lingual forms that fulfill the conditions of effectiveness, uniqueness, precision, and consonance necessary for scientific discourse among experts in the field.
3. The lingual forms must clarify in a precise and nuanced fashion the unique insights and findings of a well-defined science.
4. The lingual forms of a scientific language transcend those of the common, segmental, traditional, and prescientific metalanguages of a population. These do not yet cover the unique findings of the science in as equally distinct, precise, and finely nuanced a fashion as does the language of the science itself. Hence we use the term *meta-* or "beyond" language to imply that it operates above everyday use and common parlance.
5. Each metalingual form of a science should complement and, if necessary, clarify other forms that coform the same language system.
6. Each metalingual form should enhance the efficiency of the language system as a means of precise, theoretical, abbreviated communication between committed scientists versed in the field.
7. The metalingual forms should effectively preclude ambiguous connotations with specific usages from other sciences or from the common, segmental, or traditional language of the population at large.

Metalanguage and Popular Language

When we function in the capacity of theoreticians and researchers, we should not confuse our duty of responsible metalanguage formation with that of giving form to a postscientific popular language. Both should be done, but they cannot be done at the same time in the same type of either popular or scientific talk or paper.

At times many of us may choose to function as translators and transposers of certain practical implications of our science. This process will demand that we give form to a popular language. It is necessary also for the purpose of interviewing people who are not formed in the language of the science; for public communication, consultation, and counseling services; for dialogue with other sciences, arts, and traditions. If we engage in popularization, we should mentally keep this postscientific language distinct from the language of the science.

To prevent any confusion between the two languages, we should train ourselves to keep both types distinct, to appreciate them as modes of responsible language formation, and to use them alternatively at the proper time and in the appropriate situation.

Inherent in the scientific disposition is a kind of academic asceticism. It helps us when we function as scientists not to weaken the rigor of our language for ulterior motives, not to give in to the pressure of our needs for acclaim or remuneration. The same scientific asceticism should make us aware of our fear of not being fully understood or of being derided by colleagues, critics, or the public at large. A scientist is the servant of truth. Disclosing new facets of reality, giving form to them in an appropriate idiom—such are the privilege and burden of a true scientist.

Nonetheless, popularization of certain formationally relevant aspects of a science is a matter of social justice toward persons who cannot share directly the excitement and challenge of the scientific journey itself. This task is often performed not by scientists themselves but by popularizers or practitioners.

Fidelity to this calling implies that popularizers acquire sufficient metalingual understanding to be able to be faithful to the basic meaning of the insights they prudently select for communication. An example would be the official popularizers of religious and ideological faith and form traditions, such as preachers, orators, pamphleteers, edifying writers, retreat masters, or Sunday school teachers. The more literarily gifted they are, the more effectively, attractively, and inspirationally they can form (or deform) their audiences. To prevent distortion, popular communicators should study those aspects of the theological, philosophical, psychological and formative disciplines and sciences concerned that are relevant to their specific topic. They should especially examine or be taught the precise meaning of the languages used by these disciplines and sciences. Without this background, they may be unable to select judiciously what is useful for their audience; they will also be less capable of faithfully translating the metalanguage in a popularizing, inspirational, or edifying way that makes sense to people in general.

Criteria of Consonance and Language Formation

A number of scientists themselves have an affinity and an ability for popularization of their discipline. They should be encouraged to give some time to this interest. To be sure, scientists—in congeniality with their primary vocation—should live first of all in ascetic fidelity to the gift of research and scientific publication granted to them by the formation mystery. Their compatibility, compassion, and social presence in justice, peace, and mercy should motivate them to continue their competent labor of research in service of humanity.

When scientists are also called to spend time and energy in popularization, their main motivation should be compatibility, compassion, and social presence in regard to those who do not share their specialty. Insofar as this second calling is congenial to them and not artificially forced, or merely undertaken for cheap popularity, they remain in tune with the deepest center of their life. These efforts in regard to their primary call to research and their secondary commitment to popularization demand, of course, continual ascetic growth in competence in regard to both labors of love. To promote the growth of such gifted people in their specific calling is the responsibility of any wise superior.

Seven Principles of Popularization by Scientists

Scientists who are called to popularization should be guided in their efforts by:

1. fidelity to the distinction between scientific and popular language;
2. a growing awareness of the possibility of dialogical interaction between certain lingual forms of scientific and popular language;
3. a growth in competence in the use of common symbols, metaphors, and narratives in service of their translation of the scientific idiom into popular parlance;
4. a growth in the ability to introduce judiciously appropriate metalingual terms into the common, segmental, or traditional language of a population;
5. a growth in the capacity to appraise the needs of a population for particular insights of the science to be retold in terms of their concrete conditions of life;
6. a readiness to do scientific research when the needs of a population demand it;

7. in the case of teaching the science itself to the as yet uninitiated, the competence to alternate between metalingual and popular language without confusing the two.

An example of popularization by scientists is given by nuclear physicists or medical experts who selectively popularize some of the findings in their fields. At the same time they remain faithful to the function of the numerical or literary symbols of physics or medicine when publishing in professional journals or communicating with their colleagues.

Adoption of Metalingual Terms in Common Language

As a result of popularization, certain terms of a science may become part of a common language. For instance, some expressions of psychoanalysis (such as *unconscious, ego, superego, transference, repression,* and *defense mechanisms*) have become part of the common language of segments of the world population. Often such adoption leads to an erosion of precision. For instance, the terms *unconscious* and *repression* are less precise in meaning when used by the population at large than they are when used in psychoanalytic theory. In spite of this diminishment of precision, the adoption of scientific terms by popular language can be advantageous. There is an overall formational advantage in raising the consciousness and interconsciousness of the public in regard to disclosures of a science. These bits of knowledge taken together can significantly advance our shared formation history.

Because popular adoption may lead to corruption of original meaning, scientists should train new initiates in their field to distinguish between terms as defined in its language and as used loosely in common parlance. For instance, students of theology should be made aware of possible differences between the terms "charism" and "charismatic," as defined by theology and as used in popular or edifying media.

The longer a science has been established, the more widely its terms may have been popularized. This familiarity may be one of the sources of resistance to as yet unfamiliar expressions of new sciences. They share inevitably the initial estrangement that was typical of the beginnings of now established sciences and their languages. For instance, the medical term *myocardial infarction,* initially unfamiliar to the populace, becomes increasingly familiar in nonmedical segments.

Jargon Formation

The formation of jargon, as previously noted, involves incidental language forms that are not made a consonant part of either a coherent common, segmental, or traditional language system or of a scientific lingual system. Jargon expresses experiences in an exotic or belabored fashion that does not contribute to better understanding. In the case of jargon in common parlance what is thus communicated can be more clearly expressed in the ordinary language of people. When an accurate definition of an emotion, thought, or observation has to be elaborated, recourse to one or the other metalanguage may be necessary.

Jargon is dissonant with other lingual forms used by common, segmental, traditional, or scientific language systems. It tends to diminish the natural ease, flow, and spontaneous coherence of a language. Disruption of this flow does not serve the more accurate expression of reality. Hence jargon tends to obscure and confuse communication.

The addition of new consonant terms to a scientific language system tends to enhance it as a tool for concise, effective communication between scientists who share the same field of inquiry. Jargon does the opposite, both in scientific and in ordinary language. It makes both scientific and common parlance more cumbersome as a tool of communication. Instead of paving the way, it gets in the way of effective communication.

Sometimes jargon in ordinary language may be formed by the loose adoption of insufficiently appraised terms borrowed from scientific languages. The insertion of such terms into a different system of symbols can lead to a loss of the precise meaning of these terms. They should be understood primarily in their own context. Outside of this context, and without sufficient explanation, they deteriorate easily into jargon.

Bilingual Concern of Formation Science

One characteristic of the human sciences is their practical intent. Unlike as in, let us say, ontology or mathematics, in human sciences the selection of research topics and the unfolding of methodology, theory, and language are, from the very beginning, permeated by the intent to effect changes in conditions of life. Formation science itself is guided by the goal to gather knowledge that can concretely foster the consonant formation of human life as lived in its everydayness.

This practical intent explains why this science favors two languages: a metalanguage for its scientists and a popular language for its practitioners, who at the same time should be familiar with the science and its idiom. Ideally, both scientists and practitioners should be bilingual. Metalanguage enables precise scientific discussion, validation, and systematic integration of knowledge to be extracted from a variety of sources and to be translated and transposed by the researcher. Popular language has a twofold purpose. First, it facilitates access of scientists and practioners to the experiences of people through conversation, interview, dialogue, and discussion; this enables them to gain insight into such experiences as they are commonly lived and as they give rise to questions for scientific reflection. The second purpose of popular language is to facilitate a meaningful communication of our findings that makes sense to the population intended so that upward transcendence may occur.

Once we have established the inevitability of the formation of different languages for different sciences and other sources of formation knowledge, a question arises: How can we conduct a meaningful dialogue between formation science with its own metalanguage and its auxiliary sources with their different languages? The following chapter answers this question.

CHAPTER 25

Formation Science and
Auxiliary Sources

F ormation science requires a language comprehensive and pliable enough to integrate the formative implications of its auxiliary sources. These sources represent the results of differential perspectives, each of which may complement, correct, and expand our findings of the topic under investigation. Metalingual dialectics is the phrase we use to describe this interaction between the language of formation science and that of its auxiliary sources. We would like to discuss this relationship mainly as it exists between formation science and some of the mainline psychologies.

The variety of approaches brought to bear on the science by auxiliary sources can be categorized under familiar headings. In the light of our present paradigm of the formation field, we can identify these approaches as being mainly either pre- and intra-oriented or inter- and extra-oriented, for they may focus predominantly on the pre-, intra-, inter-, or extra-spheres of the field, and within them on one or more specific dimensions. To simplify matters in this chapter, we will use the term "outer sphere" to encompass both the inter- and extraspheres as distinct from the pre- and intraspheres. We shall also pay attention to the dimensions or regions focused upon by the psychologies or traditions we will use as examples.

Intra- and Outer Spheres

One series of perspectives emerging from auxiliary sources considers formation mainly in terms of the intrasphere of the field. Many of the metalanguages developed by different schools of psychology demonstrate this perspective. Their language differs from that found in psychologies oriented toward the outer spheres. Some of the latter, like behaviorism, tend to reduce the intrasphere to the forming influences of the outer spheres. They neglect the pre- and intraspheres in their distinctively human manifestations.

It is the province of formation science to integrate the theoretical and lingual formational insights implied in the findings of these different approaches. Ours is an open scientific model, symbolized by the paradigm of the formation field. This model operates as a provisional guide in the further disclosure and positioning of accumulating insights. We can fulfill this purpose only if our language of fundamental concepts and constructs remains open-ended, that is to say not exclusively pre-, intra-, inter-, or extra-oriented. It must transcend concentration on any one of these spheres to the exclusion of another. Hence the basic concepts and constructs we draw upon represent distinctively human qualities that pervade the field in its entirety and that are mainly expressed in the metalanguage of its underlying formation anthropology. A significant number of these theories emerge from the scientific language of its empirical body of knowledge as structured on the basis of the science's anthropological assumptions.

Dimensional Focus

Certain sciences and traditions limit their attention to chiefly one or a few dimensions within the spheres of the field. The Jungian metalanguage, for instance, concentrates mainly on the functional-transcendent dimension of the intrasphere. The Freudian metalanguage, on the contrary, moves predominantly within the vital-functional dimension of intraformation. The outer spheres are of interest to Freudians chiefly insofar as they influence the intraspheric dialectical processes occurring between these two dimensions. Certain Eastern traditions focus only on the transcendent dimension of the intrasphere. It tends to absorb all of the other spheres and dynamics of life. Victor Frankl's existential psychiatry, too, tends somewhat in that direction.

Formation science rises above these diverse perspectives while taking into account their formationally relevant implications. We consider the continual development of a wide variety of specialized sciences and form traditions to be one of the necessary conditions for the growth of formation science itself. For this science expands and differentiates itself also by utilizing the results of psychologies highly specialized in the exploration of specific spheres and dimensions of the field. These specializations become deformative only when they pretend to present the whole basis for distinctively human formation in its entirety.

In this regard the issue of one-sidedly oriented formation traditions differs from that of one-sidedly oriented auxiliary sciences. The latter concentration on one or a few facets of the whole field is in tune with their essential task as specialized sciences operating from a limited perspective. Formation traditions, however, aim at the lingual presentation of the total direction of distinctively human formation in its entirety. Some of them should widen their own paradigms to include the basic facets of the formation field for the sake of offering a more balanced approach to formation for the populations they serve. For instance, both the collectivistic Marxist and the individualistic capitalist formation traditions with their underlying belief systems should broaden their bases to cover the human formation field more adequately.

The Term "Anthropological"

The most fundamental, comprehensive lingual concepts and constructs of formation science are found in its underlying formation anthropology. These transcend the specialized languages of its auxiliary sources.

In current usage the meaning of the term *anthropology* is restricted by many people to the "science of man in relation to physical character, origin and distribution of races, environmental and social relations and culture" (*Webster's New Collegiate Dictionary*). This restriction of the term anthropology covers only the biogenetic and familial dimensions of the preformative sphere and the sociohistorical, vital, and functional dimensions of the inter- and outer spheres.

Etymologically, the term anthropology does not have this restricted meaning. It is derived from the Greek words *anthropos* ("man," or in present-day nonsexist language, "the human life-form") and *logos*, "word" or "science" about what is human. Therefore, every lingual concept, construct, or science referring to human life as a whole can properly be called anthropological.

Human life in its entirety appears under many aspects integrated into our paradigm of the formation field. Experts in cultural anthropology, for instance, refer to this life-form only insofar as it appears physically, racially, socially, and culturally. Hence, they develop the language of cultural anthropology. Other experts may focus on it in the light of their sciences or disciplines, such as medicine, history, sociology, philosophy, or theology. This concentration gives rise to the metalanguages of a medical, historical, social, philosophical, or theological anthropology. Formation scientists study human life from the perspective of distinctively human formation and its practical implications. The lingual concepts and constructs expressing the underlying assumptions of this science can thus be called a formation anthropology. In its development, we do consult the auxiliary science of philosophical anthropology to profit from what may be relevant in it for formation anthropology.

The lingual concepts and constructs we use are marked by certain characteristics. They must transcend the predominantly pre-, intra-, inter-, extra-, or dimensional connotations of the auxiliary sources of formation science. They must represent foundational human characteristics. They should be rooted in concrete appreciative apprehensions of the field in its coherent totality. They should ultimately be oriented toward transcendence, not toward function. They should be formulated in a metalanguage that goes beyond the limiting connotations of specific concepts and constructs formulated by specialized auxiliary sources.

Transcendence of the Spheres of the Formation Field

The seventeeth-century French philosopher, scientist, physiologist, and mathematician René Descartes conceived of mind and body as two distinct substances. Both mind and matter in his thinking are complete and self-sustaining. Mind is a thinking thing, body an extension thing. Toward the end of his life, Descartes attempted a reunification of the two. His original dualistic view was in tune with the temper of his times: it was destined to influence subsequent developments in philosophy and science, specifically in psychology and psychiatry.

The idea of the separation of mind and body turned attention toward the conscious subject, or to what we have called the intrasphere of our field. This intrasphere was believed to be divorced from both the inter- and extraneous spheres of the field and its horizons. The intrasphere was merely an accurate mirroring of forms emerging in the outer spheres in complete separation from it.

This view gave rise to two mutually exclusive starting points, namely, mind as unfolding within the intrasphere, on the one hand, and body as belonging to the outer spheres, on the other. Many philosophical systems that arose after Descartes adopted one of these starting points and denied or neglected the other. Idealistic philosophies stressed consciousness residing in the intrasphere, while the empiricists emphasized body and environment and considered them to be of the same order. In our terminology, they would focus exclusively on the pre-, inter-, and outer spheres, at least in the way they understood the body. For us the body is the intrasphere inevitably involved in the sensate pre-, inter-, and outer spheres of the field and its horizons.

Idealism seems to eliminate the pre-, inter-, and outer spheres as objective independent sources of apprehension and appraisal. It saw the intrasphere as pure consciousness, separated from the other spheres, as the absolute origin of clear and distinct ideas, as a kind of autarkic functional-transcendent intrasphere. Empiricism, on the contrary, held that all apprehension and appraisal originate in the outer spheres, which impose themselves on a passive consciousness in the intrasphere.

Almost every psychology became rooted in either an idealistic or an empiricist view of the field, and understandably so, because psychologists were necessarily influenced by the sociohistorical dimension of their own field, which was saturated with pulsations generated by Cartesian dualism.

Idealism, for instance, led in early psychology to introspectionism. This approach considered the contents of the intraspheric consciousness as the legitimate and exclusive object of this new science. Empiricism, on the contrary, gave rise to behaviorism. This type of psychology made its exclusive object quantifiable bodily behavior as preformed by the organism and as formed by the predictable stimuli of the outer spheres. The metalanguages of both types of psychology are filled with either idealistic or empiricistic connotations. As such they cannot be used for integral human formation without critical translation and transposition into integrative concepts or constructs useful for comprehensive formation anthropology.

Originally, neither type of psychologist seemed to understand that the restriction of attention to one or a few facets of the field should be methodological, not absolute. Many were inclined to posit this restriction of the subject matter of psychology as final and exclusive. Fortunately for formation science, this absolutized one-sided focus enhanced tremendously the development and the subsequent unique findings of the two main groups of auxiliary psychologies. The findings and theories of both idealistic and empiricistic psychologies are of value for our science insofar as they highlight implicitly important facets of formation. When translated and transposed into the wider frame of reference of our science they can expand our integrative approach to distinctively human formation.

Introspectionism, the dominant scientific psychology until 1912, holds that this science should develop means of looking into the intraspheric consciousness. This focus would reveal its "contents," which could then be described in terms of elementary sensations. Wundt and Titchener modified this development of psychology somewhat by combining the experimental method with introspection. Nevertheless the basis of their approach remained the method of looking into the mental intrasphere. All other facets of the formation field were reduced to contents of the conscious intrasphere. Accordingly an introspectionistic metalanguage was developed by these psychologists. They taught us much about significant aspects of intraspheric functioning.

Behaviorism excluded the intraspheric consciousness from the subject matter of psychology. Its one-sided yet fruitful concentration on the measurable outer spheres and dimensions of the behaving organism also gave rise to a large group of psychologies with a whole new metalanguage. They provide formation science with other substantial contributions. Some of these have formational implications and can be transposed into an integrated view of distinctively human formation. We mention here as examples only the differential theories of such psychologists as Weiss, Lashley, Hebb, Guthrie, Hull, Spence, Tolman and Skinner.

The extraspheres of the local and mondial situatedness of the intersphere became the focus of the social psychologies and gave rise to a corresponding metalanguage. They enriched our insights in interspheric formation, common and segmental as well as personal.

Differential and Comprehensive Comprehension

Each of these psychologies may claim that it is comprehensive in its own way. And in some sense they are. But they are not comprehensive in the same manner that formation science is. The distinction between *differential* and *comprehensive* comprehension may clarify what we mean.

A specific field sphere, dimension, or region on which a specialized psychology concentrates is in some limited way influential or manifest in all facets of the field. Within these limits any special psychology may explore all of the spheres and dimensions from its restrictive perspective. It errs, however, when and if it denies the validated knowledge gained from other psychologies or from other sources of cognition. The kind of comprehension that considers other knowledge only insofar as it fits within its specialized approach is *differential* comprehension. What it comprehends can be subsumed under the differential profile of research and the methodology of a specific approach.

By contrast, *comprehensive* comprehension, which is typical of formation science, gathers and formulates in a comprehensive metalanguage and from a specific practical point of view available knowledge about all the spheres, dimensions, regions, and ranges of the formation field from any reputable source.

Formation science, especially in its anthropology, develops a metalanguage that represents this kind of comprehension. In regard to the auxiliary science of psychology, the language used should be neither introspectionistic nor behavioristic. It should transcend the methodological limitations of both approaches while integrating the formational implications of their findings into a higher unity. Only such a metalanguage can create an open field of inquiry of value to distinctively human formation. It can, therefore, stimulate also a dialogue about formational findings and ideas with nonpsychological auxiliary sources as well as with various psychological schools of thought.

Formation Anthropology and Nonacademic Psychologies

Formation science cannot overlook any psychological findings that may have formational implications. To be comprehensive it must be attentive to nonacademic as well as academic psychologies. A crucial development outside the academic setting of the university was initiated by the psychoanalytically oriented psychologists. They formulated their insights and findings in a totally new metalanguage, unheard of at the time and entirely different from the metalanguage of introspectionistic and behavioristic psychologies.

The extraacademic origin of psychoanalysis is one cause among many of the disparity one sees sometimes between academic and psychoanalytic psychologists. Formation science has to transcend the mutually excluding dispositions maintained by certain representatives of both approaches. It must seek for unity in the diversity of formational implications it detects in all auxiliary sources translating and transposing these implications in an integrative metalanguage of its own.

An appraisal of Freud's metalanguage from the viewpoint of formation science leads to the conclusion that he, too, worked within the framework of Cartesian dualism. His view of human life does not seem to be based on the assumption of an original dynamic unity between all the spheres, dimensions, regions, and ranges of the formation field and its horizons.

The human life-form in Freudian anthropology is more or less fixed in the biogenetic dimension of the preformative sphere. This latter sphere manifests itself ongoingly in the intrasphere as instinctive drives. The outer spheres do not give form to the intra- in a free-flowing dialectic. Rather, they represent a collection of foreign forms to be reacted to by the fundamentally fixed vital preformation of human life.

According to Freudian anthropology, we are not primarily in open dialogue with reality as disclosing itself objectively in the spheres and dimensions of our field. We are preformed as a narcissistic, pleasure-seeking intrasphere. Libidinal and aggressive drives do not impel us to participate with increasing freedom in the transcendent horizon of our field. Rather, they use the forms emerging in the other spheres for instinctive gratification of the vital dimension of the intrasphere. The functional dimension therewith develops as a kind of compromise between the pulsions of the vital dimension and the demands of the outer spheres.

This reduction of human life led Freud to the notion that civilization was mainly a menace to the gratification of the vital intrasphere. For him, neurosis was a conflict between the instinctual intrasphere and civilization emerging in the outer spheres of our field. Not only did Freud separate the intrasphere from the other spheres; he reified it by turning it into a vital-functional apparatus. This apparatus, as described in his metalanguage, comprised a host of processes and mechanisms concerned with the quantitative regulation of instinctive tensions within the now reified intraspheric realm. Freud coined the constructs of release, repression, and sublimation to account for the economy operative within this intraspheric universe.

His metalanguage elucidated important aspects of the intrasphere and of the dialectic between its vital and functional dimensions. His analysis contains numerous implications for the formation of our life, especially in its lower formation phases. These should be critically appraised and, if relevant, integrated into formation science. Many statements that mirror his implicit anthropology are, however, open to discussion. Is destructive aggression, for example, a primary preformed instinct at the root of our intrasphere? Or should it be considered as a reaction evoked by events in the outer spheres experienced as obstructive, thwarting, and interfering? The aggressive pulsions manifested by certain counselees seem to be not merely preformed forces in isolated intraspheres. They appear more as reactions to frustrating situations whose traces are embedded in the core form of these persons during their formation history. The Freudian metalanguage often seems to suggest that these counselees are much more the victims of an urge for release of intraspheric vital tension. In reality, the human life-form as a whole is shaped as well by the outer spheres as by its intraspheric consciousness and unconsciousness.

Freud's anthropology forced him to fill the intraspheric box with all kinds of apparatus, identified in his metalanguage as *internalizations*. He needed to explain the undeniable interactions between the intrasphere and the outer spheres of the field. In all fairness, Freud could not be expected, in spite of his genius, to emancipate himself wholly from the dualism that permeated his cultural period. In spite of these sociohistorical pulsations, his acute observations compelled him to recognize the impact of significant life situations on the vital-functional formation of people. But his dualism forced him to internalize these inter- and outer influences within the intrasphere. There they lived, so to speak, a dynamic life of their own. The construct of superego in his metalanguage represented these internalized formation forces. Soon he had to expand his metalanguage with the constructs of projection and introversion to account for the contacts between the intra- and outer spheres. No integral formation worthy of its name can bypass a critical dialogue with the formative implications of Freud's significant insights.

Later Developments in Nonacademic Psychologies

Freud's theory and metalanguage—especially his later ego theory— were further developed by such analysts as Anna Freud, William Reich, Melanie Klein, Hartmann, Kris, Alexander, Loewenstein, Winnicott, and many others. These later developments reveal a considerable growth toward a less dualistic view of the human intrasphere within its dialectical formation field. Still they seem unable to transcend completely the original split. Nevertheless, the formationally relevant implications of their psychoanalytic theories and metalanguages are significant. They should be as carefully appraised as the implications of other auxiliary sources.

Carl Jung, also, is intraspherically oriented in his approach to the human person. He filled the intrasphere with other forms than Freud did and had to create his own metalanguage to account for them. He speaks, for example, about archetypes, shadows, and a collective unconsciousness. Human formation becomes for him a wholly intraspheric, somewhat mystical process, almost exclusively preoccupied with the functional-transcendent dimension of our intrasphere. One result of this one-sidedness is a kind of gnosticism bordering on a vague pantheism with little attention for social presence in justice, peace, and mercy to objective events in the outer spheres. However, Jung points to significant experiences that carry implications that can be translated and transposed into formation science after sufficient critical appraisal.

A British group of psychoanalysts, notably Melanie Klein, Fairbairn, Winnicott, and Guntrip, recognized the formative impact of culture. At the same time, their sophisticated theory of intraspheric internalization fell back on the isolated "intraspheric box theory." The Cartesian split is revived to such a degree that human life is conceived as dualistically present in intra- and outer spheres at the same time. The "internal objects-psychology" of this group is specified and intensified by their selection of the imaginative formation power of the intrasphere as one of their main perspectives.

In their theory, imagination is not considered as field-oriented and field-disclosing, but almost exclusively as part of the relatively insulated and autonomous intraspheric processes. They tend to stress internally generated conflicts, often at the expense of the formative impact of the outer spheres here and now.

Melanie Klein, for example, views the experience of the outer spheres as secondary and subordinate to the intraspheric experience. This may be true in instances of malformation, but it cannot be said without qualification of all formation all of the time. Her view and her metalanguage develop into a theory of intraspheric reality structured in terms of internal objects and object relationships. Daydreams and dreams during sleep, as well as the play of children, become expressions of this relatively autonomous intraspheric world. In the same vein, Fairbairn even concludes that the original distinction of Freud between the conscious and the unconscious is less important than the distinction between the two worlds of outer reality and inner reality. As a result of Melanie Klein's theory, the superego becomes a construct that covers a whole inner world of internalized objects.

The quality and quantity of clinical material presented by this British group compels respect. So does the quality of their theorizing. They represent an original contribution to the theory and metalanguage of psychoanalysis. Their refreshing insights and discoveries imply many formational possibilities. Their metalingual concepts and constructs are necessary and valuable within the limits of their theory. Insofar as they comprise implications for formation as a whole, they need translation into the comprehensive language of formation science. By such transposition they can be made useful for the distinctively human formation of our field of presence and action in its structured totality.

Inter- and Outer Spheric Analytic Psychology

The Cartesian split, as we have seen, led to introspectionism and behaviorism in academic psychology. An analogous development took place in nonacademic psychology. A mainly inter- and outer spheric approach in psychoanalytic theory and metalanguage was introduced by such analysts as Alfred Adler, Harry Stack Sullivan, Karen Horney, and Erich Fromm. They rejected or mitigated the anthropological assumption that human life is mainly formed by preformed instinctive drives within the vital intrasphere. They substituted the perspective of outer spheric conditions, pressures, pulsations, and patterns for the perspective of autonomous instinctual intraspheric forces of formation.

In their view, outer spheric conditions mold character. Neurosis arises from dissonances in interformative relationships. Their own metalanguages seem to point to a more or less exclusive outer spheric appraisal of human apprehension and comportment. This implies an underestimation of the relatively free dimension of the intrasphere in its all-pervading transcendence and ascendance. Their language, in comparison with that of orthodox psychoanalysis, mirrors in some way the historical development in academic psychology. There, as we have seen, introspectionism was one-sidedly concerned with the conscious processes within the intrasphere, while original behaviorism was geared to the perspective of the stimuli of the outer spheres. Certain lingual expressions of Fromm, for example, seem to suggest that the inclinations of the human intrasphere are simply the result of outer social processes that give ultimate form to the intrasphere.

Harry Stack Sullivan views the intrasphere as the product of outer formative forces acting upon it from the beginning of life. In his view, such social pressures mold the intrasphere. Sullivan recognized, however, that it is a person-integrated-in-a-situation-with-another-person-or-persons whom one should study in psychology. Such a fortunate formulation tends to go in the direction of the transcendence of the Cartesian split and to approximate our comprehensive paradigm of the formation field. However, when Sullivan further outlines this theory in his metalanguage, it becomes evident that he favors the inter- and outer spheric side of the split at the expense of the relatively free, transcendent, and rational intrasphere. His psychology is a penetrating study of mainly one facet of human life formation, namely, the compatibility accomodation of the focal and nonfocal intrasphere in interformation with the intersphere of the field. As a result, his language leaves little room for the relatively free, transcendent, and rational formation powers of the intrasphere. A typical metalingual formulation by Sullivan strikingly reveals this facet of his theory: "The self may be said to be made up of reflected appraisals." There is some truth to this statement, as we know from our own description of the apparent life-form. Its generalization, however, does not seem acceptable in view of the findings of other psychologies as well as those of other auxiliary sources. A necessary consequence of this one-sided attention to the interspheric object pole of the field is an underappreciation of the intrasphere in all its dimensions.

These psychologies initiated by the perspective of the outer spheric poles of the field illustrate strikingly the importance of auxiliary psychologies for formation science. They often clarify one or the other facet of life in a remarkable manner. They are capable of viewing the whole of life in the light of their own restricted perspective. Because such outer spheric aspects give form to human life, even in the innermost reaches of its intrasphere, they can consider each facet of the field from this viewpoint. This one-pointed attention is fruitful as a methodological principle. It should be appreciated as a source of insight into limited facets of human formation. It is impossible, however, to use the concepts and constructs of these psychologies for the comprehensive metalanguage of formation science because it must transcend the exclusivity connoted by their lingual forms.

The language of formation science thus aims to express the relative position of the formational implications of these exclusive concepts and constructs. It relativizes them in a conceptual comprehensive framework, pointing to the human formation field as a whole in service of the proximate formation, reformation, and transformation of life as lived daily.

The considerations of this chapter make it evident that the language of formation science is distinguished from that of other empirical sciences by its transcendent orientation. The next chapter will deal with this transcendent characteristic.

CHAPTER 26

Transcendent Orientation of Language

M any sciences focus on isolated profiles of human life. Insulated from human life in its transcending totality, these profiles may be marked by features, processes, and laws that can also be observed in animals, plants, or inanimate objects. These shared aspects are abstracted from human life and reified for methodological reasons of research. The metalanguage used to define them reflects this abstraction. To grasp the full formational implications of these reified features, it is necessary to devise a holistic metalanguage. Their meaning for transcendent form reception and donation becomes clear when they are apprehended and appraised in the light of the distinctively human or spiritual qualities that should permeate any and all profiles of our life.

These qualities cannot be forced into the mechanistic metalanguages of sciences like biology, physiology, chemistry, or theories like stimulus-response, punishment-reward, tension reduction, or homeostasis. Their metalingual expressions can be applied just as well to nonhuman forms of life or to matter. These sets of mechanistic constructs catch precisely facets that are not distinctively human.

By contrast, the foundational concepts and constructs that coform the language of formation science should point to the qualities that make human formation distinct from any other. Such qualities should pervade its profiles, features, patterns, and processes. They should be represented by a language that can interrelate the data and theories not only of psychologies but of other sciences, disciplines, arts, and traditions insofar as they are relevant to distinctively human life. Only such a language can facilitate the systematic apprehension, appraisal, and integration of all facets of formation.

This concern of the science for distinctively human qualities does not imply an underestimation of the methodological usefulness of mechanical models and languages in other sciences. Such an approach to abstracted aspects of the field remains methodologically justifiable, as long as the interpretation of the results does not pretend it can go beyond the restricted knowledge provided by the abstracted profile.

Metalanguages of Philosophical and of Formational Anthropologies

The language of formation science, especially in its anthropology, thus needs concepts and constructs that represent the distinctively human qualities of our life. The discipline traditionally concerned with such foundational characteristics is philosophical anthropology. This discipline studies the very being of the human life-form. It does so in the light of ontology, the study of being as such. Formation scientists, insofar as they are foundational theorists of distinctive humanness, are interested in formational implications of philosophical anthropology, and consequently in their underlying ontology.

Philosophical anthropologies and their underlying ontologies reconsider age after age the perennial questions engendered by human beings in the light of contemporary knowledge and experience. They express their insights in corresponding languages. The formation scientist has to deal with contemporary formation in research and reflection. The practitioner has to meet these issues concretely in such social institutions as the family, the schools, the workplace, the church, and the military. These issues are uppermost in the minds of directees and counselees.

To cope with the issues presented to them, practitioners must integrate past and present knowledge yielded by their own research as well as by their critical appraisal and integration of the findings of arts, sciences, disciplines, and traditions. Their effort to translate and transpose such insights into the basic language and theory of the science makes them necessarily interested in related formulations of past and contemporary philosophies. However, they do not assume these philosophical concepts lightly. They appraise them critically in the light of both historical and contemporary insights; in their applicability to this field and its auxiliary sources; and in their usefulness for the development of a comprehensive theory of proximate distinctively human formation.

One advantage of philosophical language is that it often points to qualities that can illumine the universal range of human life. Most findings of formation science are only limited generalizations, obtained by empirical study of a specific common or segmental range of the field. As such, they can only integrate the data that pertain to similar ranges. But concepts that are obtained from an explication of the essence of human life are in principle broad enough to integrate corresponding data and insights in a metalingual structure of ideas about universal formation.

Arts, sciences, disciplines, and form traditions are based on their own implicit philosophical anthropologies, which, though unspoken, permeate their language. To borrow their language uncritically is to borrow their philosophy. Often their selective anthropology is suitable only to the specific facet of life they may touch directly or indirectly. Critical appraisal of their implications for formation presupposes that the theorist makes explicit the anthropological assumptions hidden in their scientific, scholarly, aesthetic, or traditional metalanguage. Only then is dialogue possible between the assumptions of formation anthropology represented in its own language and those that underlie its auxiliary sources. The formation scientist must purify the languages of these diverse contributions of unwarranted extrapolations that arise from their implicit anthropologies.

This purifying appraisal may clarify what these scientists or traditionalists have established through observation or practice and what is merely due to their implicit anthropology. By separating the facts from the assumptions, we may find that their language points to a base of empirical data that, in its formative inferences, can be translated into the language of our own science and transposed into its theory.

This dialogical approach by formation scientists does not mean that they can call themselves professional philosophers. First of all, they usually do not create philosophical concepts and metalanguages. They only use and adapt them as another scientist might use certain concepts or constructs of physiology. A psychologist does not become a professional physiologist because of this borrowing.

Furthermore, they use only concepts of philosophical anthropology that prove relevant to the integration of the data of their own science and its auxiliary sources. Their procedure differs thus from the approach of professional philosophers. Nor do they claim a professional background that would qualify them to give form to a full-fledged philosophical anthropology with the same authority as that held by philosophers.

To return to the comparison given above, the use of philosophical language by formation theorists does not imply that they themselves are professional philosophers any more than the use of physiological language by psychologists implies that they are professional physiologists. In each case there is only a selective translation and transposition of some parts of another discipline on the basis of discoveries in one's own field of study.

The truth of the transposed concepts of philosophical anthropology cannot be proved or disproved by the methods specific to formation science itself. Formation science can only demonstrate that the transposed concepts are relevant to the appraisal and integration of the data disclosed by its own research. The same happens in other sciences. For example, the science of optics assumes that the laws of mathematics are valid. It makes use of them to support and integrate its own findings. However, optics makes no direct effort to prove or disprove the laws of mathematics.

Hence, the criterion for the selection of anthropological concepts or constructs is extrinsic to philosophical appraisal as such. It is an appraisal proper to formation science itself. The findings of this science illumine the usefulness of certain philosophical concepts for the integration of the results of its research. When we call such concepts *assumptions,* we mean only to indicate that they are assumptions for us as empirical scientists and that they are useful for us in the integrational dialogue occurring in the light of our own science. We cannot assert that they are merely assumptions. We are not competent professionally to prove such a statement by means of our own empirical methods. It may well be that various assumptions of our science are rightly considered certitudes in the disciplines from which we have transposed them.

The criterion that determines the selection and metalingual expression of such fundamental concepts is the principle of *applicability.* This principle states that *the formation scientist can translate and transpose those metalingual concepts of philosophical anthropology that can be used most adequately for the appraisal and compatible integration of the greatest number and variety of formationally relevant findings of formation science and its auxiliary sources.*

Anthropological Assumptions of Auxiliary Sciences

The argumentative appraisal concerning the usefulness of an assumption is thus formational-theoretical and not primarily philosophical. Not only formation science but also its auxiliary sciences may have borrowed philosophical assumptions. Their criterion, of course, is not the applicability of such assumptions to the integration of relevant formation insights from a variety of possible sources. They are interested in the applicability of their assumptions to the frame of reference appropriate to their specific object of research.

Hence, the assumptions borrowed by the auxiliary sciences are limited in scope. They may be adequate tools for the explanation of the field insofar as it appears in the limited perspective of their restricted object pole. A stimulus-response learning theory, for example, guides a psychology that researches the measurable stimulus-response aspects of behavior. This discipline may select as one of its anthropological assumptions the notion that human life is only a conditioned registering and reacting organism formed by the specific stimuli of its environment. In the light of this assumption, one may explain human life in all its facets in terms of stimulus and response.

As we have seen, a variety of facets of the field can indeed be considered in terms of one aspect, such as that of stimulus and response. Such a consideration of the whole field from this limited perspective may favor indirectly the unfolding and refining of formation science insofar as the science can profit for its growth from the insights of any auxiliary approach. Evidently the underlying philosophical assumption of this one type of auxiliary psychology is not necessarily applicable to other auxiliary approaches that explore different facets of the field. These cannot fully appear in the perspective of one partial theory, such as the stimulus-response learning theory. Its anthropological assumptions are useful only to a psychologist who attempts to perceive every facet of the field from this perspective.

A contrast may clarify our position. One of the implicit assumptions of the Rogerian theory seems to be that humans are capable of assuming responsibility for their own formation. This philosophical assumption has proved to be useful for Rogerians. However, stimulus-response psychologists as such cannot use Rogerian theory in their specific approach. Their restricted object pole does not imply aspects that manifest the presence of personal responsibility rooted in a relatively free intrasphere.

Metalingual Dialectics between Past and Present Sources of Formation Knowledge

Formation science fosters a dialogue between contemporary and historical resources of formation cognition. Attention to the past may preserve a metalanguage from succumbing to fascination with and uncritical adoption of a terminology that is in tune only with the passing zeitgeist.

Attentiveness to the languages of past as well as of present sources of formation knowledge protects scientists in some measure against the seduction of prevalent pulsations. The language that dominates an era may at times be mechanistic and deterministic; at other times, humanistic and personalistic, existentialistic or essentialistic, communitarian or individualistic, agnostic or transcendent, quantitative or qualitative. Each of these languages may point to one or another facet of human life. Formation science tries to interrelate them coherently by means of a transcendent language that, in principle, is applicable to as wide a variety as possible of validated findings surfacing in the past and present about distinctive humanness.

It should be clear at this point that formation science proposes its language as merely probable and provisional. The scientist knows that the lingual statements of empirical approaches are approximations at best and hence receptive to revision whenever a more probable formation cognition announces itself and demands a corresponding change in language. Experts in distinctively human living are also aware of the dynamic richness of the field of formation. They know that it can never be adequately expressed by any language, no matter its sophistication. This accounts for the essentially provisional nature of a scientific language.

Differences between the Metalanguage of Philosophies and of Formation Science

The foregoing considerations enable us to summarize the main differences between the languages of philosophies and of formation science. The difference in metalanguage is due to their differences in fundamental purposes, criteria, and methodologies.

Philosophical anthropology studies and expresses in its language the nature of human life in the light of being, whereas formation science investigates and expresses in its provisional language the human formation field in the light of empirical findings.

Formation science transposes concepts from the language of philosophy only insofar as they prove applicable to the integration of its own empirical findings and their proximate implementations.

With respect to the reliability of knowledge expressed in their language, many philosophies claim certitude. Formation science claims only that its language represents the highest probable cognition at this moment available to the best knowledge of its scientists.

The basic purpose of philosophy is not empirical praxis, whereas formation science is guided by its practical direction of disclosing and integrating empirical knowledge about distinctively human formation. Its aim in this is to find proximate directives for the more consonant formation, reformation, and transformation of human life in its upward transcendence.

The criterion for the aptness of philosophical language is its ability to express adequately the nature of human life as it discloses itself in the light of being. The criterion for the language of formation anthropology is its capacity to integrate meaningfully and consistently the empirical data, concepts, and constructs concerning human unfolding in concrete fields of presence and action.

The method of the philosophical anthropologist is a dialectical one in which the main voice is that of ontology. Philosophical anthropologists examine empirical findings in the light of ontology. They show the meaning of human life—as experientially and empirically disclosed—within the ontological view of reality expressed in their philosophical language.

The method of the formation scientist is dialectical, too, but its main voice is that of the empirically grounded concepts and constructs of its scientific language. In this light formation scientists may discover the usefulness of certain expressions of the language of philosophy for the illumination and integration of the empirical data they are examining. Such selected formulations are translated and transposed in such a way that they become an integral part of a formational frame of reference. This conceptual structure does not claim an ultimate view of the very nature of the human form of life, but only a provisional integration of empirical data regarding human formation in concrete fields as known presently.

Distinctively Human Quality of the Language of Formation Science

The object pole of this science, distinctively human formation, cannot be adequately represented by a language that is appropriate for sciences such as physiology, biology, physics, or mathematics. To do so would force insights and findings about distinctive humanness into a language that suits only the infrahuman facets of life. The language of the science takes over where such infrahuman languages leave off, that is to say, where the human formation field emerges as a unique, encompassing gestalt of distinctive transcendence. On this highest level of human integration, statistical, physical, physiological, neurological, biological, biochemical, or mathematical languages are of no avail, regardless of how well they are adapted to lower levels of integration.

The use of a mathematical language, for example, on this highest level of integration would alter the identity of the subject matter of our science. The expression of human formation in mathematical symbols would necessarily change the conception of its transcendent personal nature. Human formation is a holistic dynamic structure. It cannot be represented by an infrahuman metalanguage; it requires a distinctively human metalanguage.

The concepts and constructs that coform this language must be capable of representing appreciative apprehensions of formation as personal, transcendent, and qualitative, not as mechanical, functional, and quantitative. Our metalanguage refers to the directive presence of ascending human life in a field whose consonant formation events imply, in an ongoing way, personally formative directives.

Certain sciences must dehumanize their abstracted profiles of human life. They have to focus on the operation of specific biochemical or physical laws within this life. Such a methodological dehumanization would be impossible for formation science. It studies the human condition precisely in its distinctiveness from mere physical, biochemical, and neurological formation.

To be sure, the formation of people manifests processlike, mechanical, quantifiable features that can be abstracted and explored by sciences whose object is not the distinctively human or spiritual quality of life. These features are indispensable for the full functioning of the human organism. Therefore, their formational implications should be taken into account. They should be integrated—insofar as they are formationally relevant—into the metalingual framework of the science, but they should not dominate any aspect of its conceptual structure.

It would be unscientific and unrealistic to represent spiritual formation in languages in which the sciences of nondistinctively human object poles cast their findings and theories. These languages point to attributes the human formation process has in common with other species and with the universe of matter, but precisely for this reason these attributes are not distinctively human. Such a language would be animal-morphic, biomorphic, machine-morphic, computer-morphic. Applied to the distinctively human, it would be unduly metaphorical. While such a metaphorical use of language may be interesting from a literary point of view, it would be misleading in a science whose conceptual language must offer the best possible approximation to the reality it claims to disclose. Literary statements that suggest that what is human is somehow *like* animal life, or functions somewhat *like* a highly refined computer, or unfolds *like* a flower, are based on resemblances. They are not more than resemblances and hence should not be the basis of a scientific language, which is essentially different from literary language.

The metalanguage of, let us say, the science of the nervous systems of body and brain can effectively incorporate terms such as "electric potentials" and "neuronal circuits." It would be impossible to do justice to the distinctively human formation of our life by means of such a language alone.

The metalingual reconstruction of spiritual formation in its totality implies the incarnation of the transcendence dynamic in all facets of the field as conditioned in part by laws, processes, and patterns that as such are not distinctively human. Human formation implies always a bodily process in a formation field that is also material. An increasing number of sciences focus on the prehuman properties of these material conditions for human formation. They express their insights and findings in their own appropriate languages, augmenting immeasurably our understanding of the prehuman conditions and their possible implications for distinctively human living. Hence we can never neglect the interchange of metalingual dialectics between formation science and those auxiliary sciences that enlighten us about the prehuman conditions of our formation and their penetration of all facets of its field.

In this chapter we have focused our attention mainly on the metalanguages of auxiliary sciences. We will consider in the final chapter the languages of the auxiliary sources that we call formation traditions.

CHAPTER 27

Metalanguage of Formation Traditions

F or millennia of formation history, the records of a wide variety of formation traditions have been the only ones available regarding humanity's reflection on its distinctively human formation.

Every tradition has a language of its own, a universe of words and meanings expressing its principles and practices, its preferred directives and dispositions. This language unfolds during the history of the form tradition and is shared by its adherents. It is constantly updated and expanded. To appraise the possible contributions of a tradition and its masters is therefore, in great measure to learn their language.

The metalanguage of a tradition brings to life the experiences of men and women who reflected upon their formation from the viewpoint of a specific tradition. Critical appraisal of such a tradition cannot restrict itself to a repetition of its historical verbalization. It is necessary to analyze the language of tradition in service of its possible translation into the language of the science.

Formation scientists, therefore, engage first in affinitive and affective, then in argumentative appraisal. Usually they restrict themselves to communications of the form traditions and their masters that are relevant to their topic of research. Gaining intimate familiarity with their metalanguage enables them to resurrect the original meanings of these communications and to translate them into the more general metalanguage of the science without betraying their original message.

Personal and Segmental Modulation of Form Traditional Metalanguage

There exists not only a shared form traditional language but also a personal modulation or innovation of the common idiom. Often the adherents of a tradition give verbal form to their experiences as evoked by its teachings and practices and as communicated in a personal language that is partly their own. Some of them express a personal appreciative apprehension gained and nurtured in solitude. Others describe the formative experiences, methods, and practices that developed within an intimate group of adherents. In some instances such descriptions initiated a special school of spiritual formation within the larger tradition. The languaging of such a community or school may reveal preferences and particular ways of formation that are not as emphatically expressed in the more basic, general language of the same form tradition. For example, the Tantric school of the Buddhist and the Ignatian school of the Roman Catholic formation tradition do not cover in their metalanguages all facets of the entire form tradition that they particularize.

Metalanguage of the Masters of a Form Tradition

The language of a form tradition is significantly influenced by its acknowledged masters. In the course of the history of a tradition, these masters usually influence one another in some measure. Hence, their language may be somewhat similar. They seem to confirm each other's insights and experiences as evoked by the shared faith tradition underlying their formation tradition. The task of formation scientists is to appraise the more general relevance of their statements for the transcendent formation of a wider population that may not share the underlying faith tradition.

Formation scientists may also appraise the more personalized language of individual adherents of the tradition in their search for potentially relevant insights and experiences.

Generalization of Form Traditional Statements

The language of form traditions represents certain insights that have a general or even a universal relevance for distinctively human formation. They often generalize their statements on the basis of an approach that is different from that of auxiliary sciences. The latter may base their generalizations on logic. Many of the writers we refer to here may appeal mainly to the generality or universality of human formation experience.

Take, for instance, the *Diary of a Young Girl*, by Anne Frank, or *An Interrupted Life,* by Etty Hillesum. These diaries have a wide appeal, yet their generality is different from that of a work by Kant, Hegel, Husserl, or Rahner. The general relevance of these diaries is due to the generality of shared formation experiences. A significant number of people *can* share in facets of the formation journey of these authors because it reverberates in their own experience. Formation scientists may be able to articulate some fundamental structures of the experiences they describe, showing the probability that similar formation experiences may happen under analogous conditions.

Caution of Formation Scientists with Regard to
Generalizations of Personal Languaging

Formation scientists are cautious in regard to generalizing the personalized language of individual adherents of the form traditions they explore. They examine such language carefully to see whether it is in tune with the traditions the individuals claim to represent. If it is, then the probability seems greater that their language points to a more general formation truth. If not, one does not immediately reject the possibility that such statements may contain relevant insights for formation science, but one exercises more caution than usual.

Often the language may refer to experiences so personal that they exclude any probable generalization. Moreover, the lingual expression may be inaccurate or defective. Personal language may refer mainly to the latent residue of uniqueness that is implied in anyone's apprehension and appraisal. If it symbolizes only what is particular, it cannot be translated into the language of the science. Science, by its very nature, is about the general, not about the particular as particular. The merely unique, by definition, cannot be generalized to other situations. We can only approximate it indirectly, namely, insofar as it marginally manifests itself in more general experiences.

Caution should not lead to neglect. Individual attempts at expression may be awkward. Yet they may contain a core of general relevance. This core, when scientifically appraised, articulated, and elucidated, may lend itself to precise expression in the language of formation science. Researchers should pay attention also to the rituals of formation traditions. In many cases they are a celebration in symbols, acts, and words of formative experiences and their reenactment. They may point to more general, distinctively human directives that can be translated into formation language.

Diversification of the Metalanguage of
Formation Traditions and Their Masters

The metalanguage of formation traditions can take four main forms: experiential, formational-symbolical, faith-referential, and systematic-theoretical.

In general, experiential language directly describes formation experiences. Formational-symbolic language points to formative meanings that go beyond the mere informative meanings of its communications. Such expressions can be metaphorical or formational-relational, as we shall clarify further on.

Because form traditions are rooted in faith traditions, the researcher usually finds many expressions that root formational directives and experiences in an underlying faith tradition by means of a faith-referential language. It is important for researchers to distinguish this type of language from that which is experiential and theoretical. Language is faith-referential because of its rootedness in the faith tradition. It may introduce elements that are less apt to be generalized into directives applicable to those who do not adhere to the underlying faith tradition.

Some adherents or masters of a form tradition may have engaged in systematic reflection on its principles and practices. The results may have been expressed in traditional theory that offers scientists insights or suggestions that can correct, expand, refine, or deepen the hypothetical theory of formation science. The language of theory enables formation scientists to systematize a multiplicity of such form traditional reflections and theories. They must segregate traditional theoretical concepts and constructs from their particular faith-referential implications. This will facilitate their appraisal of potential contributions to formation science.

We shall now briefly consider the four types of metalanguage.

Experiential Language

Much spiritual writing is simply an expression in common or segmental language of formative events and the human response to them. Their quality is somewhat like that of the prescientific descriptions from which formation scientists start when they begin to examine an event. Many of these writings may already manifest some initial articulation and even elucidation of experiences. In a few writings, especially those of the masters of the form tradition concerned, we may even find a more elaborate articulation and elucidation, such as in the reflections of Saint Augustine in his *Confessions*; or in the writings of Trungpa, for instance, in his book on *Spiritual Materialism*; or in Saint John of the Cross's *Ascent of Mount Carmel*.

Formational-Symbolic Language

Words have both a symbolic informative and a symbolic formative function. Formation science and formation traditions are by their inherent direction primarily concerned with the symbolic-formational function of words.

Much experience in the realm of distinctively human formation is mystery-directed. It cannot be expressed adequately. In such a case, formational-transcendent symbols are needed that point to the inexpressible. Thus, writers of different traditions may say that the radical formation mystery is mere darkness or mere light. These words are not meant in a literal sense or as accurate descriptions. They point symbolically to ways in which the mystery can be experienced.

We call this symbolic language *formational* to express first that these symbols refer not to the informational realm of knowledge as, for instance, mathematical symbols do. Second, they may give some kind of form to the inexpressible, namely, a symbolic form. Third, when assimilated by us, they make us form receptive to what they symbolize. For example, formational symbols can help us to actualize our potency for openness to the transcendent. Fourth, they illumine and inspire form donation to our life and its field.

Formational-symbolic language can be metaphorical or relational. Without going deeper into this distinction here, we can illustrate it by an example from the writings of the Gospel. Christ is quoted as a master of transformation when he says, for instance, "I am the vine, you are the branches" (John 15:5). The symbol used here is at the same time metaphorical-symbolic and relational-symbolic. Metaphorically, it likens our oneness to the radical formation mystery as incarnated in Christ with the oneness we see between the branches and the vine. Relationally, this metaphor is used to express a formative relationship between the radical mystery as incarnated in this person and the people who adhere to it in faith. To give another example, in some Hindu traditions, the dwelling of the human being in the radical mystery is likened to a fish in the sea. This metaphor is used to express the total and continuous dependence of human life on the all embracing mystery of formation. The depth and intensity of this dependence cannot be exhaustively communicated in informative concepts alone. Hence the Hindu master resorts to a symbolic-metaphorical pointing. Again, this symbol is at the same time relational. For it symbolizes the full and uninterrupted relationship of dependency of human life on the pervading and sustaining divine presence. Thomas Aquinas and John of the Cross would express this mystery in the conceptual metalanguage of rational theology as "substantial union." This kind of language, in spite of its excellence, may be less affectively formative than the formational-symbolic language used by spiritual masters when they describe their experiences.

Faith-Referential Language

All faith traditions contain ultimate directives for human formation. Form traditions are about proximate directives. They respond to the question: How can a population or its segments live congenially, compatibly, compassionately, courageously, and competently their ultimate faith directives within a specific field?

Form traditions are a mixture of directives of our faith tradition and of those that come from our apprehension and appraisal of a concrete field in which we have to live out our ultimate faith directives. These later appraisals of ours are influenced by prescientific and scientific apprehensions and appraisals by people who do not adhere to our own faith tradition. One condition for their acceptance by us as proximate directives of our own life is that they are compatible with our own ultimate faith directives.

All formation directives are thus in some measure modulated by the underlying faith directives. This fact gives rise to a form traditional language that is totally identical neither with everyday secular language nor with the language of the science. This metalanguage refers, often implicitly and by subtle connotation, to certain underlying faith assumptions.

Consider for a moment clinical psychological faith and form traditions. These can be found in psychologies that are built on the clinical observations and personal reflections of their initiators. Unlike strictly experimental psychologists, these creators of psychological methods of healing may be inclined to develop implicitly a web of ideological assumptions about the nature, aims, and modes of human formation. Because these assumptions cannot be proven, they have to be adhered to with some kind of ideological faith or belief system.

A case in point is the Jungian ideological faith and form tradition. The Jungian tradition contains assumptions that are individualistic, panpsychic, and implicitly pantheistic. These assumptions tend to make mere functional transcendence ultimate. The Jungian faith tradition pervades implicitly the Jungian form tradition as expressed in the metalanguage of his concepts, constructs, and symbols. Concrete therapeutic experience made Jung take into account the actual formation field of his patients. Accordingly he developed a formation tradition that is a mixture of ultimate ideological faith directives and proximate, effective formation wisdom.

Formation scientists may translate the formationally relevant contributions of Jung into the language of their science. In that case they have to pay close critical attention to the ideological faith references that may be implied in Jung's language.

Systematic-Theoretical Language

The experts of certain formation traditions may reflect on the pertinent events, experiences, directives, and methods of their lived traditions in light of their religious or ideological faith assumptions. Some of them feel the need to order the results of these reflections in a coherent, consistent way. They devise for this ordering systematic and integrative concepts and constructs. These are expressed in a corresponding theoretical metalanguage. This is especially true of specific schools of formation that may develop within any foundational formation tradition.

Such systematic-theoretical concepts or constructs may be taken over from what is initially experiential, formational-symbolic, or faith-referential language only. For example, when certain Buddhist formation traditions speak of *satori*, we realize that this word first meant to express symbolically an experience the adherents of that tradition went through at particular moments of their meditation exercises. Presently, because this word seems to point for those adherents to a state of mind after which they all aspire, it has become also a kind of systematic term. The word can now be found in metalingual descriptions of the Japanese Buddhist formation tradition, outlining the path of meditation.

In the Christian formation tradition, we find the metalingual expressions *purgative, illuminative,* and *unitive.* Here again these words pointed originally to certain experiences along the way of transformation. They belonged to experiential language. Gradually, however, they were chosen also as theoretical terms to order systematically the knowledge of certain religious form traditions.

The language of the formation scientist should at least in basic intent, if not always in fact, be transdenominational, transideological, transcultural, ecumenical, and transecumenical in the widest sense. Otherwise it cannot serve a science of basic distinctively human formation applicable to the majority of people anywhere who are genuinely striving for transcendent transformation of their life. This does not mean that the science and its language can replace a consonant formation tradition. On the contrary, it should encourage people to commit themselves wholeheartedly to the consonant tradition to which they may feel called.

Formation traditions, precisely because they are rooted in faith traditions, offer a depth dimension and a motivational power the science can never offer. The science, however, can enrich such traditions with proximate practical insights into the realistic predicaments of their adherents in concrete fields of presence and action.

Relational-Symbolic Language

The paradigm of the formation field, with its interrelated ranges, regions, spheres, dimensions, integrational forms, and all-pervading relationship to the formation mystery, points to the central role of relations in human formation. In accordance with that role, we can expect in the metalanguage of form traditions many symbolic references to relationships. In this case the relationships are seen in the light of the religious or ideological faith tradition that underlies the form tradition.

To appraise relational-symbolic language in traditions, we should realize that all language is in some way relational. Take a simple word like *closet*. It can be understood only in relationship to a set of other words, such as inside and outside the closet, putting things in or out of the closet, closing or opening the closet. When infants hear the word closet for the first time, they will not fully know what it means. Gradually, they will hear how the people around them use the word closet in different sentences, such as "I put your toys in the closet," "Please, open the door of the closet," or "Let's hide in the closet." In such sentences the word closet is related to other words that express some property, possibility, or quality of the closet. They tell what closets are used for, what they look like inside, and so forth.

In and through such contexts, it becomes more and more clear to the child what people mean when they say closet. Briefly, we learn languages by learning to understand their words in relation to other words. This is one of the reasons why the learning of the metalanguage of a science or a form tradition takes time. Initially many of the words may seem exotic to us. It is only by hearing or reading them for some time in a variety of contexts that they begin to make sense.

Each word is clarified in its meaning and function by its relationship to other words. One conclusion is that students of formation, exploring the language of a tradition, must be careful not to take words out of context. They must make themselves familiar with these expressions by studious reading, extensive enough to allow these words to light up in relation to other words that clarify their meaning. Only then can such words be appraised fairly and objectively. The principle behind this appraisal of words is that a word is itself precisely in its distinction from and in its relation to many other words within the same language.

Take an original master of formation, like Kierkegaard. When we read some of his religious essays several times, words that we initially misunderstood, such as "spy for the Eternal," begin gradually to light up for us with the meaning he attaches to this expression. We discover that the metalanguage of Kierkegaard is formed around key words. Any key word he uses is related to the other words that coform his metalanguage.

Any lingual expression in a form tradition belongs to a system of words typical of that tradition. A metalingual word may sound the same as a common lingual word, yet it has a different meaning. Take, for instance, the word *dance* in the religious tradition of the population of Bali or in the context of a rock-and-roll concert.

An interesting example of taking words out of the context of a form tradition and misunderstanding them can be found in the appraisal of some reviewers of the diary of Dag Hammarskjöld, *Markings.* In the context of his Christian tradition, Hammarskjöld expressed his belief in oneness with Christ as a faithful follower and believer. He felt he had to suffer and perhaps sacrifice his life like Christ did.

Some reviewers did not take time to appraise the age-old meaning of this language by studying its traditional context. They tended to place his words in the context of the language of psychiatry. Appraising the words of his traditional metalanguage in relation to a clinical metalanguage led them to conclude that he must have been paranoid in his expectation of suffering and disturbed in his imagination insofar as it made him believe he was Christ.

Lingual Symbols of Interformative
Human and Transcendent Relationships

In any specific lingual system all words are related. Over and above this general lingual relationship, certain words express in and by themselves an essential relationship of potential or actual interformation with a human person or with the transcendent, radical formation mystery.

The word *friend*, for example can be understood only in relationship to another person who is one's friend. Insofar as this relationship is actualized, interformation will happen between the friends. The word also announces indirectly one's less intimate relationship to those who are not friends. Not only that, such words of human relationship carry symbolic-formative meanings that may be partly nonfocal, either for a population or for a segment or an individual within that population. For some populations the word may have no deeper meaning than acquaintance; for others it may mean something more than acquaintance and less than intimate friendship; it may mean comrade. For certain people friendship may carry a bitter taste, with the idea that you cannot really depend on it when you are in trouble.

In other words, the history of interformation in regard to friendship coforms its symbolic-formative meaning. Therefore, words mean different things to different populations, segments, and individuals because of their differences in formation history. Hence formation scientists, examining the language of a specific form tradition, should bracket what its words of human or transcendent relationships mean to themselves dependent on their own formation history. They should study with an unprejudiced mind the different meanings that similar words may have in the language of the tradition they are exploring.

This principle applies to all words such as father, mother, husband, wife, superior, inferior, brother, sister, family, teacher, minister, or student. Those who experienced respect and love from the people thus named will not attach the same meaning to such words as those who felt misunderstood, disrespectfully treated, oppressed, discriminated against, or ridiculed. For many people, or for whole segments of the population, such words may be crystalizations of contradictory meanings dependent on how they experienced the relationships conveyed by them. For oppressed black minorities in certain populations, the word *boss* may have a pejorative connotation.

Lived relationships color each word we use. Words are literally filled with formative-symbolic meanings. This is one of the reasons why scientists and professionals coin scientific words or a metalanguage that is not subject to the ongoing variation of emotional meanings attached to words as used in everyday parlance.

In form traditions certain words of ordinary language may be used also to signify relationships to the transcendent. For example, certain traditions may call God "Father." Others may speak about female deities. These words may have different meanings for different persons at various times of their life. During the transition period in which people have to free themselves from a child-parent relationship, the words father and mother may have a less attractive meaning than during childhood (presupposing that children experience a good relationship with their parents).

Therefore, formation scientists, investigating the formative meaning of such words in a tradition, must pay close attention also to the phasic segment in which the tradition is trying to give form to life, for instance, childhood, adolescence, young adulthood, midlife, or old age.

The term "relational-symbolic" in formation science means, as noted previously, that a word signifying human or transcendent relationships is not merely informing us about that relationship but carries over and above this a system of interrelated symbolic meanings that are formative.

Think, for instance, of the word *superior*. Such a word conveys the information that a person has some position of control in relation to ourselves or other persons in particular areas of life. But over and above this information, the word carries a wealth of other symbolic meanings regarding our concrete apprehensions, appraisals, memories, images, anticipations, affects, acts, and dispositions in relation to anyone who is called superior. These symbols are not merely informational; they are formative. They give form to our concrete relationships with the persons who are our superiors. Hence words are powerful means that can give form to the acts and dispositions of people. Preachers and politicians often play on these dynamic formational-symbolic meanings.

Even before a word is filled with personal experiential meanings during our formation history, it already carries symbolic power due to the formative impact of those who communicate the word to us in the first place. A word must come from somewhere. It is communicated by a language community that initiates us into the meaning to be given to a word, not only in its informational signification but also in its multiple symbolic potencies. People speak the word in a special way in various contexts, often accompanied with meaningful sign language, gestures, and facial expressions.

Take for instance, the difference with which an Indian tribe speaks about the elders and the way in which contemporary Americans may speak about the old man. Their words signify informationally the same genetic relationship, but there is a difference between the symbolic-formational meanings of the same expression.

Formative Power of Words

The formative power of a word comes initially from the community in which we live, and it can give form to our relationships for a lifetime. This power can, of course, be modulated by later personal experiences.

The same applies to our relationship to the transcendent mystery. Take, for example, the litany of names used in the Islamic formation tradition for Allah. There is no doubt that hearing these names spoken from childhood in a religious setting may form in a worshipful way the relationship between the Muslim and Allah. This example points also to the formative meaning of meditation on holy names. By naming the transcendent in such ways, the radical formation mystery may come alive for us in a forming fashion. These insights have to be taken into account when we explore the impact of a form traditional language.

We should be aware that, unlike the language of formation science itself and its auxiliary sciences, the languages of formation traditions are filled with common words. These traditions assign to these words different informative and formative meanings. Because of the latter, it becomes a metalanguage.

For example, the word *Father* as used in various Christian traditions for God has a different meaning than the word father as used in ordinary parlance to signify the biological relationship to a parent and to the many symbolic, formative relationships included in that word, dependent as they are on the speaking community. There is an analogy, but the word Father as given to the radical formation mystery has a transcendent meaning that we do not find in our everyday relationship to our biological father. Confusion between the two different realms of meaning can lead to serious religious misunderstandings.

Relational-Symbolic Quality of Mythical Metalanguages

So far we have spoken about symbolic expressions that are relational because they symbolize formative relationships between people and between them and the formation mystery. We find another kind of symbolic-formative relation in the language of the traditions we study, namely, relationships between words that belong to the same verbal constellation. We refer here more specifically to those constellations of words in traditions that coform their mythical language.

Metalingual mythical narratives are symbolic constellations about a specific formative subject of the traditions concerned, for example, about the creation of the world. The mythical story is a unified symbolic constellation because each word in the language derives its specific meaning from the mythical constellation as a whole and from its interformation with the rites and religious relationships that have been formed around this myth. A number of faith and form traditions gave form to the metalingual myths about the origin of the world. Each word in such a mythical metalanguage is interwoven with and receives its specific symbolic meaning from the other metalingual forms in the myth. Formation scientists must carefully appraise each word in relation to all other words of this specific language. They must resist the temptation to appraise them in light of other languages, such as those of genetics, anthropology, geology, astronomy, or physics. The same applies to stories that in mythical language describe mystical formation experiences. Uncritical transposition of such words into, for example, the language of psychiatry or clinical psychology will necessarily lead to their misapprehension.

Formative Implications of Relational Metalanguage

As we have seen, certain words in the languages of traditions, may first of all *inform* us about relationships. They may also have the potency to express and make such relations *formative* for people. Insofar as they can do so, we call them formative-relational words. They give a certain form to our intrasphere as appreciatively apprehending its unique relationship to other forms in its pre- and outer spheres. Conversely, the same relational words endow the forms to which we relate with new formative meanings in relation to us and to themselves.

For example, one may identify a person as a spiritual director. Let us say he or she has been appointed by a school or community as the person available to counsel others spiritually in accordance with the directives of the form tradition to which they adhere. While the institution concerned has informed people about this appointment, the relational expression "spiritual director" may remain merely informative. In that case they neither relate to this director in a formative fashion nor fully apprehend and appreciate what the expression "spiritual director" or "direction" means in their tradition. The formative depth dimension of this use of language may not yet be fully appreciated by them. They may never have had the experience of spiritual direction in their life.

Imagine now, that you seriously ask this appointed person to see you in spiritual direction. Gradually, during the process of direction, you begin to appreciate what this formative relationship in terms of your shared faith and form tradition can mean for you. You may find yourself speaking with respect, genuine appreciation, and more depth and docility about this facet of your tradition. The term "spiritual direction" and related words as used in your tradition begin to be filled with formative-relational meanings. You realize that this relationship discloses something new about yourself as a committed adherent to this tradition and its language.

The formative relationship of the director to you makes you aware in a new and deeper way of who you are as a cared-for participant in this tradition, as a person called uniquely by the formation mystery within this specific historical setting.

In other words, the relational symbol cultivated by the language of your tradition points to a graced relationship that can give form to your life as illumined by the deeper sources of the tradition that you share with your spiritual director. Similarly you begin to look with new eyes on the spiritual director who, in his or her own way, interforms with you. The director cannot give form to your life without disclosing something of who he or she is. Hence you see your director in a new light. Somehow, your trust and docility, the communication of your problems, and your response to counsel make you *be* in a new way. This relationship also discloses to the director some previously unknown facet of who you are.

Later on when you hear or read about spiritual direction, the words themselves have gained the power to revive an experiential awareness of what this special forming relationship means in your life. Indeed, the metalingual expression begins to exercise some power of its own. It has become a dynamic expression, rich with meanings that somehow affect you inwardly.

Hence, students of the languages of formation traditions must try to probe the formative potencies of relational words as used uniquely in each tradition. As scientists of formation, they cannot be satisfied with the merely informative meanings of these words. This meaning is admittedly easier to detect and define. The dynamic form potencies of the living language of any tradition can be appreciated only by evaluation of the specific relational formative power of the words used by the adherents with the unique shades of meaning each tradition may give to them. We should always remember that metalanguages are not only defined by new words not found in the common language, but also by common words used by the adherents of a tradition in a special fashion somewhat different from their use in everyday parlance.

Part of the task of the researcher is to articulate and elucidate objectively these fine nuances of formative-relational meanings insofar as they touch on a research topic and event. Only then can one do justice both to the tradition he or she explores and to the translation of its language into that of the science of formation.

Afterword

T he afterword to this book can be read as a transition to our next volume, which will treat the topic of transcendent formation. In that final volume we will consider the dynamics of what we have called our *integrational forms* of life. We will relate these dynamics to our aspiration for transformation. We will also relate them to consonant formation traditions, rooted in belief systems. For they are supreme sources of enlightenment and power for our transcendent integration. At the end of that volume the basics of this relationship to traditions will be illustrated in one of many traditions, that of the Christian, familiar to most of us.

Our question at the end of this book must be: Are the scientific methodology we expounded and its results compatible with the transcendent integration to which we feel called in our personal and social life?

To answer this question, we shall retrace some of our steps. At the beginning of Volume 1, we began by looking at the split in human formation. We saw that this split was deepened by opposite materialistic or idealistic, behavioristic or existentialistic, views of human life and its ways of knowing. We proposed formation thinking as one possible contribution to the healing of this dissonance. Accordingly, in Volumes 1, 2, and 3, we worked out a transmaterialistic and transidealistic, a transbehavioristic and transexistentialistic, theory of distinctively human formation in its main features. We described our field of life in its pre-, intra-, and extrastructures of formative consciousness as well as in the infra-, trans,-and prefocal, and focal regions of the same consciousness.

Finally, in this fourth volume we indicated how the split between materialistic and idealistic formation, discussed in Volume 1, generated a similar split in the social, psychological, and educational sciences. Hence our main concern in this volume was the development of a scientific methodology that would transcend this split within the human sciences while saving their methods and findings insofar as they could be made relevant to

277

distinctively human formation. Our earlier attempt in the psychology department of Duquesne University to transcend both behavioristic and existentialistic psychologies by an anthropological psychology influenced the development of this dialogical-integrational methodology for formation science. The initiation of formation science required that we transcend psychology itself.

The question that now emerges can be formulated as follows: Can this new holistic understanding of our field of formative consciousness and the scientific results of this proposed empirical methodology for the exploration of this field bring about a transcendent integration of human life as formative? If so, to what degree? Do we have to add something to the outcomes of empirical scientific exploration to make our transcendent integration of life possible? Our next volume will present an answer to this question. By way of transition to that volume we give here only a few pointers to an answer.

We have seen in this volume, specifically in the chapters on language, that our everyday common or segmental, form traditional versions of thought and expression are not adequate to the most central timeless problems of formation as modulated by our actual formation field as a whole. Our syncretic form traditional apprehensions and appraisals, as pragmatically selected and prescientifically applied by us to the emergencies of everyday formation, are not sufficient. Their routine use tends to neglect the historical, scientific, theoretical, and metalingual perspectives that we have seen are necessary. We need the latter for a coherent in-depth understanding of human formation as a whole and as an unfolding self-correcting knowledge by ongoing dialogue in the course of the history of human formation. Hence a first condition for transcendent integration of our life from a critical scientific perspective will be sufficient acquaintance with certain basic findings of the science of formation. This science can help us to rise above our everyday pragmatic versions of our unexplored syncretions of religious and secular form traditions by which many of us live today prefocally in our pluriform societies.

We have also seen that existing positive and human sciences rarely deal adequately with the basic problems of distinctively human formation. One reason for this is that they have not articulated and elucidated sufficiently the field of formative consciousness in its main structures, dynamics, and conditions. Nor have they developed a methodology that is rooted in the experienced, evident, and successive operations of the human mind. These are our certain anchors into reality. From this certain self-evident ground, we can safely venture forth into our wider field of increasing probability. Other sciences failed, moreover, to give sufficient attention to their underlying anthropologies. They did not examine to what degree these might be contaminated by the split between materialistic and idealistic, behavioristic and existentialistic, perspectives. This is why the economic, political, social, therapeutic, or inspirational-edifying solutions they propose do not necessarily touch the deepest problematics of life's formation. They may effect working compromises among tensions in and between different dimensions, ranges and regions of personal and social life. Such effective compromises may be helpful, yet they may detour us from the path toward transcendent integration in depth if they are not complemented and modulated by transcendent approaches.

Therefore, in our treatment of the methodological category of dialogical consulation we outlined methods of reflection of both the methods of the auxiliary sciences and of their findings before and during the translation and transposition of some of them into our own methodology or into our integrational frame of reference.

Another basic concept to which we continually referred is that of the formation mystery, cosmic and radical. We pointed to this all-embracing presence as drawing us out in saving consonance or love. We described its operation as suffusing us with its own consonance or love so that it may radiate in and through our personal and social presence. In Volume 3 we saw that this gift of transcendent consonance or love generates faith, hope, and charity, which become concretized in their subordinated dispositions of congeniality, compatibility, compassion, courage, and competence. These were shown to express themselves further in loving confirmation, collaboration, concelebration, and in social presence in justice, peace, and mercy.

The gift of consonant love is the ultimate source of transcendent integration. As has been pointed out in the beginning of Volume 3, it lights up for us the *appreciable* truth, goodness, and beauty of the original founding forms granted by the mystery to people, animals, plants, events, and things. It integrates our life of formative apprehension, of affinitive and affective appreciation, of affirmation, of functional vital and sociohistorical incarnation; it generates in us faith, hope, and charity. All of these supreme epiphanies of the formation mystery counteract our pseudo-foundational pride-form—the autarkic, self-centering, isolating form of life. Accordingly they liberate us from our self-encapsulating personal, ethnic, or cultural prejudices and pulsations. The subordinated dispositions mentioned above enable us, after this intraspheric liberation, to strive effectively for a more integrated social field of just, peaceful, and merciful interformation.

The more we progress on this road toward transcendent integration, the more we can withstand what we have described as dissonant deformative pulsations, pulsions and accretions.

Transcendent integration strives to embrace all appearances in our field of formative consciousness. We have argued in this volume that the emergence of the empirical sciences and their impact on the empirical way of thought in educated people, on the historical sciences, on the humanities, on philosophies, and on theologies signified a revolution in formation thought and practice. Transcendent integration of all appearances cannot succeed if it neglects this major impact on contemporary formation. Nor can it blindly subject itself to this appearance alone. For the emergence of empirical thought is only one, albeit a major, epiphany of the mystery of formation in our history. Our tentative response has been that transcendent consonance—or the dynamic love of the mystery, as expressed in faith, hope, charity and their subordinated dispositions—must enter through us into the scientific enterprise itself. It will enhance its dynamism, purify its intentionality and motivation, deepen the asceticism of scientific dedication, inspire mutual confirmation, collaboration, and concelebration among scientists, and foster the relevance of science to social presence in justice, peace, and mercy.

We have stressed throughout this book that distinctively human formation in its upward ascendance to transformation is historical. The historical ascent of humanity toward transformation is precisely an ascent because it is a journey with an uncertain empirical outcome, with ups and downs, victories and defeats, peaks and valleys. We cannot know for certain whether humanity will fulfill this aspiration empirically in formative fidelity to the mystery that draws it out over the past millennia and the millennia to come. Historical development is by definition a dialogical development. Hence our emphasis in this volume on *dialogical* dispositions and *dialogical* methods of inquiry. The only way to play our part in the awe-inspiring saga of human transformation is by means of critical creative dialogue with the popular syncretic form traditional versions of life as expressed in ordinary parlance. This should be followed by a respectful dialogue of experts with the theoretical expressions of the particular formation traditions that influence this everyday syncretism. For great formation traditions have their own legitimate authorities and their spiritual masters who, in dialogue with their own acknowledged scholarly experts and practitioners, formulate critically in their own metalanguages what is basic for each tradition of practical formation.

This critical creative dialogue must extend itself to the sciences, arts, and disciplines that probe methodically, with the refined tools of their metalanguages and methods, the formation events vaguely apprehended, appraised, and formulated by means of ordinary form traditional languages.

Without such continual dialogue, an ongoing preparation of humanity for transcendent integration or transformation will be delayed unnecessarily.

The attentive reader may realize that we have touched, in this summation of preparatory approaches to the transformation of humanity, upon all successive phases of the methodology of formation science. The dialogical attention of our scientists leads to a selection of a specific formation topic. This is followed by a first articulation and initial elucidation—by means of ordinary lingual symbols—of this selected topic as lived in a concrete formation event, apprehended in everyday life. This first articulation lays the groundwork for an emergent awareness of the ambivalence and of the sociohistorical pulsations, accretions, personal subjectivistic affinities, and affects that obscure the essence of this first kind of uncritical apprehension. Yet it makes us appreciate the hidden core of truth that initially can only be approached implicitly in this way. A second dialogical articulation and initial elucidation, now in terms of scientific language and theory, grants us a higher perspective. The theory used and expanded during these theoretical considerations needs the guarantee of methodical correctness to assure us that the highest probability available at this moment of history can be approximated—hence the consultative dialogue with relevant theories and findings in other sciences.

All this prepares us for a deeper elucidation, by means of the categorical elucidation methodology, of hidden dynamics and their facilitating and hindering conditions, expressions, and consequences. This deeper elucidation of dynamics enables us also to disclose our inherent transcendence dynamic and the way our striving for integration within this dynamic can integrate the conflicting dissonances in our field. In this regard, formation science enables human reason to glimpse the promised land. However, it is not sufficient by itself alone to make us enter it. As we shall see in the final volume, this preparation has to be completed by the mystery as it discloses itself in transscientific ways in the great faith and formation traditions of humanity. Their sacred writings disclose to our higher reason facets of transformation that transcend scientific functional rationality without becoming irrational. Formation scientists cannot prove by their own empirical methods the truth or falsehood of such transrational disclosures. That is the supreme task of philosophers and theologians. What formation scientists can and should do is to investigate empirically the observable consequences of such disclosures and their implementations in the transcendent formation of various populations.

What is this transcendent integration? It is the activation of the gift of our transformation potency. This potency enables us—through the drawing power of the mystery—to participate congenially, compatibly, courageously, and competently in formation wisdom and knowledge that come to us directly or indirectly via both popular and expert form traditional knowledge and via formation science insofar as it has gathered for us relevant findings and insights from all its auxiliary sources.

At present we need a basic familiarity with this wisdom and knowledge, communicated to us if necessary in ordinary language. A person or population on the way to transcendent integration may grow through this understanding beyond the dissonance of contemporary mind and heart. This progress on the path of transcendence readies us for communication with our unique foundational and potentially integrative form of life. In the hidden source of this foundational form dwells the formation mystery drawing us out lovingly. This transcendent integrative source strives to realize our transcendent integration concretely over a lifetime via the integrational life-forms: the foundational, core, current apparent, and actual forms of life. Their dynamics will be discussed in our final volume. The same mystery discloses itself in the great formation traditions of humanity insofar as they are consonant. Hence the necessity to deal in the next volume also with the dialogical interaction between the dynamics of the integrational forms and the transcendent disclosures of the consonant formation traditions.

Bibliography

Books

Acham, K. *Philosophie der Sozialwissenschaften*. Freiburg i.B.: Alber, 1983.

Achinstien, P. *Concepts of Science*. Baltimore: Johns Hopkins University Press, 1968.

Adorno, T. W., and others, *Der Positivismusstreit in der deutschen Soziologie*. Edited by Heinz Mauz and Friedrich Fürstenberg. Neuwied and Berlin: Luchterhand, 1969.

Alexander, F., and S. Selesnick. *The History of Psychiatry*. New York: Harper and Row, 1966.

Allport, G. W. *Becoming*. New Haven, Conn.: Yale University Press, 1955.

_____ . *Pattern and Growth in Personality*. New York: Holt, Rinehart & Winston, 1961.

_____ . *Personality*. New York: Henry Holt and Co., 1957.

_____ . *Personality and Social Encounter*. Boston: Beacon Press, 1960.

Alquier, F. *Le désir de l'éternité*. Paris: University of France, 1947.

Anderson, H., ed. *Creativity and Its Cultivation*. New York: Harper, 1959.

_____ , and L. Savary. *Passages: A Guide for Pilgrims of the Mind*. New York: Harper and Row, 1972.

Angyall, A. *Foundations for a Science of Personality*. New York: Commonwealth Fund, 1941.

_____ . *Foundations for a Science of Personality*. Cambridge, Mass.: Harvard University Press, 1941.

Apel, K. O. *Analytic Philosophy of Language and the "Geisteswissenschaften."* Dordrecht: Reidel, 1976.

_____ . *Hermeneutik und Ideologiekritik*, Frankfurt: Suhrkamp, 1972.

Arasteh, A. *Toward Final Personality Integration*. New York: Halsted Press, 1975.

Arendt, H. *The Life of the Mind*. Vol. 2. New York and London: Harcourt Brace Jovanovich, 1978.

Argyle, M. *The Scientific Study of Social Behavior*. London: Methuen and Company, Ltd., 1957.

Argyris, C. *Inner Contradictions of Rigorous Research*. New York: Academic Press, 1980.

Arieti, S. *The Intrapsychic Self*. New York: Basic Books, 1967.

Arnold, M. *Emotion and Personality*. 2 vols. New York: Basic Books, Inc., 1961.

_____ , and J. Gasson. *The Human Person*. New York: Ronald Press, 1954.

Assagioli, R. *Psychosynthesis*. New York: Hobbs, Dorman, 1965.

283

Atkinson, R. F. *Knowledge and Explanation in History: An Introduction to the Philosophy of History.* Ithaca, N.Y.: Cornell University Press, 1978.

Ayer, A. J. *Language, Truth and Logic.* 2nd ed. New York: Dover, 1952.

Barber, M. *The Foundations of Phenomenology.* Cambridge, Mass.: Harvard University Press, 1943.

Barnett, H. G. *Innovation: The Basis of Cultural Change.* New York: McGraw-Hill Book Co., Inc., 1965.

Barral, M. R. *Merleau-Ponty: The Role of the Body Subject in Interpersonal Relations.* Pittsburgh, Pa.: Duquesne University Press, 1965.

Barrett, W. *Irrational Man: A Study in Existential Philosophy.* Garden City, N.Y.: Doubleday, 1958.

Bateson, G. *Mind and Nature: A Necessary Unity.* New York: E. P. Dutton, 1979.

Becker, E. *The Revolution in Psychology,* New York: The Free Press, 1964.

Berdiaev, N. *The Meaning of the Creative Act.* Translated by D. A. Lowrie. New York: Harper, 1955.

Berger, P. *The Sacred Canopy.* Garden City, N.Y.: Doubleday and Company, Inc., 1967.

_____, B. Berger, and H. Kellner. *The Homeless Mind.* New York: Vintage Books, 1973.

_____, and H. Kellner. *Sociology Reinterpreted: An Essay on Method and Vocation.* Garden City, N.Y.: Anchor Books, 1981.

_____, and T. Luckmann. *The Social Construction of Reality.* Garden City, N.Y.: Doubleday and Company, Inc., 1966.

Bergson, H. *Creative Evolution.* Translated by A. Mitchell. New York: Random House, 1944.

_____. *The Creative Mind.* Translated by M. L. Anderson. New York: The Philosophical Library, Inc., 1946.

_____. *The Two Sources of Morality and Religion.* Translated by R. Audra, C. Brereton, and the assistance of W. Carter. New York: Henry Holt, 1935.

Bernard, L. L. *Instinct, A Study in Social Psychology.* New York, 1924.

Bertocci, P., and R. Millard. *Personality and the Good.* New York: David McKoy Co., 1963.

Binswanger, L. *Grundformen und Erkenntnis menschlichen Daseins.* Zurich: MaxNiehans, 1942.

Black, M. *Margins of Precision: Essays in Logic and Language.* Ithaca, N.Y.: Cornell University Press, 1970.

Bleicher, J. *Contemporary Hermeneutics: Hermeneutics as Method, Philosophy and Critique.* London: Routledge & Kegan Paul, 1980.

Boelen, B. *Existential Thinking.* New York: Herder and Herder, 1971.

_____. *Philosophical Orientation.* Pittsburgh, Pa.: Duquesne University, 1958.

Bollnow, O. F. *Studien zur Hermeneutik.* Vol. 1, *Zur Philosophie der Geisteswissenschaften.* Freiburg i.B.: Alber. 1982.

Bosanquet, B. *Knowledge and Reality.* St. Clair Shores, Mich.: Scholarly Press, 1976.

Braithwaite, R. B. *Scientific Explanation: A Study of the Function of Theory, Probability and Law in Science.* Cambridge: Cambridge University Press, 1955.

Brentano, F. *Psychologie vom empirischen Standpunkte.* Leipzig: Duncker and Humblot, 1947.

_____ . *Psychology from an Empirical Standpoint.* Edited by L. L. Mc-Alister and translated by A. C. Rancurello, D. B. Terrell, and L. L. McAlister. New York: Humanities Press, 1973.

Brody, B. A., ed. *Readings in the Philosophy of Science.* Englewood Cliffs, N.J.: Prentice-Hall, 1970.

Brown, C. W., and E. E. Ghiselli. *Scientific Method in Psychology.* New York: McGraw-Hill Book Co., Inc., 1955.

Brown, H. I. *Perception, Theory and Commitment: The New Philosophy of Science.* Chicago: University of Chicago Press, 1977.

Brown, J. *Mind, Brain and Consciousness: The Neuropsychology of Cognition.* New York: Academic Press, 1977.

Brown, R. H. *A Poetic for Sociology: Toward a Logic of Discovery for the Human Sciences.* Cambridge: Cambridge University Press, 1977.

Buber, M. *Between Man and Man.* Translated by R. G. Smith. New York: Macmillan, 1965.

_____ . *I and Thou.* New York: Charles Scribner's Sons, 1970.

Bubner, R. *Handlung, Sprache und Vernunft.* Frankfurt: Suhrkamp, 1976.

Buhler, K. *Die geistige Entwicklung des Kindes.* 6th ed., Jena: G. Fischer, 1930.

Bulhof, I. *Wilhelm Dilthey: A Hermeneutical Approach to the Study of History and Culture.* The Hague: Nijhoff. 1980.

Bunge, M. *Causality and Modern Science.* 3rd rev. ed. Cleveland: World, 1963.

Burtt, E. A. *The Metaphysical Foundations of Modern Physical Science.* Garden City, N.Y.: Anchor Books, 1954.

Buytendijk, F. J. J. *Phenomenologie de la rencontre.* Paris: Desclée de Brouwer, 1952.

_____ . *De Vrouw. Haar Verschijning, Natuur en Bestaan.* Utrecht: Spectrum, 1951.

_____ . *La Femme.* Bruges: Editions Desclée de Brouwer, 1954.

Campbell, D. T., and J. C. Stanley. *Experimental and Quasi-Experimental Designs for Research.* Chicago: Rand McNally, 1963.

Campbell, N. R. *What Is Science?* New York: Dover, 1953.

Capek, M. *Philosophical Impact of Contemporary Physics.* Princeton, N.J.: Van Nostrand, 1961.

Carnap, R. *An Introduction to the Philosophy of Science.* Edited by M. Gardner. New York: Basic Books, 1966.

Caruso, I. *Psychoanalyse und Synthese der Existenz, Beziehungen zwischen psychologischer Analyse und Daseinswerten.* Vienna: Herder, 1952.

Casey, E. S. *Imagining: A Phenomenological Study.* Bloomington: Indiana University Press, 1976.

Cassirer, E. *The Logic of Humanities.* New Haven, Conn.: Yale University Press. 1961.

Castaneda, C. *Tales of Power.* New York: Pocket Books, 1976.

Chang, G. *Teachings of Tibetan Yoga.* New Hyde Park, N.Y.: University Books, 1963.

Chapman, H. M. *Sensations and Phenomenology.* Bloomington: Indiana University Press, 1966.

Child, I. L. *Humanistic Psychology and the Research Tradition: Their Several Virtues.* New York: John Wiley, 1973.

Chomsky, N. *Reflections on Language.* 2nd ed. New York: Random House, 1976.

Clebsch, W., and C. Jaekle. *Pastoral Care in Historical Perspective.* Association for Pastoral Care and Counseling, Constitution Papers. New York: Aronson, 1975.

Colaizzi, P. F. *Reflection and Research in Psychology.* Dubuque, Iowa: Kendall Hunt, 1973.

Collingwood, R. G. *The Idea of History.* Oxford: Oxford University Press, 1946.

Combs, A. W., A. C. Richards, and F. Richards. *Perceptual Psychology: A Humanistic Approach to the Study of Persons.* Rev. ed. New York: Harper and Row, 1976.

Cook, T. D., and D. T. Campbell. *Quasi-Experimentation: Design and Analysis Issues for Field Settings.* Chicago: Rand McNally, 1979.

Cunningham, F. *Objectivity in Social Sciences.* Toronto: University of Toronto Press, 1973.

Davidson, D. *Essays on Actions and Events.* Oxford: Clarendon Press, 1980.

Davis, L. H. *Theory of Action.* Englewood Cliffs, N.J.: Prentice-Hall, 1979.

De Boer, T. *Foundations of a Critical Psychology.* Pittsburgh, Pa.: Duquesne University Press, 1983.

—————. *Wijsgerige en wetenschappelijke antropologie* Assen: Van Gorcum, 1969.

de Groot, A. D. *Methodology: Foundations of Inferences and Research in the Behavioral Sciences.* Translated from the Dutch by J. A. A. Spiekerman. The Hague: Mouton and Co., 1969.

Denzin, N. K. *Sociological Methods: A Source Book.* 2nd ed. New York: McGraw Hill, 1978.

de Rivera, J. *A Structural Theory of the Emotions.* Psychological Issues Monograph 40. New York: International Universities Press, 1977.

—————, ed. *Conceptual Encounter.* Washington, D.C.: University Press of America, 1981.

Descartes, R. *Discourse on Method.* Translated by L. J. Lafleur. New York: The Liberal Arts Press, 1956.

De Waelhens, A. *Existence et Signification.* Louvain and Paris: Nauwelaerts, 1958.

—————. *Une philosophie de l'ambiquité. L'Existentialisme de Maurice Merleau-Ponty.* Louvain: Publs. Universitaires de Louvain, 1957.

Diel, P. *Psychologie de la motivation, theorie et application therapeutique.* Paris: University of France Press, 1948.

Dondeyne, A. *Contemporary European Thought and Christian Faith.* Translated by E. McMullin and J. Burnheim. Pittsburgh, Pa.: Duquesne University Press, 1958.

Duhem, P. *Aim and Structure of Physical Theory.* New York: Atheneum, 1962.

Dunne, J. *A Search for God in Time and Memory.* New York: The Macmillian Company, 1967.

Dunne, T. *Lonergan and Spirituality.* Chicago: Loyola University Press, 1985.

Durant, W. *The Story of Philosophy* Garden City, N.Y.: Garden City Publishing, 1927.

Durkheim, E. *The Rules of Sociological Method.* Translated by S. A. Solovay and J. H. Mueller. Introduction by G. E. G. Catlin. Chicago: University of Chicago Press, 1938. New York: Macmillan, 1964.

Edwards, T. *Living Simply Through the Day.* New York: Paulist, 1977.

Eliade, M. *The Sacred and the Profane.* New York: Harper and Row, 1961.

Ermarth, M. *Wilhelm Dilthey: The Critique of Historical Reason.* Chicago: University of Chicago Press, 1978.

Ey, H. *Consciousness: A Phenomenological Study of Being Conscious and Becoming Conscious.* Translated by J. H. Flodstrom. Bloomington: Indiana University Press, 1978.

Fairbairn, R. *Object Relations Theory of the Personality.* New York: Basic Books, 1952.

Feigl, H., and M. Brodbeck, eds. *Readings in the Philosophy of Science.* New York: Appleton-Century-Crofts, 1953.

Feyerabend, P. K. *Against Method.* 2nd ed. London: Verso, 1978.

Filmer, P., M. Phillipson, D. Silverman, and D. Walsh. *New Directions in Sociological Theory.* London: Collier-Macmillan, 1972.

Fingarette, H. *The Self in Transformation.* New York: Harper Torchbooks, 1965.

Foucault, M. *The Order of Things: An Archaeology of the Human Sciences.* New York: Pantheon Books, 1971.

Frankl, V. E. *The Doctor and the Soul: An Introduction to Logotherapy.* Translated by R. and C. Winston. New York: Alfred A. Knopf, 1955.

Freire, P. *Pedagogy of the Oppressed.* New York: Seabury Press, 1970.

Freud, S. *The Interpretation of Dreams.* Translated by James Strachey. New York: Science Editions, 1961.

_____. *Psychologie des Unbewussten.* Studienausgabe 3. Frankfurt am Main: Fischer, 1975.

_____. *Vorlesungen zur Einfuhrung in die Psychoanalyse.* Studienausgabe 1. Frankfurt am Main: Fischer, 1969.

Frings, M. S. *Max Scheler.* Pittsburgh, Pa.: Duquesne University Press, 1965.

Fromm, E. *The Art of Loving.* New York: Harper and Bros., 1956.

Gadamer, H.-G. *Philosphical Hermeneutics.* Edited and translated by D. E. Lings. Berkeley: University of California Press, 1976.

_____. *Reason in the Age of Science.* Translated by F. G. Lawrence. Cambridge, Mass.: MIT Press, 1981.

_____. *Truth and Method* New York: Crossroad Publishing Co., 1975.

Gard., R., ed. *Buddhism.* New York: George Braziller, 1962.

Gardner, J. *Self-Renewal: The Individual and the Innovative Society.* New York: Harper and Row, 1963.

Garfinkel, H. *Studies in Ethnomethodology.* Engelwood Cliffs, N.J.: Prentice-Hall, 1967.

Gendlin, E. T. *Focusing.* New York: Bantam Books, 1981.

Geurts, J. P. M. *Feit en theorie.* Assen: Van Gorcum, 1978.

Giddens, A. *New Rules of Sociological Method: A Positive Critique of Interpretative Sociologies.* New York: Basic Books, 1976.

Giorgi, A. *Psychology as a Human Science: A Phenomenologically Based Approach.* New York: Harper and Row, 1970.

Glucksmann, M. *Structuralist Analysis in Contemporary Social Thought: A Comparison of the Theories of Claude Levi-Strauss and Louis Althusser.* London: Routledge & Kegan Paul, 1974.

Glymour, C. *Theory and Evidence.* Princeton, N.J.: Princeton University Press, 1980.

Goffman, E. *Asylums.* Garden City, N.Y.: Anchor Books, 1961.

_____. *Stigma.* Englewood Cliffs, N.J.: Prentice-Hall, 1963.

Goldstein, K. *Human Nature in the Light of Psychopathology.* Cambridge, Mass.: Harvard University Press, 1947.

_____ . *The Organism.* Boston: Beacon Press, 1963.

Gruhle, H. W. *Verstehende Psychologie. Erlebnislehre.* Stuttgart: Georg Thieme Verlag, 1956.

Gurwitsch, A. *Field of Consciousness.* Pittsburgh, Pa.: Duquesne University Press 1964.

Gusdorf, E. G. *Speaking.* Chicago: Northwestern University Press, 1965.

Gusdorf, G. *Mythe et Metaphysique.* Paris: Flammarion, 1953.

Habermas, Jürgen. *Erkenntnis und Interesse.* Frankfurt am Main: Suhrkamp, 1968. (The Fourth edition, 1973, has a new epilogue, pp. 367–417.)

_____ . *Knowledge and Human Interests.* Translated by J. J. Shapiro. Boston: Beacon Press, 1971.

_____ . *Technik und Wissenschaft als "Ideologie."* Frankfurt: Suhrkamp, 1968. (Contains Habermas's inaugural address, "Erkenntnis und Interesse," pp. 146–69.)

_____ . *Theorie und Praxis.* 4th rev. ed. Frankfurt am Main: Suhrkamp, 1971.

_____ . *Zur Logik der Sozialwissenschaften. Materialien.* Frankfurt am Main: Suhrkamp, 1970.

Hacking, I. *Why Does Language Matter to Philosophy?* Cambridge: Cambridge University Press, 1975.

Hall, C., and G. Lindzey. *Theories of Personality.* New York: John Wiley and Sons, 1978.

Hampden-Turner, C. *Radical Man.* Cambridge, Mass.: Schenkam, 1970.

Hanson, N. R. *Patterns of Discovery: An Inquiry into the Conceptual Foundations of Science.* Cambridge: Cambridge University Press, 1958.

Hare, R. M. *The Language of Morals.* 2nd ed. Oxford: Oxford Paperbacks. 1967.

Harre, R. *The Philosophies of Science: An Introductory Survey.* Oxford: Oxford University Press, 1972.

Havighurst, R. *Human Development and Education.* New York: Longmans, Green. 1953.

Hebb, D. O. *The Organization of Behavior.* New York: John Wiley and Sons, Inc., 1949.

Hegel, G. W. F. *Phanomenologie des Geistes.* Edited by J. Hoffneister. Hamburg: Meiner. 1952.

_____ . *Science of Logic.* 2 vols. Translated by W. H. Johnston and L. G. Struthers. New York: Macmillan, 1929.

Heidegger, M. *Being and Time.* Translated by J. Macquarrie and E. Robinson. New York: Harper and Row, 1962.

_____ . *Poetry, Language, and Thought.* New York: Harper and Row, 1971.

Heider, F. *The Psychology of Interpersonal Relations.* New York: John Wiley and Sons, 1958.

Hempel, C. G. *Aspects of Scientific Explanation, and Other Essays in the Philosophy of Science.* London: Collier MacMillan, 1965.

Hengstenberg, H.-E. *Philosophische Anthropologie.* Stuttgart: W. Kohl-Hammer Verlag. 1957.

Heschel, A. *Who Is Man?* Stanford, Calif.: Stanford University Press, 1965.

Hoffman, H. F. *Die Schichtentheorie.* Stuttgart: F. Enke, 1935.

Holzner, B. *Reality Construction in Society.* Cambridge, Mass.: Schenkman Publishing Co., 1968.

Homas, G. C. *The Nature of Social Science.* New York: Harcourt, Brace, and World, 1967.

Honigswald, R. *Die Grundlagen der Denkpsychologie.* 2nd ed. Berlin and Leipzig: m.p. 1925.

Hora, T. *Existential Metapsychiatry.* New York: Seabury, 1979

Horney, K. *Neurosis and Human Growth.* New York: W. W. Norton, 1950.

Hugh of Saint Victor, *Selected Spiritual Writings.* New York: Harper and Row, 1962.

Husserl, E. *Cartesian Meditations.* Translated by D. Cairns. The Hague: Martinus Nijhof, 1960.

_____ . *The Crisis of European Sciences and Transcendental Phenomenology.* Evanston, Ill.: Northwestern University Press, 1970.

_____ . *Erfahrung und Urteil, Untersuchungen zur Genealogie der Logik.* Edited by L. Landgrebe. Hamburg: Claassen & Goverts. 1948.

_____ . *Ideas Towards a Pure Phenomenology and Phenomenological Philosophy.* Translated by W. R. Boyce Gibson. New York: Macmillan, 1931.

_____ . *Logische Untersuchungen.* Vol. 2, Pt. 1, 4th ed. Halle a.d. Saale: Niemeyer, 1928.

Ihde, D. *Experimental Phenomenology: An Introduction.* New York: Putnam's, 1977.

_____ . *Hermeneutic Phenomenology: The Philosophy of Ricoeur.* Evanston, Ill.: Northwestern University Press, 1971.

James, W. *Essays in Radical Empiricism.* New York: Longmans, Green, 1940.

_____ . *The Principles of Psychology.* New York: Holt, 1890.

_____ . *The Varieties of Religious Experience.* New York: Modern Library, 1936.

Jaspers, K. *Existenzerhellung.* Berlin: J. Springer, 1932.

_____ . *Man in the Modern Age.* Translated by E. and C. Paul. London: Routledge & Kegan Paul, 1951.

_____ . *Vernunft und Existenz.* Bremen: Storm, 1949.

_____ . *Way to Wisdom: An Introduction to Philosophy.* Translated by R. Manheim. New Haven, Conn.: Yale University Press, 1951.

Jay, M. *The Dialectical Imagination: the History of the Frankfurt School and the Institute of Social Research 1923–1950.* London: Heinemann, 1973.

Johnston, W., ed. *The Cloud of Unknowing.* New York: Doubleday/Image, 1973.

Jourard, S. *Disclosing Man to Himself.* Princeton, N.J.: Van Nostrand, 1968.

_____ . *The Transparent Self.* Princeton, N.J.: Van Nostrand, 1964.

Jung, C. *The Integration of the Personality.* Translated by S. M. Dell. London: Routledge & Kegan Paul, 1940.

_____ . *Memories, Dreams and Reflections.* Recorded and edited by A. Joffé. Translated by R. and C. Winston. New York: Pantheon Books, 1963.

_____ . *Modern Man in Search of a Soul.* Translated by W. S. Dell and C. F. Baynes. New York: Harcourt, Brace & Co., 1933.

_____ . *The Undiscovered Self.* Translated by R. F. C. Hull. Boston: Little, Brown and Co., 1958.

Kant, I. *Prolegomena to Any Future Metaphysics.* Indianapolis: Bobbs-Merrill, 1950.

Kapleau, P. *Zen: Dawn in the West.* Garden City, N.Y.: Doubleday/Anchor Press, 1979.

Kelly, G. A. *The Psychology of Personal Constructs.* New York: W. W. Norton & Co., 1955.

Kelsey, M. *Discernment—A Study in Ecstasy and Evil.* New York: Paulist, 1978.

Kemeny, J. G. *A Philosopher Looks at Science.* Princeton, N.J.: Van Nostrand, 1959.

Kenny, A. *Action, Emotion and Will.* London: Routledge & Kegan Paul, 1963.

Kierkegaard, S. *Concluding Unscientific Postscript.* Princeton, N.J.: Princeton University Press, 1968.

Kirchberger, C. *Richard of St. Victor: Select Writings on Contemplation.* New York: Faber & Faber, 1957.

Knowles, R. *Human Development and Human Possibility: Erikson in the Light of Heidegger.* Lanham, Md.: University Press of America, 1985.

Kockelmans, J. *Phenomenology and Physical Science.* Pittsburgh, Pa.: Duquesne University Press, 1966.

Köhler, W. *Gestalt Psychology.* New York: Liveright, 1929.

Kolakowski, L. *Husserl and the Search for Certitude.* New Haven, Conn.: Yale University Press, 1975.

Krech, D., and S. G. Klein, eds. *Theoretical Models and Personality Theory.* Durham, N.C., 1952.

Kuenzli, A. E., ed. *The Phenomenological Problem.* New York: Harper and Bros., 1959.

Kuhn. T *The Structure of Scientific Revolutions.* 2nd ed. Chicago: University of Chicago Press, 1970.

Kunz, H. *Die Anthropologische Bedeutung der Phantasie.* 2 vols. Basel: Verlag für Recht und Gesellschaft, 1946.

Kwant, R. C. *Encounter.* Translated by R. C. Adolfs. Pittsburgh, Pa.: Duquesne University Press, 1960.

_____. *Phenomenology of Language.* Pittsburgh, Pa.: Duquesne University Press, 1965.

_____. *Phenomenology of Social Existence.* Pittsburgh, Pa.: Duquesne University Press, 1965.

Ladrière, J. *L'articulation du sens.* Paris: Aubier/Cerf, 1970.

Laing, R. D. *The Divided Self.* Chicago: Quadrangle Books, Inc., 1960.

Laszlo, E. *Introduction to Systems Philosophy: Toward a New Paradigm of Contemporary Thought.* New York: Gordon & Breach, 1972.

Lauer, Q. J. *The Triumph of Subjectivity.* New York: Fordham University Press, 1958.

Lavelle, L. *La conscience de soi.* Paris: B. Grasset, 1933.

Leckey, D. "Growing in the Spirit: Notes on Spiritual Direction and Sexuality." Washington, D.C.: Alban Institute, 1976.

Lee, D. *Freedom and Culture.* Englewood Cliffs, N.J.: Prentice-Hall, 1959.

Leech, K. *Soul Friend.* New York: Harper and Row, 1980.

Lepp, I. *The Psychology of Loving.* Translated by B. B. Gilligan. Baltimore: Helicon, 1963.

Le Senne, R. *Obstacle et valeur.* Paris: University of France Press, 1934.

Levi-Strauss, C. *Structural Anthropology.* Translated by C. Jacobson and B. G. Schoepf. New York: Basic Books, 1963.

Levinas, E. *Humanisme de l'autre homme.* Montpellier, Vt.: Fata Morgana, 1972.

Levy-Bruhl, L. *Primitive Mentality.* Translated by L. A. A. Clare. New York: Macmillan, 1923.

Liddy, G. G. *Out of Control.* New York: St. Martin's Press, 1979.

_____ . *Will.* New York: St. Martin's Press, 1980.

Litt, T. *Die Wiedererweckung des geschichtlichen Bewusstseins.* Heidelberg: Quelle u. Meyer, 1956.

Lonergan, B. *Insight: A Study of Human Understanding.* San Francisco: Harper and Row, 1958.

_____ . *Method in Theology.* London: Darton, Longman and Todd, 1972.

Luckmann, T., ed. *Phenomenology and Sociology: Selected Readings.* New York: Penguin Books, 1978.

Luijpen, W. A. *De psychologie van de verveling.* Amsterdam: H. J. Paris, 1951.

_____ . *Existential Phenomenology.* Translated by H. J. Koren. Pittsburgh, Pa.: Duquesne University Press, 1960.

_____ . *Phenomenology and Metaphysics.* Pittsburgh, Pa.: Duquesne University Press, 1965.

MacDougall, C. *Interpretive Reporting.* New York: Macmillan, 1972.

MacGill, V. J. *Emotions and Reason.* Springfield, Ill.: Thomas, 1954.

McKay, D. M. *Information, Mechanism and Meaning.* Cambridge, Mass., and London: MIT Press, 1969.

Macksey, R., and E. Donato, eds. *The Structuralist Controversy: The Languages of Criticism and the Sciences of Man.* Baltimore: Johns Hopkins University Press, 1970.

MacMurray, J. *Reason and Emotion.* New York: Barnes and Noble, 1962.

Macquarrie, J. *Three Issues in Ethics.* New York: Harper and Row, 1970.

Makkreel, R. A. *Wilhelm Dilthey: Philosopher of the Human Studies.* Princeton, N.J.: Princeton University Press, 1975.

Mandler, G., and W. Kessen. *The Language of Psychology.* New York: John Wiley and Sons, Inc., 1959.

Manninen, J., and R. Tuomela, eds. *Essays on Explanation and Understanding.* Dordrecht: Reidel, 1976.

Marcel, G. *Being and Having.* 1935. Translated by K. Farrer. London: Collins, 1965.

_____ . *Creative Fidelity.* Translated by R. Rosthal. New York: Farrar, Strauss, 1964.

_____ . *L'homme problematique.* Paris: Aubier, 1955.

_____ . *Man Against Mass Society.* Translated by G. S. Fraser. Chicago: Regnery, 1952.

Marcuse, H. *One Dimensional Man: The Ideology of Industrial Society.* London: Sphere Books, 1969.

Maslow, A. *The Farther Reaches of Human Nature.* New York: Viking, 1971.

_____ . *Religions, Values and Peak-experiences.* New York: Viking, 1970.

_____ . *Toward a Psychology of Being.* New York: Van Nostrand, 1968.

May, G. G. *Care of Mind/Care of Spirit.* San Francisco: Harper and Row, 1982.

_____ . *Open Way.* New York: Paulist, 1977.

_____ . *Simply Sane.* New York: Paulist, 1977.

_____ . *Will and Spirit.* New York: Harper and Row, 1982.

May, R., and others, eds. *Existence: A New Dimension in Psychiatry and Psychology.* New York: Basic Books, Inc., 1958.

_____ . *Existential Psychology.* New York: Random House, 1961.

_____ . *Man's Search for Himself.* New York: W. W. Norton, 1953.

_____ . *Power and Innocence.* New York: Norton, 1972.

McCleary, R., and R. Moore. *Subcortical Mechanisms of Human Behavior.* New York: Basic Books, 1965.

McClelland, D. *The Achievement Motive*. New York: Appleton-Century-Crofts, 1953.

Merleau-Ponty, M. *Phenomenology of Perception*. Translated by C. Smith. New York: Humanities Press, 1962.

_____. *The Structure of Behavior*. Translated by A. L. Fisher. Boston: Beacon Press, 1967.

_____. *The Visible and the Invisible*. Evantson, Ill.: Northwestern University Press, 1968.

Merton, R. K. *Social Theory and Social Structure*. Rev. ed. Glencoe, Ill.: Free Press, 1957.

Merton, T. *Zen and the Birds of Appetite*. New York: New Directions, 1968.

Minkowski, E. *Lived Time: Phenomenological and Psychopathological Studies*. Translated by N. Metzel. Evanston, Ill.: Northwestern University Press, 1970.

Mounier, E. *The Character of Man*. Translated by C. Rowland. New York: Harper, 1956.

Moustakas, C. E., ed. *The Self: Explorations in Personal Growth*. New York: Harper and Brothers, 1956.

Murray, E. *Imaging Our Life*. Pittsburgh, Pa.: Duquesne University Press, 1986.

Nagel, E. *The Structure of Science*. 2nd ed. London: Routledge & Kegan Paul, 1968.

Naranjo, C. *On the Psychology of Meditation*. New York: Viking, 1972.

Natanson, M. *The Journeying Self*. Reading, Pa.: Addison-Wesley Publishers, 1970.

Nédoncelle, M. *La reciprocité des consciences. Essai sur la nature de la personne*. Aubiers: Editions Montaigne, 1942.

Needleman, J. *A Sense of the Cosmos—The Encounter of Modern Science and Ancient Truth*. New York: Doubleday, 1975.

Neihardt, J. *Black Elk Speaks*. Lincoln, Neb.: University of Nebraska Press, 1961.

Nicholl, D. *Scientia Cordis*. Santa Cruz, Calif.: William James Press, 1975.

Nixon, R. *The Art of Growing*. New York: Random House, 1962.

Nouwen, H. J. M. *Making All Things New*. San Francisco: Harper and Row, 1981.

Nuttin, J. *Psychoanalysis and Personality*. New York: Sheed and Ward, 1953.

Nygren, A. *Agape and Eros*. Translated by P. S. Watson. New York: Harper and Row, 1969.

O'Brien, E. *Varieties of Mystic Experience*. New York: Holt, Rinehart and Winston, 1964.

Ogilvy, J. *Many Dimensional Man: Decentralizing Self, Society, and the Sacred*. New York: Oxford University Press, 1977.

Olafson, F. A. *The Dialectic of Action: A Philosophical Interpretation of History and the Humanities*. Chicago: University of Chicago Press, 1979.

Ornstein, R. *The Nature of Human Consciousness*. New York: Viking, 1973.

Otto, R. *The Idea of the Holy; An Inquiry into the Non-Rational Factor in the Idea of the Divine and its Relation to the Rational*. Translated by J. W. Harvey. London: Oxford University Press, 1950.

Palmer, R. E. *Hermeneutics: Interpretation Theory in Schleiermacher, Dilthey, Heidegger, and Gadamer*. Evanston, Ill.: Northwestern University Press, 1969.

Peck, S. *The Road Less Traveled*. New York: Simon and Schuster, 1978.

Peters, R. S. *The Concept of Motivation*. 2nd ed. New York: Humanities Press, 1960.

Phillips, D. C. *Holistic Thought in Social Science*. Stanford, Calif.: Stanford University Press, 1976.

Piaget, J. *The Origins of Intelligence in Children.* New York: International Universities Press, 1952.

_____. *Structuralism.* Edited and translated by C. Maschler. New York: Basic Books, 1970.

Pico della Mirandola, G. *Oration on the Dignity of Man.* Translated by A. R. Caponigri. South Bend, In.: Gateway Editions, 1956.

Pieper, J. *Happiness and Contemplation.* Translated by R. and C. Winston. Chicago: Henry Regnery Co., 1958.

_____. *In Tune with the World: A Theory of Festivity.* Chicago: Franciscan Herald Press, 1973.

_____. *Leisure, the Basis of Culture.* Translated by A. Dru. New York: Pantheon Books, Inc., 1952.

Pirsig, R. M. *Zen and the Art of Motorcycle Maintenance.* New York: Bantam Books, 1974.

Planck, M. *Philosophy of Physics.* New York: Norton, 1936.

Plantinga, T. *Historical Understanding in the Thought of Wilhelm Dilthey.* Toronto: University of Toronto Press, 1980.

Ploanyi, M. *Personal Knowledge: Toward a Post-Critical Philosophy.* Chicago: University of Chicago Press, 1958.

Polkinghorne, D. *Methodology for the Human Sciences.* Albany: State University of New York Press, 1983.

Popper, K. *The Logic of Scientific Discovery.* New York: Basic Books, 1959.

_____. *Objective Knowledge: An Evolutionary Approach.* 2nd rev. ed. Oxford: University Press, 1973.

_____. *The Poverty of Historicism.* 3rd ed. London: Routledge & Kegan Paul, 1961.

_____, and J. C. Eccles. *The Self and Its Brain.* Berlin: Springer, 1977.

Pratt, C. C. *The Meaning of Music.* New York: McGraw-Hill, 1931.

Putnam, H. *Meaning and the Moral Sciences.* London: Routledge & Kegan Paul, 1978.

Radcliffe-Brown, A. R. *Structure and Function in Primitive Society.* Glencoe, Ill.: Free Press, 1952

Radnitzky, G. *Contemporary Schools of Metascience.* Chicago: Henry Regnery, 1973.

_____, and G. Andersson, eds. *Progress and Rationality in Science.* Dordrecht: Reidel. 1978.

Rahner, K. *Spirit in the World.* Translated by W. Dych. New York: Herder and Herder, 1968.

Reichenbach, H. *Experience and Prediction.* Chicago: University of Chicago Press, 1938.

_____. *The Rise of Scientific Philosophy.* Berkeley: University of California Press, 1951.

Reilly, F. E. *Charles Peirce's Theory of Scientific Method.* New York: Fordham University Press, 1970.

Rickert, H. *Kulturwissenschaft und Naturwissenschaft.* 6th and 7th rev. ed. Tubingen: J. C. B. Mohr, 1926.

Ricoeur, P. *The Conflict of Interpretations: Essays in Hermeneutics.* Evanston, Ill.: Northwestern University Press, 1974.

_____. *Fallible Man.* Translated by C. Keley. Chicago: H. Regnery, 1965.

_____. *Freedom and Nature: The Voluntary and the Involuntary.* Translated by E. V. Kohak. Evanston, Ill.: Northwestern University Press, 1966.

_____. *Freud and Philosophy: An Essay on Interpretation.* Translated by D. Savage. New Haven, Conn.: Yale University Press, 1970.

_____. *Hermeneutics and the Human Sciences.* Translated by J. B. Thompson. Cambridge: Cambridge University Press, 1981.

_____. *Interpretation Theory: Discourse and the Surplus of Meaning.* Fort Worth: Texas Christian University Press, 1976.

_____. *The Rule of Metaphor: Multi-Disciplinary Studies of the Creation of Meaning in Language.* Translated by R. Czerny. Toronto: University of Toronto Press, 1977.

Riesman, D. *The Lonely Crowd.* New Haven, Conn.: Yale University Press, 1961.

Roche, M. *Phenomenology, Language and the Social Sciences.* London: Routledge & Kegan Paul, 1973.

Rogers, C. *On Becoming a Person.* Boston: Houghton Mifflin, 1961.

Romanyshyn, R. *Psychological Life: From Science to Metaphor.* Austin: University of Texas Press, 1982.

Rosenstock-Huessy, E. *Speech and Reality.* Norwich, Vt.: Argobooks, 1970.

Rychlak, J. F. *The Psychology of Rigorous Humanism.* New York: John Wiley, 1977.

Sampson, G. *Schools of Linguistics: Competition and Evolution.* London: Hutchinson, 1980.

Sanford, R. N. *Self and Society.* New York: Atherton, 1966.

Sarason, S. B. *Psychology Misdirected.* New York: Free Press, 1981.

Sartre, J. P. *The Emotions: Outline of a Theory.* Translated by B. Frechtman. New York: Philosophical Library, 1948.

_____. *The Psychology of Imagination.* Translated by B. Frechtman. New York: Philosophical Library, 1948.

_____. *Search for a Method.* New York: Vintage Books, 1968.

_____. *Sketch for a Theory of the Emotions.* Translated by P. Mairet. London: Methuen. 1971.

Saussure, F. de. *Course in General Linguistics.* Edited by C. Bally and A. Sechehaye. Translated by W. Baskin. New York: McGraw-Hill, 1966.

Schachtel, E. *Metamorphosis.* New York: Basic Books, 1959.

Scheler, M. *Formalism in Ethics and Non-Formal Ethics of Value.* Translated by M. S. Frings and R. L. Funk. Evanston, Ill.: Northwestern University Press, 1973.

_____. *Man's Place in Nature.* Boston: Beacon Press, 1961.

_____. *The Nature of Sympathy.* Translated by P. Heath. New York: Archon Books, 1970.

_____. *Ressentiment.* New York: The Free Press of Glenco, 1954.

_____. *Wesen und Formen der Sympathie, Gesammelte Werke.* Vol. 7. Bern: Francke. 1974.

Schrag, C. O. *Radical Reflection and the Origin of the Human Sciences.* West Lafayette, Ind.: Purdue University Press, 1980.

Schutz, A. *Collected Papers.* 3 vols. Edited by M. Natanson. The Hague: Martinus Nijhoff, 1973.

_____. *Reflections on the Problem of Relevance.* New Haven, Conn.: Yale University Press, 1970.

Schwemmer, O. *Theorie der rationalen Erklarung: zu den methodischen Grundlagen der Kulturwissenschaften.* Munich: Verlage H. Beck, 1976.

Searle, J. R. *Speechacts: An Essay in the Philosophy of Language.* London: Cambridge University Press, 1969.

Seung, T. K. *Structuralism and Hermeneutics*. New York: Columbia University Press, 1982.

Severin, F. T. *Humanistic Viewpoints in Psychology*. New York: McGraw-Hill Book Co., 1965.

Shaffer, J. B. P. *Humanistic Psychology*. Englewood Cliffs, N.J.: Prentice-Hall, 1978.

Shorf, B. L. *Language, Thought, and Reality: Selected Writings of Benjamin Lee Shorf*. Edited by J. B. Carroll. Cambridge, Mass.: MIT Press, 1956.

Skinner, B. F. *Beyond Freedom and Dignity*. New York: Knopf, 1971.

_____ . *Science and Human Behavior*. New York: Macmillan, 1953.

Snygg, D., and A. W. Combs. *Individual Behavior*. New York: Harper, 1949.

Sorokin, P. *The Crisis of Our Age*. New York: E. P. Dutton and Co., Inc., 1941.

Spicker, S., ed. *The Philosophy of the Body*. Chicago: Quadrangle Books, 1970.

Spiegelberg, H. *The Phenomenological Movement: A Historical Introduction*. 2 vols. 2nd ed. The Hague: Martinus Nijhoff, 1976.

Spranger, E. *Lebensformen Geisteswissenschaftliche Psychologie und Ethik der Personlichkeit*. Halle a.d. Salle: Max Niemeyer Verlag, 1930.

Squire, A. *Asking the Fathers*. 2nd American ed. New York: Paulist; Wilton, Conn.: Morehouse-Barlow, 1976.

Strasser, S. *Das Gemut. Grundgedanken zu einer Phänomenologischen Philosophie und Theorie des Menslichen Gefühlslebens*. Utrecht: Het Spectrum; Freiburg: Verlag Herder, 1956.

_____ . *The Idea of Dialogical Phenomenology*. Pittsburgh, Pa.: Duquesne University Press, 1969.

_____ . *Phenomenology and the Human Sciences*. 2nd ed. Translated by H. Koren. Pittsburgh, Pa.: Duquesne University Press, 1974.

_____ . *Phenomenology of Feeling: An Essay on the Phenomena of Heart*. Translated by R. E. Wood. Pittsburgh, Pa.: Duquesne University Press, 1977.

_____ . *The Soul in Metaphysical and Empirical Psychology*. Translated by H. J. Koren. Pittsburgh, Pa.: Duquesne University Press, 1957.

_____ . *Understanding and Explanation*. Pittsburgh, Pa.: Duquesne University Press, 1985.

Sullivan, H. S. *Conceptions of Modern Psychiatry*. Washington, D.C.: William Alanson White Foundation, 1947.

_____ . *The Interpersonal Theory of Psychiatry*. New York: W. W. Norton and Co., 1953.

Sullivan, J. W. N. *The Limitations of Science*. New York: The New American Library, 1933.

Sutherland, J. W. *A General Systems Philosophy for the Social and Behavioral Sciences*. New York: George Braziller, 1973.

Suzuki, S. *Zen Mind, Beginner's Mind*. New York: Weatherhill, 1970.

Szasz, T. *The Myth of Mental Illness*. New York: Hoeber/Harper, 1961.

Tart, C. *Transpersonal Psychologies*. New York: Harper and Row, 1975.

Tauber, E. S., and M. R. Green. *Prelogical Experience*. New York: Basic Books, Inc., 1959.

Thomas, D. *Naturalism and Social Science: A Post-Empiricist Philosophy of Social Science*. Cambridge: Cambridge University Press, 1979.

Thompson, J. B. *Critical Hermeneutics: A Study in the Thought of Paul Ricoeur and Jurgen Habermas*. Cambridge: Cambridge University Press, 1981.

Tillich, P. *The Courage to Be*. New Haven, Conn.: Yale University Press, 1963.

_____ . *Theology of Culture*. New York: Oxford University Press, 1959.

Topitsch, E. *Sozialwissenschaft zwischen Ideologie und Wissenschaft.* Neuwied: Luchterhand. 1961.

Tournier, P. *The Meaning of Persons.* New York: Harper and Row, 1957.

Trungpa, C. *Cutting Through Spiritual Materialism.* Berkeley, Calif.: Shambala, 1973.

_____ . *The Myth of Freedom.* Berkeley, Calif.: Shambala, 1976.

Tulku, T. *Gesture of Balance.* Emeryville, Calif.: Dharma Publishing, 1977.

_____ . *Time, Space and Knowledge.* Emeryville, Calif.: Dharma Publishing, 1977.

Tymieniecka, A. T., ed. *The Phenomenology of Man and the Human Condition in Communication with the Human Sciences.* Boston: D. Reidel, 1983.

Underhill, E. *Mysticism.* New York: Dutton, 1911.

Valle, R., and R. von Eckartsberg. *The Metaphors of Consciousness.* New York: Plenum Press, 1981.

van Croonenburg, E. J. *Gateway to Reality (An Introduction to Philosophy).* Pittsburgh, Pa.: Duquesne University Press, 1964.

van de Hulst, H. C., and C. A. van Peursen. *Phaenomenologie en natuurwetenschap.* Utrecht: Erven J. Byleveld, 1953.

van den Berg, J. H. *The Changing Nature of Man.* Translated by H. F. Croes. New York: Norton, 1961.

_____ . *Divided Existence and Complex Society.* Pittsburgh, Pa.: Duquesne University Press, 1974.

_____ . *The Phenomenological Approach to Psychiatry. An Introduction to Recent Phenomenological Psychopathology.* Springfield, Ill.: Charles C. Thomas, 1955.

_____ , and J. Linschoten. *Persoon en Wereld.* Utrecht: Erven J. Bijleveld, 1953.

van der Horst, L. *Anthropologische psychiatrie.* Amsterdam: van Holkema and Warendorf, 1946.

van Kaam, A. *The Art of Existential Counseling.* Denville, N.J.: Dimension Books, 1966.

_____ . *The Emergent Self.* 4 vols. Denville, N.J.: Dimension Books, 1968.

_____ . *Existential Foundations of Psychology.* Lanham, Md.: University Press of America, Inc., 1983.

_____ . *Foundations of Personality Study: An Adrian van Kaam Reader.* Denville, N.J.: Dimension Books, 1983.

_____ . *In Search of Spiritual Identity.* Denville, N.J.: Dimension Books, 1975.

_____ . *Living Creatively.* Denville, N.J.: Dimension Books, 1981.

_____ . *On Being Yourself: Reflections on Originality and Spirituality.* Denville, N.J.: Dimension Books, 1972.

_____ . *The Participant Self.* 2 vols. Denville, N.J.: Dimension Books, 1969.

_____ . *Personality Fulfillment in Spiritual Life.* Denville, N.J.: Dimension Books, Inc., 1966.

_____ . *Religion and Personality.* Denville, N.J.: Dimension Books, 1980.

_____ . *The Science of Formative Spirituality* Vol. 1. *Fundamental Formation.* New York: Crossroad/Continuum, 1983.

_____ . *The Science of Formative Spirituality.* Vol. 2. *Human Formation.* New York: Crossroad/Continuum, 1985.

_____. *The Science of Formative Spirituality*. Vol. 3. *Formation of the Heart*. New York: Crossroad/Continuum, 1986.

_____. *The Third Force in European Psychology*. Greenville, Del.: Psychosynthesis Research Foundation, 1960.

_____. *The Transcendent Self*. Denville, N.J.: Dimension Books, 1979.

_____. *The Vocational Director and Counseling*. Derby, N.Y.: St. Paul Publications, 1962.

_____, and S. A. Muto. *Catholic Traditions of Foundational Formative Spirituality*. Cassette (8 tapes). Canfield, Ohio: Alba House, 1984.

_____, and S. A. Muto, eds. *Creative Formation of Life and World*. Lanham, Md.: University Press of America, 1982.

_____, and K. Healy. *The Demon and the Dove: Personality Growth Through Literature*. Lanham, Md.: University Press of America, 1982.

van Laer, H. *Philosophico-Scientific Problems*. Pittsburgh, Pa.: Duquesne University Press, 1964.

_____. *The Philosophy of Science*. Part 2. "A Study of the Division and Nature of Various Groups of Sciences". Pittsburgh, Pa.: Duquesne University Press, 1964.

van Melsen, A. G. *From Atomos to Atom*. Pittsburgh, Pa.: Duquesne University Press, 1952.

_____. *The Philosophy of Nature*. Pittsburgh, Pa.: Duquesne University Press, 1952.

_____. *Science and Technology*. Pittsburgh, Pa. Duquesne University Press 1961.

van Peursen, C. A. *Phenomenology and Analytical Philosophy*. Pittsburgh, Pa.: Duquesne University Press, 1972.

Verhoeven, C. *The Philosophy of Wonder*. Translated by M. Foran. New York: Macmillan, 1972.

von Bertalanffy, L. *General System Theory: Foundations, Development, Applications*. New York: George Braziller, 1968.

_____. *Modern Theories of Development*. New York: Harper and Row, 1962.

_____. *Robots, Men and Minds*. 2nd ed. New York: George Braziller, 1969.

von Eckartsberg, R. *Life-World Experience*. Lanham, Md.: University Press of America, 1986.

von Wright, G. H., *Explanation and Understanding*. London: Routledge & Kegan Paul; Ithaca, N.Y.: Cornell University Press, 1971.

Wallace, W. L. *The Logic of Science in Sociology*. Chicago: Aldine, 1971.

Wann, T. W., ed. *Behaviorism and Phenomenology: Contrasting Bases for Modern Psychology*. Chicago: University of Chicago Press, 1964.

Weber, M. *Methodologische Schriften*. Edited by J. Winckelmann. Frankfurt am Main: Fischer, 1968.

_____. *The Protestant Ethic and the Spirit of Capitalism*. London: George Allen & Unwin, 1930.

_____. *The Theory of Social and Economic Organization*. Edited by T. Parsons. New York: Free Press, 1964.

Weingartner, R. H. *Experience and Culture: The Philosophy of Georg Simmel*. Middletown, Conn.: Wesleyan University Press, 1962.

Wertheimer, M. *Productive Thinking*. New York: Harper and Bros., 1959.

Wheelwright, P. *The Burning Fountain: A Study in the Language of Symbolism.* Bloomington: Indiana University Press, 1954.

Williams, D. D. *The Spirit and the Forms of Love.* New York: Harper and Row, 1968.

Winch, P. *The Idea of a Social Science and its Relation to Philosophy.* 6th ed. London: Routledge & Kegan Paul, 1970.

Wittgenstein, L. *Philosophical Investigations.* 3rd ed. Translated by G. E. M. Anscombe. New York: Macmillan, 1968.

——————. *Tractatus Logico-Philosophicus.* 3rd ed. New York: Humanities Press, 1961.

Zaner, R. M. *The Context of Self: A Phenomenological Inquiry Using Medicine as a Clue.* Athens: Ohio University Press, 1981.

——————. *The Problem of Embodiment: Some Contributions to a Phenomenology of the Body.* The Hague: Martinus Nijhoff, 164.

Articles

Aanstoos, C. A. "A Phenomenological Study of Thinking." In *Duquesne Studies in Phenomenological Psychology.* Vol. 4. Edited by Giorgi, and others. Pittsburgh, Pa.: Duquesne University Press, 1983.

Albert, H. "Hermeneutik und Realwissenschaft." In *Pladoyer fur einen kritischen Realismus,* by H. Abel. Munich: Piper, 1971.

——————. "Konstruktivismus oder Realismus?" In *Kritik der kritischen Psychologie,* edited by H. Albert and H. Keuth. Hamburg: Hoffmann und Campe, 1973.

——————. "Theorie und Prognosen in den Sozialwissenschaften." In *Logik der Socialwissenschaften,* edited by E. Topitsch. Cologne and Berlin: Kiepenhever and Witsch, 1967.

Allport, G. W. "The Psychology of Participation." *Psychological Review* 53 (1945): 117–32.

——————. "Scientific Models and Human Morals." *Psychological Review* 54 (1947): 182f.

Beck, S. J. "Emotional Experience as a Necessary Constituent in Knowing." In *Feelings and Emotions.* The Mooseheart Symposium, edited by M. L. Reymert. New York: McGraw-Hill, 1950.

Bell, D. R. "The Ideal of a Social Science." In *Proceedings of the Aristotelian Society* 41 (1967): 115–33.

Bergmann, G. and K. W. Spence. "Operationism and Theory Construction." In *Psychological Theory,* edited by M. H. Marx. New York: The Macmillan Company, 1951.

Betti, E. *Hermeneutics as the General Methodology of the Geisteswissenschaften.* In *Contemporary Hermeneutics: Hermeneutics as Method, Philosophy and Critique,* edited by J. Bleicher. London: Routledge & Kegan Paul, 1980.

Boring, E. G. "A History of Introspection." *Psychological Bulletin.* 50 (1953): 169–89.

Brodbeck, M. "Explanation, Prediction, and 'Imperfect' Knowledge." In *Minnesota Studies in the Philosophy of Science.* Vol. 3. Edited by H. Feigl and G. Maxwell. Minneapolis: University of Minnesota Press, 1962.

Bubner, R. "Is Transcendental Hermeneutics Possible?" In *Essays on Explana-*

tion and Understanding, edited by J. Manninen and R. Tuomela. Dordrecht: Reidel, 1976.

Buytendijk, F. J. J. "The Phenomenological Approach to the Problem of Feelings and Emotions." In *Feelings and Emotions*. New York, Toronto, London: McGraw-Hill Book Co., Inc., 1950.

Campbell, D. T. "Evolutionary Epistemology." In *The Philosophy of Karl R. Popper*. 2 vols. Edited by P. Schilpp. LaSalle, Ill.: Open Court, 1974.

Carnap, R. "Logical Foundation of the Unity of Science." In *Readings in Philosophical Analysis*, edited by H. Feigl and W. Sellars. New York: Appleton-Century-Crofts, 1953.

_____. "Testability and Meaning." In *Readings in the Philosophy of Science*, edited by H. Feigl and M. Brodbeck. New York: Appleton-Century-Crofts, 1953.

Casey, E. S. "Comparative Phenomenology of Mental Activity: Memory, Hallucination, and Fantasy Contrasted with Imagination." *Research in Phenomenology* 6 (1976): 1-25.

Colaizzi, P. "Learning and Existence." In *Existential Phenomenological Alternatives for Psychology,* edited by R. Valle and M. King. New York: Oxford University Press, 1978.

Crites, S. "The Narrative Quality of Experience." *Academy of Religion* 39 (1971): 291-311.

Czikszentmihalyi, M. "Attention and the Holistic Approach to Behavior." In *The Stream of Consciousness,* edited by K. Pope and J. Singer. New York: Plenum Press, 1978.

de Boer, T. "Werkelijkheid, waarden en wetenschap." In *Waarden en Wetenschap,* edited by T. de Boer and A. F. J. Kobben. Bilthoven: Ambo, 1974.

Denzin, N. K. "The Research Act." In *Symbolic Interaction: A Reader in Social Psychology,* edited by J. G. Manis and B. N. Meltzer. Boston: Allyn & Bacon, 1978.

Dilthey, W. "Der Aufbau der geschichtlichen Welt in den Geisteswissenscaften." In *Gesammelte Schriften*. Stuttgart-Gottingen: Teubner and Vandenhoek & Ruprecht, 1958.

_____. "The Rise of Hermeneutics." Translated by T. Hall. In *Critical Sociology*, edited by Paul Connerton. New York: Penguin Books, 1976.

_____. "Die Wissenschaften vom Menschen, der Gesellschaft und der Geschichte. Vorarbeiten zur Einleitung in die Geisteswissenschaften." In *Gesammelte Schriften,* Stuttgart-Gottingen: Teubner and Vandenhoek & Ruprecht. 1977.

_____. "Einleitung in die Geisteswissenschaften." In *Gesammelte Schriften*. Vol. 1, 4th ed. Stuttgart-Gottingen: Teubner and Vandenhoek & Ruprecht. 1959.

Egan, H. "Christian Apophatic and Kataphatic Mysticisms." In *Theological Studies* 38 (Fall 1978): 399ff.

Fischer, C. T., and F. J. Wertz. "Empirical Phenomenological Analysis of Being Criminally Victimized." In *Duquesne Studies in Phenomenological Psychology*. Vol. 3. Edited by A. Giorgi, R. Knowles, and D. L. Smith. Pittsburgh, Pa.: Duquesne University Press, 1979.

Fischer, W. "On the Phenomenological Mode of Researching 'Being Anxious.'" *Journal of Phenomenological Psychology* 4 (1974): 405-23.

Fokkema, S. D. "Methodologie en 'voorwetenschappelijkheid' in de psychologie." *Nederlands Tijdschrift voor de Psychologie* 15 (1960): 266-95.

Gadamer, H. G. "Rhetorik, Hermeneutik, und Ideologiekritik." In *Hermeneutik und Ideologiekritik*, edited by J. Habermas, D. Henrich, and J. Taubes. Frankfurt: Suhrkamp, 1971.

_____. "Rhetorik, Hermeneutik und Ideologiekritik: Metakritische Erorterungen zu 'Wahrheit und Methode'." In *Hermeneutik und Ideologiekritik*, edited by J. Habermas, D. Henrich, and J. Taubes. Frankfurt: Suhrkamp, 1971.

Gellner, E. "The New Idealism—Cause and Meaning in the Social Sciences." In *Proceedings of the International Colloquium in the Philosophy of Science: Three Problems in the Philosophy of Science*, edited by I. Lakatos and A. Musgrave. Amsterdam: North Holland, 1968.

Gendlin, E. T. "Experiential Phenomenology." In *Phenomenology and the Social Sciences*, edited by M. Natanson. Evanston, Ill.: Northwestern University Press, 1973.

Giorgi, A. "The Experience of the Subject as a Source of Data in a Psychological Experiment." *Review of Existential Psychology and Psychiatry* (Fall 1967): 169–76.

_____. "Convergence and Divergence of Qualitative Methods in Psychology." In *Duquesne Studies in Phenomenological Psychology*. Vol. 2. Edited by A. Giorgi, C. Fischer, and E. Murray. Pittsburgh, Pa.: Duquesne Univerity Press, 1975.

Globus, G. "On 'I': The Conceptual Foundations of Responsibility." *American Journal of Psychiatry* 137 (April 1980): 417–22.

Grof, S. "Theoretical and Empirical Basis of Transpersonal Psychology." *Journal of Transpersonal Psychology* 5 (1973): 15–54.

Habermas, J. "Knowledge and Interest." *Inquiry* 9 (1966): 285–300.

Hanson, N. R. "Is There a Logic of Scientific Discovery?" In *Current Issues in the Philosophy of Science*, edited by B. A. Brody. Englewood Cliffs, N.J.: Prentice-Hall, 1970.

Hebb, D. O., and W. R. Thompson. "The Social Significance of Animal Studies." In *Handbook of Social Psychology*. Vol. 1. Edited by G. Lindzey. Cambridge, Mass.: Addison-Wesley Publishing Co., Inc., 1954.

Heidbreder, E. "Functionalism." In *Schools of Psychology: A Symposium*, edited by D. L. Krantz. New York: Appleton-Century-Crofts, 1969.

Hempel, C. G. "On the Standard Conception of Scientific Theories." *Minnesota Studies in Philosophy of Science* 4 (1970): 142–70.

_____, and P. Oppenheim. "Studies in the Logic of Explanation." *Philosophy of Science* 15 (1948): 135–75.

_____. "Studies in the Logic of Explanation." *Philosophy of Science* 15 (1948): 135–75.

Hertzberg, L. "On Deciding." In *Essays on Explanation and Understanding,* edited by J. Manninen and R. Tuomela. Dordrecht: Reidel, 1976.

Hesse, M. "Theory and Observation." In *Revolutions and Reconstructions in the Philosophy of Science*. Bloomington: Indiana University Press, 1980.

Hitt, W. D. "Two Models of Man," *American Psychologist* 24 (1969): 651–59.

Hofstee, W. K. B. "De betrekkelijkheid van sociaalwetenschappelijke uitspraken." *Nederlands Tijdschrift voor de Psychologie* 30 (1975): 573–600.

Horkheimer, M. "Traditionelle und kritische Theorie." In *Kritische Theorie*. Vol. 2. Frankfurt: Suhrkamp, 1969.

Jager, B. "Theorizing, Journeying, Dwelling." In *Duquesne Studies in Phenomenological Psychology*. Vol. 2. Edited by A. Giorgi, C. Fischer, and E. Murray. Pittsburgh, Pa.: Duquesne University Press, 1975.

James, W. "Does Consciousness Exist?" *Journal of Philosophy, Psychology and Scientific Methods* 1 (1904).

Jarvie, I. C. "Understanding and Explanation in Sociology and Social Anthropology." In *Explanation in the Behavioral Sciences*, edited by R. Borger and F. Cioffi. Cambridge: Cambridge University Press, 1970.

Jourard, S. M. "Experimenter-Subject Dialogue: Paradigm for a Human Science of Psychology." In *Disclosing Man to Himself*, edited by S. M. Jourard. Princeton, N.J.: Van Nostrand, 1968.

Jung, C. G. "Psychological Commentary." In *The Tibetan Book of the Dead*, edited by Evans-Wents. New York: Oxford University Press, 1960.

Kaplan, B. "Radical Metaphor, Aesthetic and the Origin of Language." *Review of Existential Psychology and Psychiatry.* 2 (February 1962): 75-84.

Katz, D. "Connective Inhibitions During Thought Processes." In *Feelings and Emotions*, edited by M. L. Reymert. The Mooseheart Symposium. New York: McGraw-Hill, 1950.

Kessel, F. S. "The Philosophy of Science as Proclaimed and Science as Practiced, 'Identity' or 'Dualism'?" *America Psychologist* 24 (1969): 999-1006.

Klinger, E. "Modes of Normal Consciousness Flow." In *The Stream of Consciousness,* edited by K. Pope and J. Singer. New York: Plenum Press, 1978.

Kockelmans, J. J. "Theoretical Problems in Phenomenological Psychology." In *Phenomenology and the Social Sciences.* Vol. 2. Edited by M. Natanson, Evanston, Ill.: Northwestern University Press, 1973.

Krueger, F. "Theorie der Konsonanz." *Psychologische Studien* 1 (1906), 4 (1908).

_____ . "Differenztone und Konsonanz." *Archiv für die Geschichte Psychologie,* Vol. 1, 1903 and Vol. 2, 1904.

Kuhn, T. S. "History of Science," *The Essential Tension: Selected Studies in Scientific Tradition and Change.* Chicago: University of Chicago Press, 1977.

Kwant, R. C. "De ambiguiteit van het feit." *Gawein* 1 (1954): 9-23.

Leary, D. E. "Wundt and After: Psychology's Shifting Relations with the Natural Sciences, Social Sciences, and Philosophy." *Journal of the History of the Behavioral Sciences* 15 (July 1979): 231-41.

MacLeod, R. B. "The Place of Phenomenological Analysis in Social Psychological Theory." In *Social Psychology at the Crossroads*, edited by J. H. Rohre and Sherif. New York: Harper, 1951, 215-41.

_____ . "The Phenomenological Approach to Social Psychology." *Psychological Review* 54 (1947): 193-210.

Maes, C. "Listening, Silence and Obedience." *Studies in Formative Spirituality* 5 (May 1984): 211-17.

Maslow, A. H. "A Theory of Motivation." *Psychological Review* 50 (1943): 370-96.

May, G. G. "The Psychodynamics of Spirituality." *Journal of Pastoral Care* 28 (June 1974): 84-91.

May, R. "Toward the Ontological Basis of Psychotherapy." *Existential Inquiries* 1 (September 1959): 5-7.

McCarthy, T. A. "A Theory of Communicative Competence." *Philosophy of the Social Sciences* 3 (1973): 135-56.

McNamara, W. "Psychology and the Christian Mystical Tradition." In *Transpersonal Psychologies*, edited by C. Tart. New York: Harper and Row, 1975.

Merleau-Ponty, M. "Indirect Language and the Voices of Silence." In *Signs.* Evanston, Ill.: Northwestern University Press, 1964.

Nijk, A. J. "Beheersing en emancipatie." In *Waarden en Wetenschap*, edited by T. de Boer and A. J. Kobben. Bilthoven: Ambo, 1974.

Orth, E. W. "Externe Bestimmung der Geisteswissenschaften?" In *Die politische Herausforderung der Wissenschaften*, edited by K. Heubener, and others. Hamburg: Meiner, 1976.

Piaget, J. "The Place of the Sciences of Man in the System of Science." In *Main Trends of Research in the Social and Human Sciences*. Vol. 1. Paris: UNESCO, 1970.

Plessner, H. "Das Lacheln." In *Zwischen Philosophie und Gesellschaft*. Bern: Francke, 1953.

—————. "Die Deutung des mimischen Ausdrucks: Ein Beitrag zur Lehre vom Bewusstsein des anderen Ichs." In *Zwischen Philosophie und Gemeinschaft*. Bern: Francke Verlag, 1953.

Popper, K. R. "Die Logik der Sozialwissenschaften." In *Der Positivismusstreit in der deutschen Soziologie,* edited by T. Adorno, and others. Neuwied and Berlin: Luchterhand, 1969.

—————. "The Myth of the Framework." In *The Abdication of Philosophy: Philosophy and the Public Good. Essays in Honor of Paul Arthur Schilpp,* edited by E. Freeman. LaSalle, Ill.: Open Court, 1976.

Ricoeur, P. "Hermeneutique et critique des ideologies." In *Demythisation et ideologie,* edited by E. Castelli. Paris: Aubier-Montaigne, 1973.

—————. "The Human Experience of Time and Narrative." *Research in Phenomenology* 9 (1979): 17-34.

—————. "The Model of the Text." *Social Research* 38 (1971): 529-62.

—————. "The Model of the Text: Meaningful Action Considered as a Text." In *Hermeneutics and the Human Sciences,* edited and translated by J. B. Thompson. Cambridge: Cambridge University Press, 1981.

—————. "Structure and Hermeneutics." In *The Conflict of Interpretations: Essays in Hermeneutics*, edited by D. Ihde. Evanston, Ill.: Northwestern University Press, 1974.

—————. "What Is a Text? Explanation and Understanding." In *Hermeneutics and the Human Sciences*, edited and translated by J. B. Thompson. Cambridge: Cambridge University Press, 1981.

Robinson, J. M. "Hermeneutic Since Barth." In *The New Hermeneutic,* edited by J. M. Robinson and J. B. Cobb, Jr. New York: Harper and Row, 1964.

Rogers, C. "Some Observations on the Organization of Personality." *American Psychologist* 2 (1947): 358-68.

—————, and B. F. Skinner. "Some Issues Concerning the Control of Human Behavior." *Science* 124 (1956): 1057-66.

Schachter, S., and J. E. Singer. "Cognitive, Social and Physiological Determinants of Emotional State." *Psychological Review* 69 (1962): 121-28.

Schutz, A. "The Problem of Social Reality." In *Collected Papers*. Vol. 1. The Hague: Nijhoff, 1962.

Smith, D. "Freud's Metapsychology." In *Duquesne Studies in Phenomenological Psychology*. Vol. 2. Edited by A. Giorgi, C. Fischer, and E. Murray. Pittsburgh, Pa.: Duquesne University Press, 1975.

Stein, E. "Beitrage zur philosophischen Begrundung der Psychologie und der Geisteswissenschaften." In *Jahrbuch für Philosophie und Phänomenologische Forschung* 5 (1922):1F.

Taylor, C. "Understanding and Explanation in the Geisteswissenschaften." In

Wittgenstein: To Follow a Rule, edited by S. H. Holtzman and C. Leigh. London: Routledge & Kegan Paul, 1981.

Thouless, R. H. "The Affective Function of Language." In *Feelings and Emotions,* edited by M. L. Reymert. The Mooseheart Symposium. New York: McGraw Hill, 1950.

Van Breemen, P. "De mens en de Moderne natuurwetenschap." *Streven* 3 (1956): 212–20.

_____. "De Natuurwetenschap zelfgenoegzaam?" *Streven* 3 (1957): 635–44.

van den Berg, J. H. "Phenomenology and Metabletics." *Humanitas* 7 (1971): 279–90.

van Kaam, A. "The Addictive Personality." *Humanitas* 1 (Fall, 1965): 183–93.

_____, and L. V. Pacoe. "Anthropological Psychology and Behavioristic Experimentation." in *Festschrift Dr. Straus,* edited by R. M. Griffith and V. von Baeyer. Berline, Heidelberg, New York: Springer-Verlag, 1966.

_____. "Assumptions in Psychology." *Journal of Individual Psychology* 14 (1958): 22–28.

_____. "Commentary on 'Freedom and Responsibility Examined.'" In *Behavioral Science and Guidance, Proposals, and Perspectives,* edited by E. Lloyd-Jones and E. M. Westervelt. New York: Columbia University Press, 1963.

_____. "Counseling and Existential Psychology." *Harvard Educational Review* 32 (Fall 1962): 403–15.

_____. "Differential Psychology." In *The New Catholic Encyclopedia.* Washington, D.C.: The Catholic University of America, 1966.

_____. "The Existentential Approach to Human Potenialities." In *Explorations in Human Potentialities,* edited by H. A. Otto. Springfield, Ill.: Charles C. Thomas, 1966.

_____. "Existential Psychology." In *The New Catholic Encyclopedia.* Washington, D.C.: The Catholic University of America, 1966.

_____. "Existential and Humanistic Psychology." *Review of Existential Psychology and Psychiatry* (Fall 1965): 291–96.

_____. "Existential Psychology as a Comprehensive Theory of Personality." *Review of Existential Psychology and Psychiatry* 3 (Winter 1963): 11–26.

_____. "Die existentielle Psychologie als eine Theorie der Gesamtpersonlichkeit." *Jahrbuch für Psychologie und medizinische Anthropologie* 12.

_____. "The Fantasy of Romantic Love." In *Modern Myths and Popular Fancies.* Pittsburgh, Pa.: Duquesne University Press, 1961.

_____. "The Field of Religion and Personality or Theoretical Religious Anthropology." *Insight* 4 (Summer 1965): 1–7.

_____. "The Goals of Psychotherapy from the Existential Point of View." In *The Goals of Psychotherapy,* edited by A. R. Mahrer. New York: Appleton-Century-Crofts, 1966.

_____. "Humanistic Psychology and Culture." *Journal of Humanistic Psychology* 1 (Spring 1961): 94–100.

_____. "The Impact of Existential Phenomenology on the Psychological Literature of Western Europe." *Review of Existential Psychology and Psychiatry* 1 (1961): 63–92.

_____. "Motivation and Contemporary Anxiety." *Humanitas* 1 (Spring 1965): 59–75.

_____. "Phenomenal Analysis: Exemplified by a Study of the Experience of 'Really Feeling Understood.'" *Journal of Individual Psychology* 15 (1959): 66–72.

_____ . "A Psychology of the Catholic Intellectual." In *The Christian Intellectual,* edited by S. Hazo. Pittsburgh, Pa.: Duquesne University Press, 1963.

_____ . "A Psychology of Falling-Away-From-the-Faith." *Insight* 2 (Fall 1963): 3–17.

_____ . "Religion and Existential Will." *Insight* 1 (Summer 1962): 2–9.

_____ . "Religious Counseling of Seminarians." In *Seminary Education in a Time of Change,* edited by J. M. Lee and L. J. Putz. Notre Dame, Ind.: Fides Publishers, Inc., 1965.

_____ . "Sex and Existence." *Review of Existential Psychology and Psychiatry* 3 (Spring 1963): 163–82.

_____ . "Sex and Personality." *The Lamp* 63 (July 1965).

_____ . "Structures and Systems of Personality." In *The New Catholic Encyclopedia.* Washington, D.C.: The Catholic University of America, 1966.

von Bertalanffy, L. "General System Theory: A Critical Review." In *Modern Systems Research for the Behavioral Scientist,* edited by W. Buckley. Chicago: Aldine, 1968.

von Eckartsberg, E. "God Conscious and the 'Poetry of Madness.'" In *The Metaphors of Consciousness,* edited by R. Valle and R. von Eckartsberg. New York: Plenum Press, 1981.

_____ . "On Experiential Methodology." In *Duquesne Studies in Phenomenological Psychology.* Vol. 1. Edited by A. Giorgi, W. Fischer, and R. von Eckartsberg. Pittsburgh, Pa.: Duquesne University Press, 1971.

_____ . "Experiential Psychology: A Descriptive Protocol and Reflection." *Journal of Phenomenological Psychology* 2 (1972): 161–73.

_____ . "Maps of the Mind: The Cartography of Consciousness." In *The Metaphors of Consciousness,* edited by R. Valle and R. von Eckartsberg. New York: Plenum Press, 1981.

_____ . "Validity and the Transpersonal Ground of Psychological Theorizing." In *Duquesne Studies in Phenomenological Psychology.* Vol. 4. Edited by A. Giorgi, A. Barton, and C. Maes. Pittsburgh, Pa.: Duquesne University Press, 1983.

von Gebsattel, V. E. "The World of the Compulsive." Translated by S. Koppel and E. Angel. In *Existence: A New Dimension in Psychiatry and Psychology,* edited by R. May, E. Angel, and H. F. Ellenberger. New York: Basic Books, 1958.

von Wright, G. H. "Determinism and the Study of Man." In *Essays on Explanation and Understanding,* edited by J. Manninen and R. Tuomela. Dordrecht: Reidel, 1976.

_____ . "Replies to Commentators. Second Thoughts on Explanation and Understanding." In *Essays on Explanation and Understanding,* edited by J. Manninen and R. Tuomela. Dordrecht: Reidel, 1976.

Weber, M. "Wissenschaft als Beruf." In *Gesammelte Aufsatze sur Wissenschaftslehre.* 2nd ed. Tubingen: J. C. B. Mohr, 1922.

Wertheimer, M. "Gestalt Theory." In *A Source Book of Gestalt Psychology,* edited by W. Ellis. London: Routledge & Kegan Paul, 1938.

Windelband, W. "Geschichte und Naturwissenschaft." In *Präludien.* Vol 2. Tubingen: J. C. B. Mohr, 1921

Wolff, H. G. "Life Situations, Emotions and Bodily Disease." In *Feelings and Emotions*, edited by M. L. Reymert. The Mooseheart Symposium. New York: McGraw Hill, 1950.

Unpublished Theses

Agnew, U., SSL. "Originality and Spirituality: The Art of Discovering and Becoming Oneself." Master's thesis, Institute of Formative Spirituality, Duquesne University, Pittsburgh, Pa., 1974.

Balawejder, M. F., CCSF. "Spirituality and Journeying in the Freedom-Structure of Daily Life." Master's thesis, Institute of Formative Spirituality, Duquesne University, Pittsburgh, Pa., 1978.

Bendewald, A., O.Carm. "Spirituality and Technical Environment." Master's thesis, Institute of Formative Spirituality, Duquesne University, Pittsburgh, Pa., 1977.

Blank, G., SDR. "On the Relationship of Embodiment to Spiritual Unfolding." Master's thesis, Institute of Formative Spirituality, Duquesne University, Pittsburgh, Pa., 1976.

Bomberger, R., SSJ. "Tradition: A Way to Creative Original Living." Master's thesis, Institute of Formative Spirituality, Duquesne University, Pittsburgh, Pa., 1981.

Byrne, R., OCSO. "Living the Contemplative Dimension of Everyday Life." Master's thesis, Institute of Formative Spirituality, Duquesne University, Pittsburgh, Pa., 1973.

_____ . "The Science of Foundational Human Formation and Its Relation to the Christian Formation Traditions." Doctoral dissertation, Institute of Formative Spirituality, Duquesne University, Pittsburgh, Pa., 1982.

Carfagna, R., OSU. "Empathy and Personal Responsiveness: The Way of Spirit-Enlightened Relatedness." Master's thesis, Institute of Formative Spirituality, Duquesne University, Pittsburgh, Pa., 1976.

_____ . "Formative Teaching as Interformation." Doctoral dissertation, Institute of Formative Spirituality, Duquesne University, Pittsburgh, Pa., 1984.

Copps, M., OFM. "Spirituality and Silence as a Condition for Listening." Master's thesis, Institute of Formative Spirituality, Duquesne University, Pittsburgh, Pa., 1980.

Earner, M. A., SDR. "Life as Communication: Saying, Silence, and the Spiritual Life." Master's thesis, Institute of Formative Spirituality, Duquesne University, Pittsburgh, Pa., 1972.

Foley, J. P. "Remember Who You Most Deeply Are: The Role of Memory in the Unfolding of Foundational Identity and Commitment." Doctoral dissertation, Institute of Formative Spirituality, Duquesne University, Pittsburgh, Pa., 1984.

Gadoury, M. R. C., SSA. "Conversion and the Life of Spirit." Master's thesis, Institute of Formative Spirituality, Duquesne University, Pittsburgh, Pa., 1973.

Greiner, D. "Anthropological Psychology and Physics." Master's thesis, Duquesne University, Pittsburgh, Pa., 1962.

Jordan, G. "The Dynamics or Human Longing and Their Relationship to the Cosmic Epiphany." Doctoral dissertation, Institute of Formative Spirituality, Duquesne University, Pittsburgh, Pa., 1986.

Kelly, M., SSL. "Spirituality and Human Spatial Surroundings." Master's thesis, Institute of Formative Spirituality, Duquesne University, Pittsburgh, Pa., 1973.

_____. "Reformation of the Disposition of Formative Appraisal in the Service of Consonant Life Direction." Doctoral dissertation, Institute of Formative Spirituality, Duquesne University, Pittsburgh, Pa., 1984.

Kleppner, J. "Becoming More Wholeheartedly Committed: The Role of Commitment in the Unfolding of the Foundational Life-Form and the Formation of the Heart." Doctoral dissertation, Institute of Formative Spirituality, Duquesne University, Pittsburgh, Pa., 1985.

Kraft, W. F. "Anthropological Psychology and Phenomenology." Master's thesis, Duquesne University, Pittsburgh, Pa., 1962.

Leavy, M., OSB. "Reforming Dispositions: A Formative Approach to Habit Change." Doctoral dissertation, Institute of Formative Spirituality, Duquesne University, Pittsburgh, Pa., 1981.

Linschoten, J. "Das Experiment in der phaenomenologischen Psychologie." (Paper read in Bonn, Germany, 1955).

Mahoney, M., OSF. "Spirituality and Growth in Affirmative Presence." Master's thesis, Institute of Formative Spirituality, Duquesne University, Pittsburgh, Pa., 1978.

Mester, M., RSM. "Spiritual Awakening and a Sense of Wonder." Master's thesis, Institute of Formative Spirituality, Duquesne University, Pittsburgh, Pa., 1975.

Noonan, P., CFC. "Spirituality and Symbolic Presence." Master's thesis, Institute of Formative Spirituality, Duquesne University, Pittsburgh, Pa., 1978.

Pacoe, L. V. "Anthropological Psychology and Behavioristic Animal Experimentation." Master's thesis, Duquesne University, Pittsburgh, Pa., 1963.

Reeves, J. C. "An Introduction to the Methodology of Anthropological Psychology." Master's thesis, Duquesne University, Pittsburgh, Pa., 1962.

Richardt, S., DC. "Towards an Understanding of Human Receptivity: Implications for Religious Formation." Master's thesis, Institute of Formative Spirituality, Duquesne University, Pittsburgh, Pa., 1972.

Satala, M., DC. "Compassionate Living." Master's thesis, Institute of Formative Spirituality, Duquesne University, Pittsburgh, Pa., 1972.

Schaut, M. R., OSB. "Spirituality and the Role of the Family." Master's thesis, Institute of Formative Spirituality, Duquesne University, Pittsburgh, Pa., 1973.

Sharpe, M. J., RSM. "Life-Form and Its Transforming Influence upon the Person." Master's thesis, Institute of Formative Spirituality, Duquesne University, Pittsburgh, Pa., 1971.

Sheehan, W., OMI. "The Ongoing Movement of Integration and the Spiritual Life." Master's thesis, Institute of Formative Spirituality, Duquesne University, Pittsburgh, Pa., 1973.

Smith, D. "Anthropological Psychology and Ontology." Master's thesis, Duquesne University, Pittsburgh, Pa., 1960.

Tracy, M. F., CDP. "Man Responding to Changes: Implications for Spirituality." Master's thesis, Institute of Formative Spirituality, Duquesne University, Pittsburgh, Pa., 1973.

van Kaam, A. "The Experience of Really Feeling Understood by a Person." Doctoral dissertation, Western Reserve University, 1958.

Whelan, M., SM. "Confronting Truth in the Negative Movement." Master's thesis, Institute of Formative Spirituality, Duquesne University, Pittsburgh, Pa., 1978.

_____ . "The Process of Moving from an Idealizing Stance towards a Consonant Formation of Ideals." Doctoral dissertation, Institute of Formative Spirituality, Duquesne University, Pittsburgh, Pa.,1984.

Index

Note: In general this index does not repeat chapter or sectional titles. Please use the table of contents in conjunction with this index.

309